1987

THE ORIGINS OF ENGLAND 410–600

THE ORIGINS
OF ENGLAND
410 - 600

Martyn J. Whittock

BARNES & NOBLE BOOKS
Totowa, New Jersey

© 1986 Martyn Whittock
First published in the USA 1986 by
Barnes & Noble Books
81 Adams Drive
Totowa, New Jersey, 07512
Printed in Great Britain

Library of Congress Cataloging-in-Publication Data

Whittock, Martyn.
    The origins of England, 410-600 A.D.

    Bibliography: p.
    Includes index.
    1. Great Britain — History — Anglo-Saxon period, 449-
1066. 2. Great Britain — History — Roman period, 55 B.C.-
449 A.D. 3. Anglo-Saxons — England — History. 4. Romans —
England — History. 5.England — Antiquities. I. Title.
DA152.W48 1987   942.01′4   86-20659
ISBN 0-389-20682-2

CONTENTS

INTRODUCTION

This book has been written to give an overview of the current thinking concerning the origins of the English nation. It examines the migration of English people, from Europe to Britain and the establishment of their kingdoms in the period AD410–600. This period of history has become a particularly popular topic of discussion in schools, universities, television documentaries and private study. This is hardly surprising as it is a challenging area — full of controversies and intriguing problems. The observer is faced with interesting and fundamental questions: What are the literary sources of information and what can be relied on? Who were the great personalities of the era and what can confidently be said about them? Why have we remembered Vortigern or Hengest? What can archaeology tell us about the day-to-day experiences and lifestyles of early English men and women? Why did the English come to Britain and how did Roman Britain turn into England and Wales? These questions lie at the very heart of this study. Faced with such matters the historian must adopt the skills of the detective: primary and secondary sources must be classified and tested for reliability; the clues must be sifted and related to one another; bias must be detected and explained; gaps must be filled with careful and honest opinions; the overall mass of evidence must be fitted together like a gigantic and sometimes incomplete jigsaw puzzle. The need for an overview is essential. It prevents the reader from being swamped and lost in a mass of material.

Many published works tend to fall into one of two categories:

(1) General books on Roman Britain (55BC–AD410) or on Anglo-Saxon England (AD410–1066).
(2) Specialist books on archaeology, pottery, place names, weapons, art, regional history, etc.

Both approaches have shortcomings. The first approach treats the establishment of England as either a conclusion to Roman Britain or an introduction to later Anglo Saxon history, which ended at the battle of Hastings. In such books the vital migration period is dominated by either earlier or later events. This is particularly problematic when one considers that King Harold in 1066 was as far removed from his Germanic ancestors as we are from Richard III and the battle of Bosworth (1485). The same is true of Julius Caesar and the time between the first Roman interest in Britain and the loss of it from the empire. In such books the problems and controversies of the migration period are often glossed over or simplified. This is a pity as the period deserves study in its own right. It repays such study by providing a wealth of stimulating debates.

The second, specialist, approach is vital to the serious advance of knowledge but fails to give overviews and on its own constitutes not one approach but many. Indeed so many that each can become an individually overwhelming project without ever linking into other areas.

What is needed is a manageable text that will act as a springboard to further study but can also be read, in its own right, as a one-volume history book. Such a book would suit the student, or teacher, who wishes to gain a deeper knowledge of the era *and* the amateur historian who wants to discover where the roots of England lie. Such a book should provide a general view of current historical and archaeological opinion whilst introducing the reader to specialist sources and the latest books by way of notes in the text.

This book has been written with such aims in mind. In its writing the latest ideas on the literary sources, archaeology, place name study, etc. have been consulted and synthesised. New methods and discoveries have been outlined and their significance discussed (for example, the technological skills practised in the analysis of 'Wilmslow Man' in 1984, or at the Sutton Hoo Research Project in 1984–5, or the latest excavations at Silchester, Verulamium and the early English cemeteries on the east coast). This is necessary because archaeological finds have increased and revolutionary interpretations have been advanced in all fields. Current opinions differ widely from some held even 10 or 20 years ago. The literary sources have been subjected to closer scrutiny; pottery dates and sequences have been revised; the question of the relationship between the English immigrants and late Roman society has undergone drastic reconsideration. Now is the time to bring these great currents of thought together under one heading. In short the aim of this book is that it could be placed in someone's hands with the words, 'this will give you an understanding of modern ideas concerning this period and will introduce you to the great debates. This is the "state of play" as we approach the end of the twentieth century.' In order to achieve this each of the chapters examines an area of study crucial to an understanding of the early English. Their origins in northern Europe are traced; how, why and when they arrived in this country is considered; how they related to the existing society is examined; the lifestyles of the early English are explored along with their beliefs; the circumstances surrounding the founding of the first kingdoms are studied. In this way a period and its people are brought under the spotlight. The work begins with the arrival of the first pagan English and ends with the establishment of the great monarchies and the arrival of Christianity. In addition to this, appendices provide genealogies of the early English ruling houses (otherwise unavailable in books now in print), a concise analysis of early English personal names and an outline of English tribes and the survival of their names in later place names.

The writing of this book has constituted something of a personal journey. It is the product of many months of varied work — from using university facilities to measuring the Wansdyke ditch in the company of my wife, my brother and a dog more interested in chasing rabbits; from handling Romano Saxon pottery in St Albans museum to probing the moss green ruins of Spoonley Wood villa; from surveying the Cirencester and Silchester amphitheatres to walking fields of sugar beet in order to explore the cremation cemeteries of Norfolk. To do all this has been to 'look' into the lives of people who lived in a distant age. It has been immensely rewarding to attempt this insight into the social fabric of such people. If there is empathy or drama or modern parallels in this book it is because it was written by a person about people. Intellectual study is dry without a measure of empathy. By empathy is meant not fantasy but the disciplined exercise of the imagination under the constraints of the available evidence. To stand at Compton Beauchamp (Oxfordshire) and search for the burial mound of a Dark Age Hwituc (mentioned in a land grant in AD955) or to pick fragments of cremation urns out of the turmoil of a ploughed field is as much a part of an intellectual search for the past as is the study of books and periodicals in a university library. However, empathy alone is not enough. It must be accompanied by painstaking research. It also has a great limitation. As Aristotle remarked, 'fire burns in Persia as in Greece, but the laws are different'. In other words, whilst much of human experience is common to all ages the way in which we respond to it and interpret its significance is not. The student of the past follows an Ariadne's thread of common humanity but it often leads through 'passages' and 'places' unfamiliar to twentieth-century eyes. Aubrey Burl, in his examination of the building of prehistoric Avebury, concluded:

> . . . the thinking of people ignorant of physics, chemistry, meteorology, astronomy, is often allusive and symbolic. Just as they find it difficult to follow our reasoning so we, in turn, cannot easily understand the poetic images that explain the world in which they live. (*Prehistoric Avebury*, London, 1979, p. 82)

The student of history should not be afraid to admit that sometimes, in the study of ancient peoples, it is easier to understand *their* world than to comprehend how they themselves understood their own world. L. P. Hartley grasped this nettle, in his book *The Go-Between*, when he admitted that 'The past is a foreign country: they do things differently there.' Hence there will be times when important questions cannot be met with absolutely watertight answers. There will be occasions when a number of options need to be considered when attempting to understand why some ancient person did this or that. In some instances the reasoning behind an action will only be dimly perceived, if at all. These are important balances to those things that *can* be empirically stated. They also help to keep a historian humble and always eager to discover new insights into difficult situations. It is better to adopt this stance than to embark on reading back one's own thoughts and prejudices into the minds of ancient people, whilst the great mass of those being studied must remain poignantly dumb, unable to concur or contradict. At all times the available evidence must be paramount in our thinking. The past must be allowed to speak through its own literary sources and our interpretation of the dumb evidence of archaeology must be careful, precise and open to constructive criticism. Where the clues are elusive, or ambiguous, we should not be afraid to admit this. Only in this way will a study of the past uncover reality.

Having completed this work I owe special thanks to a number of people. I am grateful to the staff of Bristol University library and those of the Dorset Library Service for providing me with huge quantities of reading matter (or chasing it up for me!). I am grateful to the various museums (staff and directors) who have answered my enquiries and allowed me to examine the primary sources in their collections, and to those academics who have offered me advice. I must also thank the farmers who have allowed me to visit sites now under the plough. For help with the typing and presentation of the manuscript I owe thanks to Mrs M. Allen, Mr J. Chantry, Mrs M. Hodgson, Mrs E. Lloyd, Mrs J. Rendell and Mrs J. Shand. My especial thanks are reserved for my wife Chris and for my father, mother and two brothers. They have never objected to (indeed have encouraged) the fact that so much of my present is spent living in the past!

Martyn John Whittock
Canford Heath.

1 THE COMING OF THE ENGLISH

(A) THE ENGLISH BEFORE ENGLAND

The beginnings of English history lie in the so-called 'Dark Ages'. This term has become a popular way of describing the period of time in which Roman rule, in Britain, ended and Anglo Saxon rule began. It is not a very satisfactory term. In the way that Victorian writers lumped together African cultures as the 'Dark Continent', it covers over a complex and exciting story with a blanket name. More than this it is a defeatist term. It celebrates ignorance and almost encourages the eager researcher to give up before he, or she even starts! The term conveys an almost breathless hurry to get from the tidiness of Roman history to that of the Middle Ages, all in between being murky, indistinguishable and dark! This is a pity because the reality was so vibrant, dynamic, tragic and intriguing. Perhaps the only good thing about the term is the fact that at least it does admit that light would help the situation. Light is available. It has been provided by archaeologists winning back clues long lost to the past and the ground. It has been provided by the careful study of old manuscripts in order to piece together the fragments of written evidence. Whilst it would be foolish to declare that the gloom is anything like dispersed, there are, as it were, countless 'glow-worms' glinting in the dark. As the work continues the 'Dark Ages' yield more information. They give up details about kings and peasants. Something of the personal experiences and tragedies of individuals can be traced. This is vital because not only did the period seem so dark — its inhabitants seemed so mute. As discoveries mount they have begun to find 'voice'. This does not mean that the story told is always coherent or plausible. At times lone voices express feelings or memories. At other times it is the babble of a distant crowd and only the odd word can be heard. The story which they tell is the story of the origins of England.

To find the original English we must look towards northern Europe as it was in the four centuries after the birth of Christ. It is here that we will find them before they emigrated to this country. The general name 'English' is a better one than the more popular

1

one of 'Anglo Saxons'. When we refer to the English before they travelled to Britain we shall call them proto English. The decision to use these terms is a deliberate one and rests on good foundations:

1. The name Anglo Saxons implies that only two tribes took part in the invasion of Britain, at the end of Roman rule, in the fifth century AD. This was not the case. Many other tribes were also involved.

2. The name Anglo Saxon was not used by the early English. It first appeared, in the forms 'Angli Saxones'[1] or 'Engel Saxon'[2] in continental writings of the eighth and ninth centuries. These names never became rooted in England. While Asser's biography of Alfred the Great used the title 'Anglorum Saxonum Rex' ('King of the Angles and Saxons') in its introduction[3] there is much debate about whether this truly represented a constitutional title. The more usual form was 'Rex Anglorum' ('King of the English') and not the one which Asser used.[4]

3. The English themselves were very inconsistent in their use of their so-called national names. Wilrid, Bishop of York, called himself a Saxon although he lived in an area traditionally colonised by Angle tribesmen; the Abbot Hwaetbert called Northumbria 'Saxonia' despite its Angle origins; the Angle ruler Penda of Mercia was known to the Welsh as 'Panta the Saxon'; the venerable Bede identified the fifth century arrivals in Kent as Jute tribesmen. Afterwards he described them as Angles and Saxons!

If any form of national title is appropriate it is that of English (and England). There is historical backing for this. The Angles, Saxons and Jutes who lived south of the river Humber were often described in ancient sources as the 'Sutangli' or 'Southern English'. Those parts of Britain inhabited by these Germanic tribesmen became known as Angelcynn, Englaland and eventually England.[5] The collective name English is clearly much more appropriate than the alternative one of Anglo Saxon.[6] In this study the names Angle and Saxon will only be used when describing particular groups among the English, or when a source quoted uses these specific titles. When particular groups are so described it will be because those under discussion originally came from the continental homeland of one of these tribes. All this talk of what to call people may sound tedious and pedantic. It is not as, unless the ground is cleared from the beginning, it will soon be impossible to tell the wood from the trees. Too many studies have perished in this way and the last thing that the Dark Ages need is more confusion!

The original home of the English was in northern Germany and in Scandanavia. Perhaps the most famous analysis of their origins was written by the Englishman Bede in the eighth century. Bede was a Northumbrian churchman who (*c*.AD731) finished a book entitled *A History of the English Church and People*. In it he described the history of the English in Britain up to his own day. He also referred to the ultimate homes of the English:

> These newcomers were from the three most formidable races of Germany, the Saxons, Angles, and Jutes. From the Jutes are descended the people of Kent and the Isle of Wight and those in the province of the West Saxons opposite the Isle of Wight who are called Jutes to this day. From the Saxons — that is, the country now known as the land of the Old Saxons — came the East, South and West Saxons. And from the Angles — that is, the country now known as Angulus, which lies between the provinces of the Jutes and Saxons and is said to remain unpopulated to this day — are descended the East and Middle Angles, the Mercians, all the Northumbrian stock (that is, those peoples living north of the river Humber), and the other English peoples.

In short, the Saxons came from the estuary of the river Elbe; the Angles came from Angeln, in Schleswig; the Jutes came from Jutland. However, there is now much debate about at least two elements central to the description of Bede. The first is a nagging doubt about whether many other tribes were also involved in the invasions. The second concerns the geography of Bede's account. Before any conclusions can be reached it is necessary to examine what other evidence has survived concerning the proto English tribes in their European homes.[7]

Bede was not the first writer who attempted to describe the origins of the English nation. The Byzantine historian Procopius, writing in the second half of the sixth century, assumed that the population of Britain was then made up of 'Angiloi, Frissones and Britons'.[8] Whilst he omitted the Saxons his inclusion of Frisians should not be ignored. The Old English and the Old Frisian languages were closely related and the two peoples must have had close ties, both of culture and of blood. It is likely that Frisians accompanied their English cousins in their travels.

The evidence provided by Bede and Procopius is vital but it does not provide us with a detailed description of the proto English. Neither does it furnish us with enough geographical intelligence. To get more information it is necessary to turn to the surviving works of older Roman authors. The earliest account of the proto English was written in the late first century AD by Cornelius Tacitus. This writer made no mention of the Saxons but he did refer to the Angles. He called them 'Anglii' and placed them among the tribes of north west Europe — the 'Ingaevones'. These tribes of the North Sea coast were, according to his work *The Germania*, part of a larger confederation of peoples whom he called 'Suebi',[9] 'who are not comprised of one tribe . . . for they occupy the greater part of Germany . . .'[10] Among the Ingaevones[11] were the following tribes:

> . . . the Reudigni and the Aviones and the Anglii and the Varini, the Eudoses and the Suardones and the Nuithones. These tribes are protected by forests and rivers and there is nothing noteworthy about them except their common worship of Nerthus or Mother Earth. They consider that she intervenes in human affairs and rides in procession through the cities of men. In an island of the ocean is a holy wood and in it a consecrated chariot covered with robes: a single priest is permitted to touch it. He interprets the presence of the goddess in her shrine and follows with deep reverence as she rides away drawn by cows. Then follow days of rejoicing . . . they make no war, take up no arms, every weapon is put away . . . until the same priest returns the goddess to her temple . . . After this the chariot and the robes and, if you are willing to credit it, the deity in person are washed in a secluded wood. Slaves are the servants and immediately are swallowed by the same lake . . .[12]

This is the earliest surviving record that we have. Tacitus' Anglii[13] appear to have been situated in modern Schleswig-Holstein. This idea was later reinforced by Bede. The ocean referred to by Tacitus was probably intended to be the North Sea. It is unlikely that he meant the Baltic as he usually called this the 'Mare Suebicum' ('Sea of the Suebi'). His text implies that the Angles lived around the mouth of the river Eider and in the area around Svavsted.

Something of the religious beliefs of the tribes, mentioned by

Tacitus, can be seen in the objects and people sacrificed in peat bogs and recovered by archaeologists in Denmark. At the bog at Rappendam the find included a cart complete with draught animals.[14] Finds at other sites have ranged from garrotted corpses (Tacitus' slaves?) to plaited nooses and neck rings associated with the sacrificial rite. To what extent the Angles were involved in these activities is open to question. Tacitus clearly believed that they were and at least three of the excavated sites[15] are far enough south in Denmark to suggest that they may once have been in Angle territory.

Tacitus' book can be used to gain a glimpse into other social customs of the proto English peoples. His work does have to be read with a little care though. Some of it is very general. At other times one cannot help but get the impression that he was more concerned with making a point, regarding the shortcomings of his own society, than with simply recording facts. Sometimes those whom he described sound just a little bit too much like 'noble savages' and the modern reader may wonder whether he or she has been left with a 'warts and all' picture, or with the equivalent of a touched-up picture postcard addressed to Roman society with the message 'wish you were here'. Despite these misgivings many of his details can be relied on. He mentioned a custom of tying the hair in a knot which '. . .distinguishes the Suebi from other Germans'.[16] This fashion of wearing a Suebian knot was evident on the head of a bog victim found in a peat marsh at Osterby.[17] Similarly *The Germania* account suggests that the German tribes armed themselves with spears but that swords, helmets and armour were rarities.[18] This pre-eminence of the spear was clearly seen in excavations at Nydam. Over 500 spear heads and ashwood shafts were found in this bog deposit. Archaeological work in England has also shown that the commonest weapon, in the fifth and sixth centuries, was the spear. Tacitus also mentioned the nature of authority among the Germans. He wrote how 'They take their kings on the grounds of birth, their generals on the basis of courage.'[19] It will be necessary to return to this dichotomy of political authority when discussing the nature of English monarchy in Britain. As well as the rulers Tacitus also mentioned the 'comitatus' or warband of a warrior chief. They were a '. . .glory in peace, a protection in war'.[20] These warbands were central to Germanic society. They were richly rewarded by their patrons and were often made up of warriors from more than one tribe. They helped make their society one that was centred on warfare. The very existence of the warbands encouraged chiefs to turn to violence, for

> . . .you cannot keep up a great retinue except by war and violence, for it is to the generous chief that they look for that war horse, for that murderous and masterful spear . . . The material for this generosity comes through war . . .[21]

Having briefly looked at this sketch of proto English society it now remains to put Tacitus' tribes into some kind of geographical setting. It is likely that he described them in a list that ran from south to north. If this is what he did, the Reudigni must have lived north of the river Elbe with the Aviones, Anglii, Varini and Eudoses to the north of them. There is reason to believe that the Suardones and the Nuithones lived to the east of the Reudigni, on the southern shore of the Baltic (Figure 1.1).

A major omission from the text of *The Germania* is the whereabouts of the tribe known to later Roman writers as the Saxons (this is accepting that Tacitus' Eudoses were the same as the Jutes who were mentioned by Bede). Tacitus clearly had not heard of them by that name. In the second century AD this was rectified by the geographer Ptolemy. He described the Saxons as a Germanic people who lived on the neck of the Cimbric peninsular in modern Holstein. It is possible that what he called Saxons, Tacitus had previously called Reudigni. Ptolemy also mentioned the Angles but claimed that they were an inland people.His information at this point was probably faulty. If the Saxons were previously called by a different name we are justified in asking how and why such a change came about. The name used by Ptolemy was originally derived from the Old English 'seax' and the Old High German 'sahs', meaning 'short sword'. The Old Frisian form was 'sax' and the collective name Saxon corresponded to the Old English 'Seaxan' and the Old High German 'Sahso'. It was a general name used by Roman writers. It was used to describe a number of tribes who lived on the coast of north-western Europe. These Saxons were more of a confederacy of peoples than a clearly recognised tribe. From the third century onwards these Saxons began pirate raids against Roman provinces, on both sides of the channel. The name became a synonym for piracy and barbarism. Those who suffered their raids were not fussy in describing the cultural characteristics of their tormentors. That the Saxons were made up of many peoples

Figure 1.1: The Northern Tribes of Tacitus, with Some Mentioned in Old English Poetry (Swaefa, Myrgingas)

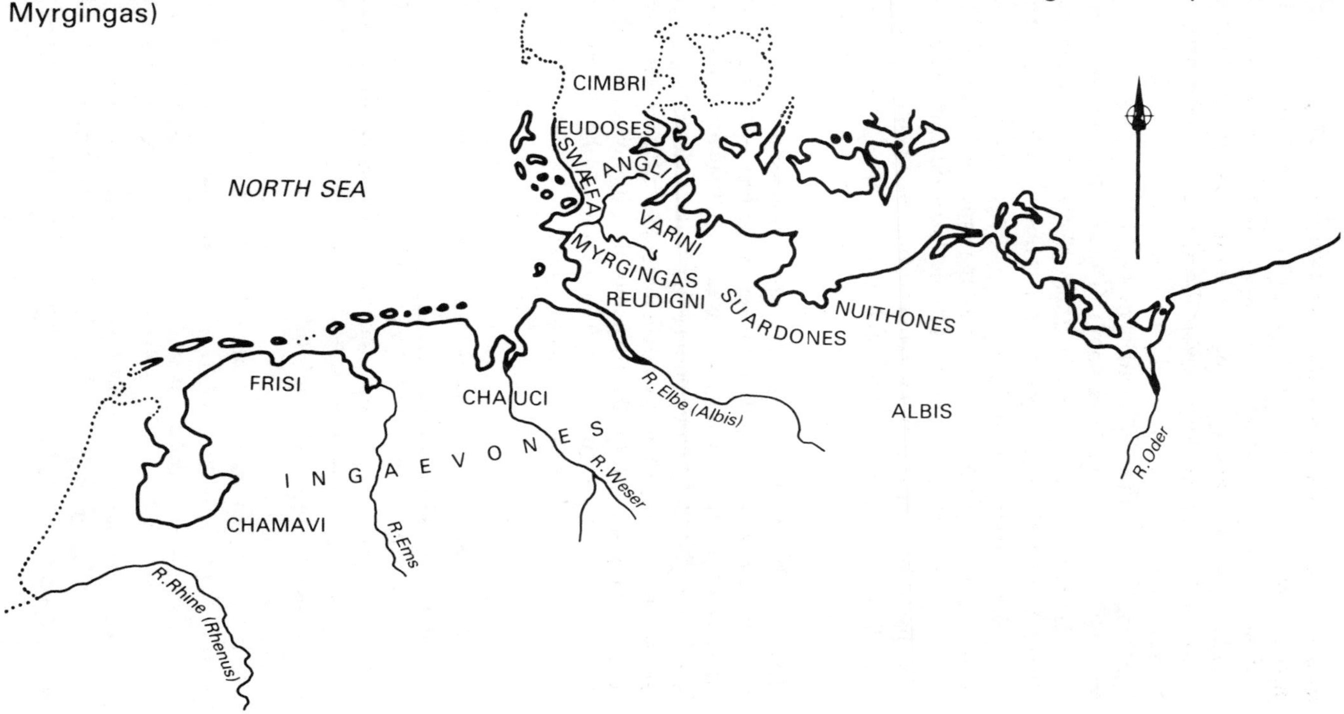

(probably including those once known as Reudigni) would have been irrelevant semantics to those whose houses were burnt. The victims of such activities did not engage in detailed anthropological discussion with, or about, their enemies. To the victims the equation was simple — Saxons were the enemy and the enemy were all Saxons. The situation would have been not unlike that in the American west in the nineteenth century. Many Roman provincials must have paraphrased the cowboy slogan that 'the only good Saxon was a dead one', although many of them, like the later coiners of the phrase, were not averse to employing groups of the 'enemy' when it suited their purpose![22]

By the fifth century the 'curved longships of the Saxons' had become an ever-present menace. The historian Sidonius, who wrote this, also commented that 'everyone of them is an arch pirate' and reminded his readers that 'your enemy is the most ferocious of all enemies'.[23] These raids were accompanied by an expansion of peoples from the original Saxon homeland, as described by Ptolemy. This westward folk movement began in the mid third century. It involved a drift from the region of the Elbe, in the direction of the river Weser. This was an encroachment onto land which according to Tacitus belonged to a tribe called the Chauci. According to him, they occupied the coast between the Frisian tribes and the neck of the Danish peninsular. It may be more than a coincidence that the first Roman references to the Saxons were written at about the time of the last references to the Chauci. This may mean that:

1. The Chauci were a Saxon people and their name was lost in that of the confederacy.
2. Alternatively the Saxons and the Chauci may have been two separate peoples. Ptolemy mentioned them as such and there is some evidence to suggest that the Chauci (or some of the tribe) migrated southward towards the river Rhine.

Of these alternatives the second is the most likely explanation of what took place. If the Chauci migrated it is likely that the Saxons took their place. Indeed it is quite possible that the Chauci were pushed out by the expanding Saxons. Part of the incentive to the Saxons to expand was provided by a sharp growth of population in their original homeland. This growth is represented by the excavated cemeteries of the so-called Bordesholm–Nottfeld culture in Holstein. Here and later, in the region of Stade on the western edge of the Elbe flood plain, thriving communities grew up and expanded. In one of the 45 cemeteries around Stade — that of Westerwanna — over 4,000 cremation urns have been unearthed.

Between AD250 and 450 the Saxons drove on westward, along the coast. Soon Saxon villages were established west of the mouth of the Ems. Some groups migrated as far as Drenthe, Veluwe and Rijnsburg in the modern Netherlands. These communities, however, were small ones. The main thrust was directed against the Frisian coast. The villages of the Frisians were soon swamped by waves of their Saxon cousins. The Frisians lived on mounds which had been built up over generations to protect their inhabitants from the encroaching sea. The Saxon groups who came to live on these inspired the ancient historian Orosius to describe the Saxons as '. . .a people of the ocean, settled. . .on the sea shore'.[24] However, these mound villages cannot have sufficed the newcomers for long or have provided the kind of environment and luxury desired by the aristocratic warbands. The Saxo Frisian settlements — with their mixed culture — constituted nothing more than one more stage in the westward coastal expansion. The next obvious move was either into the Roman land of Gaul or that of Britain.

The mound villages, which acted as staging points, are variously known today as terps, warf, werft, wierde or wurt. These elements are common in a number of place names to be found on the North Sea coast of Germany and the Netherlands. Many mound villages, or terpen, were constructed on the German coast between the mouth of the Elbe and that of the Ems. They can still be found as far north as the area around Marne, west of Brunsbuttel. There was a notable concentration of such communities between the Ems and the Weser. This area (now known as Ostfriesland) was sheltered by a group of islands including the islands of Borkum, Juist, Norderney, Langeoog, Spiekeroog and Wangeroge. One of the larger Saxon villages in this area was sited at Feddersen Wierde. This village was abandoned about 450, and its inhabitants probably came to Britain. Another group of terpen were constructed on the Dutch coast facing the islands of Ameland, Schiermonnikoog, Texel, Terschelling and Vlieland. One of these terpen now lies under the modern village of Ezinge. Situated on an inlet of the sea, this site was occupied from c.300 BC to the fifth century AD. Today the mound, on which the modern village is built, measures 457.2 m in diameter and is 5.1 m above the natural soil level. This height has been built up over time by layers of clay, dung, and the remains of turf walls, wattle and hut floors. In its late Roman phase the mound was 152.4 m in diameter and stood 3.5 m tall. Excavations have revealed a uniform layout of oblong buildings constructed by the original Frisian tribesmen. However, by c. AD 400 the village was swamped by Saxon colonists. Crude square pits are evidence of proto English huts which were constructed over the earlier structures. Such an occurrence must have been common at many coastal sites (see Figure 1.2).

The experiences of generations of movements must have assisted cultural intermixing between different groups. The rigidity of tribal groupings must have become plastic in this situation. From many areas of north-west Europe archaeology has revealed something of this confusion. Between the Elbe and the Weser (and in Frisia) Angle and Saxon cultures mixed. Although this was largely speaking a Saxon area some of the proto English dead were buried with Anglian cruciform brooches alongside others buried with Saxon saucer brooches and equal arm brooches (shaped like a letter 'H'). Burial rituals were not uniform either. Along the Rhineland, tribes practised inhumation; in the Elbe Weser region, and in Angeln, cremation was the norm; in east and north Jutland (and on the Baltic islands of Fyn and Langeland) some groups buried their dead unburnt; in the fifth and sixth centuries cremation replaced inhumation rituals (common in the fourth and early fifth centuries) in the area north of Limfjorden, whilst east of Hamburg (at Hamfelde) the rites were mixed, and at Deutsch Evern (south of Luneburg) inhumations have been found, in fourth century contexts, in this otherwise cremating area.[25] In this great period of flux many smaller groups were absorbed. The Old English author of the seventh-century poem *Widsith* recorded a folk memory of an earlier encounter, in Europe, between the Angles and two smaller tribes. In some form of boundary dispute the Angle king, Offa, settled the matter in heroic fashion:

> With single sword he struck the boundary
> against the Myrgings, where it marches now,
> fixed it at Fifeldor. Thenceforward it has
> stood between Angles and Swaefe . . .[26]

The poem tells us something about the extent of Angle territory, assuming that by Fifeldor the poet meant the river Eider. It also

Figure 1.2 : Mound Villages in the Netherlands, which show signs of English settlement

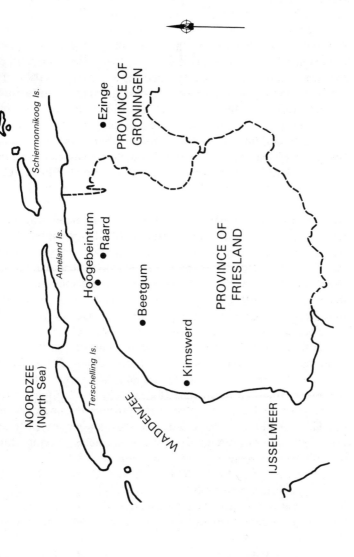

confirms the idea of close political relations between the tribes. The Myrgings (or Myrgingas) were probably a member of the Saxon confederacy, whilst the name Swaefe represents an Old English form of the name Suebi. Sharing a common boundary such people would either have turned to co-operation or to conflict. History decided in favour of the former.[27] It was clearly in all of their interests to work together in the same sphere of influence. Similar occurrences, at the southern end of the migration, were noted by the writer Eunapius who categorised the low countries tribe of the Chamavi as Saxon. They had clearly come into the orbit of the confederation. In this complex situation it becomes even more apparent why Roman provincials used simple terms in an attempt to clarify such a fluid and shifting mass of tribal names and peoples. This clearly is part of the root of the ubiquitous name Saxon, which was considered earlier. This tendency has survived in the Celtic habit of classifying all English people as 'Saesnaeg' or 'Sasanach' (both words derived from Saxon!). The curious fact is that while the Romans and Celts used Saxon as the 'catch all' name, the Saxons took that of the Angles and eventually called themselves English. Perhaps this was because they understood how imprecise a term Saxon was; perhaps it was because the Angles had a more rigid hierarchy which enabled proportionally more of them to be transported to Britain compared to their Saxon allies.In this case the term English might have meant 'the English Saxons' as opposed to those Saxons left behind, in what came to be called Old Saxony. Either way it is one of the more curious ironies of history.

So far the surviving evidence has been examined regarding the proto English peoples of the Angles and the Saxons. This examination has revealed that whilst Bede's account of English origins clearly preserved genuine folk traditions it would be unwise to think that his account cannot be added to. The situation was clearly much less tidy than Bede pretended it to be. Nevertheless, having allowed for cultural intercourse, Bede's opinion that Schleswig was the *original base* of the Angles and north-west Germany the *original base* of the Saxons was a fairly sound one.[28] However, the evidence is clear that between leaving those original bases and arriving in Britain many English men and women travelled large distances, through other areas.

In following the clues so far the historical detective will have realised how difficult it is to make hard and fast statements until all the shreds of evidence have been gathered up together and examined. If this is true in the case of the Angles and Saxons it is doubly true in the case of the Jutes. This member of Bede's three-way division has provoked more controversy than the other two combined.[29] Two basic questions have arisen concerning the Jutes: firstly, was Bede right in his location of their homeland? and secondly, was Bede right in his description of the Jutish colonisation of specific parts of southern Britain? The second question must wait until another chapter. The first question cannot be put off any longer.

Bede was clearly of the opinion that the Jutes played an important part in the fifth-century conquest of Britain. He suggested that they had their original home north of the Angles — in what is now Jutland. Because of this it is tempting to identify the Eudoses (mentioned by Tacitus) as Jutes.[30] This assumption has been challenged for a number of reasons.

1. The archaeology of the so-called Jutish county of Kent is, in the opinion of some experts, more in keeping with Frankish tribes who lived in the Rhineland. The field system used in Kent was very similar to the layout of fields in the territories of the Ripuarian Franks. The legal codes issued by early English rulers of Kent were similar (in subject matter if not in form) to the laws issued by the Salian Franks. In addition, in the 540s the Frankish King Theudebert[31] claimed authority over a tribe known as the 'Saxones Eucii' (Jutes?) and Pope Gregory I (pope from 590-604) used the phrase 'your subjects', of the people of Kent, when writing to the Frankish monarchs Theuderic and Theuderbert.
2. The name Jutland (or Jylland), it has been claimed, is derived not from the name of the Jutes but from the Scandanavian word 'Jotar'[32] The similarity between 'Jutland' and 'Jutes' being purely coincidental.
3. A further problem for those who would like to connect the Jutes with the name of Jutland is the fact that from the late fifth century onwards the area was invaded by Danish folk who came from what is now southern Sweden. Some scholars believe that it is unlikely that the conquering tribe would have adopted the regional name that had been coined by those that they replaced or vanquished.[33]

Against these assertions it is possible to raise a number of counter objections in an attempt to balance the argument or even tip it in favour of a Jutish homeland as described by Bede. These counter proposals are as follows:

1. Similarities between Kent and the Rhineland do not prove that this was the original home of the Jutes, anymore than parallels between pottery found in eastern Britain and that found in Frisia prove that this was the original home of the Angles and the Saxons.

2. Frankish claims to authority over Kent need not have been based on the fact that the county was colonised from Frankish territory. The claim could have been prompted by at least two other factors: the Frankish King Chilperich (ruled 567–84) extended his authority over a continental people called the Euthiones.[34] This people lived on the northern border of the lands of the Franks and may well have been Jutes. This conquest may have led to claims over Jutish people living elsewhere in 'Greater Jutish Territory' (that is, in Kent); secondly, the historian Procopius, in his analysis of the sixth-century population of Britain, added the comment that 'There was such overpopulation that every year large numbers migrated . . . to the Franks, who settled them in the emptier parts of their territory . . . by these means they [that is, the Franks] are winning over the island.'[35] While the significance of this reverse migration will be discussed in another section, this passage could suggest a different reason for Frankish claims over the whole Jutish nation, based more on sixth-century power politics and reverse migration than on fifth-century migrations from an original Frankish homeland.

3. There is continued argument, among historians, over whether the 'Frankish culture' in Kent was the result of fifth-century migrations or of trade in the sixth century. Until this is finally settled (and the answer seems to point more towards trade as the major factor) this cannot be used as a reason for discounting Bede's ideas.

4. The problem over relating the Jutish name to that of Jutland may not be as problematic as some writers have thought. Bede called the Jutes by the Latin form of their name — 'Iutae'. This form was most probably based on an Old English form such as 'Iotas' or 'Eotas'. These forms must have arisen from originals such as 'Juti-z' or 'Euti-z'. The former name is very hard to

reconcile with the name of Jutland but may have given rise to the Danish word 'Jyder' or 'inhabitant of Jutland'. The name Jyder may have developed from the word 'Jeuti' and this would have been derived from the word Juti-z. However, the latter possibility (Euti-z) is the most likely candidate for the original form of the Jutish national name. In the form 'Eutii' it would have given rise to the second element in the name Saxones Eucii — who came under Theudebert's sway in the sixth century. The name Eutii would have developed into the Iutae of Bede and the Old English Iotas. By way of the medieval Latin form 'Jutae/Juti' this name reached us as Jute.[36] The names based on Eutii can be related to the original appearance of the name of Jutland.

5. The idea that a conquering people would not adopt the proper name used by the previous inhabitants does not stand up to careful scrutiny. It should be noted that while the cemeteries of west Jutland appear to demonstrate massive folk departures, from the second century onwards, this does not mean that the entire peninsular was evacuated. Remnants of the tribe may have remained behind to pass on the name of the area to incoming peoples. This idea would be more tenable if a historic example of such an occurrence could be cited. One example of this type of name retention can be found in the extreme north of the Danish peninsular. Around the year 120 BC the Cimbri, Teutones and Ambrones tribes took part in a large-scale migration southwards. Nevertheless the modern regional names of Thy and Himmerland probably represent something of the regional names used by these ancient folk. If this could happen in these cases there is no reason to suppose that it could not have happened in the case of the Jutes.[37]

Having examined the arguments the most balanced conclusion would seem to be that the original home of the Jutes *was* in Jutland. They probably occupied the land north of the Anglian villages in Schleswig. The modern town name of Eutin, in eastern Holstein, may point to a southerly extension of this Jutish territory. This homeland was probably vacated by the Jutes from the second century onwards. It is highly likely that when the Saxons expanded into Chauci territory they did so in the company of Jutes. This connection with the Saxons probably helped give rise to the later composite name of Saxones Eucii or Saxon/Jutes. If the Saxons were a mongrel people, the Jutes revealed from the earliest times an ability to mix and adapt themselves out of existence as a recognisable social group! This racial confusion helps explain why there is no evidence of the use of the name in Kent.[38] Bede of course wrote in Northumberland and clearly used technical terms which the people of Kent had long discarded (there is some evidence that the Jutes of the New Forest kept alive some use of their national name for a much longer period). This is in direct contrast to the Saxon use of their tribal title which did survive in the names Essex, Middlesex and Sussex. When one considers how loose a term 'Saxon' was it only serves to illustrate how the Jutish name had become even more dilute and meaningless.

The most probable route of the Jutes to Britain was via the Frisian coast, although some migrants may have come by way of the Rhineland.[39] This movement was probably in the company of both Angles and Saxons for large parts of the journey. This would have meant that the communities between the Elbe and Frisia included Jutish elements as well as the previously mentioned tribes of the proto English. Here some Jutes remained — the Euthiones, or Saxones Eucii — until the sixth century when others had left for Britain in the previous century. In these great folk wanderings many different cultures were involved and borne along. A law code produced at the end of this migration period, known as the Lex Anglorum et Werinorum, revealed Varni tribesmen far from their homes on the Baltic and, along with scattered Angle communities, on the borders of Frankish territory.[40]

Some proto English groups did not make the sea crossing to this country. Some remained in northern Europe, others emigrated towards the Rhine or into south-eastern Germany; yet others found a home along the coast of what is now France. The actual mechanisms in operation which propelled them were many and varied. Some of them were long-term stimuli that affected much of the Germanic world. Others were shorter-term triggers which produced the particular movements in the fourth and fifth centuries. These must now be considered. They were the 'midwives' that brought the new world to birth and dispatched the old.

Among long-term stimuli the proto English experienced something of the westward movement which classical writers recorded as the lot of many northern and eastern folk. The Germans were at the end of a chain which stretched back into the Eurasian steppe country. This was coupled with the attractions offered by the rich imperial provinces and the increasing difficulties faced by the imperial authorities in defending their frontiers from Germanic incursions. This westward movement has been called the 'Volker-wanderung', or 'folk wanderings', by continental historians. It was caused by a number of factors and is a fascinating subject in its own right. Suffice it to say that in the years around AD350 a huge confed-eracy of Mongolian nomads had extended its authority from Outer Mongolia to the region about lake Balkash. Known as the 'Juan Juan' this mighty group of peoples shunted many other Asiatic tribes westward. By the 370s the most famous of these — the Huns — had exploded onto the Euxine steppe of southern Russia. In the face of this intrusion the Visigoths (a Germanic people) were driven into the territory of the Roman empire. Under their leader, Alaric, they sacked Rome itself in the year 410. The Huns, who had helped cause all this chaos, moved on to a new home in the Hungarian plain. From there they raided as far as the Roman prefecture of Gaul in 451. As a result of these upheavals many other tribes were pushed from their traditional homes. Like a stone thrown into a pond, the ripples spread far from the point of impact. The proto English were on one of the most western ripples.

Many historians have stressed how tempting a target the rich Roman empire was to these displaced persons of Germanic Europe. The villa economy and the urban markets, it is argued, offered vast possibilities of spoil. However, while this may explain the urge towards piracy it does not, of itself, explain the need to colonise. The attractions of luxury villas to pirate bands might well be rooted in the social structures and expectations of the comitatus society but more fundamental reasons, of a more localised type, must be sought to explain the movement of farming people. In short, the ploughman probably emigrated for different reasons from those of the warrior chief and his warband. As J. M. Roberts has noted: 'The prospects of booty might animate a raiding party but could hardly bring down an empire.'[41] For a people to engage in wholesale movement, over a number of generations, vital demographic and economic factors need to be in operation. The risks to a basically subsistence economy must have been great. No farmer abandons cultivated land without good reason. He invests too much sweat in the land. The proto English peoples were farming people.For them to move, the risks to the economic well-being of the community involved in moving must have been marginally outweighed by the disadvantages of staying where they were! It is to the immediate reasons that persuaded these ploughmen to disrupt their traditional lifestyle that we now must turn.

As we have seen the ancestors of the English were under a lot of pressure in their continental homes. Although many of the long- and short-term stimuli were related it was the most localised and immediate factors which forced the proto English from their homes. The pressure of increasing population clearly strained resources over time and acted as a dynamic force which drove the excess population on to 'pastures new'. This developed into a national search for land which was already cultivated but could be wrested from those who owned it. This clearly presented an easier choice than the alternative of clearing virgin forest in the uncultivated areas of northern and central Germany. To this end the proto English sought the lines of least resistance — where they could expand at the smallest cost and effort to themselves. This led them to stream along the North Sea coast. It also led them elsewhere. In the late fourth century Anglian settlers established themselves throughout eastern Holstein and into Mecklenburg. Others of their tribe travelled as far as the upper Elbe and Saale. For those who chose the coastal route geographical factors added themselves to the problems of overpopulation. It is an established fact that at the same time as north German immigrants arrived on the terpen an encroaching sea was already threatening these impoverished sites. A Saxon or Angle farmer might well have exclaimed, in the words of Shakespeare's Hamlet, 'How all occasions do conspire against me'! The only option left to those on the terpen was to move on into Gaul or cross to Britain. The growth of Frankish power in Gaul meant that this route was soon cut off. The only real alternative left was the sea crossing to Britain. It was this option which was finally taken by thousands of peasant farmers and their families. It was the culmination of generations of movement and can only have served to further fragment the English, both culturally and politically.

So far all of the particular emphasis has been on population and geography. These were the most striking, and local, forces which drove the peoples of Schleswig-Holstein firstly from the Danish peninsular and secondly from the North Sea coast to Britain. However, it would be short-sighted to leave the story here. These movements were, after all, the outer ripples on a great pond. These outer ripples were related to the great impacts that shook the European continent. That they were far removed from the immense dramas being enacted on the European plains cannot be denied.

Nevertheless distance does not nullify causation! The over populated and land hungry proto English *had* to move *westward* along with numberless other footloose people. The route to the east was not open to a mass migration. It had been shut by the inroads of other settlers. These people were the Slavs. These folk had been on the move, from their original home in the Carpathians, for almost two millenniums. They had established themselves between the rivers Vistula and Dnieper and it was from here that they threatened the north German tribes in the fifth and sixth centuries. They drove on to the river Oder and on again to the Elbe. Historians have given these Baltic Slavs a number of names including Polabians, Pomeranians, Sorbs and Sorbians. By the sixth century they had crossed the Elbe in a number of places.[42] However, long before this they had shut off the route to the east. The Slavs themselves were under pressure from the fiercer tribes sweeping into eastern and central Europe. The Slavs had as great an incentive to migrate as the proto English. By the sixth century the Slavs occupied the areas around Erfurt, Gotha, Hamburg, Luneburg and Magdeburg.[43] Some advanced to the river Saale. The tribe known as the Vilci (or Ljutici) occupied the land between the Elbe and Varnava. Around Mecklenburg the newcomers were the Obodrites; in Holstein they were called the Vagrians;[44] on Luneburg heath the tribe was the Dreviane. On the banks of the mid-lower Elbe the Slavic Cervelii confronted the Germanic Swaefe.[45] Ceramic evidence for Slavic settlement in north Germany can be fitted into flexible date boundaries from the fourth to the sixth centuries AD. In Hamburg excavations have produced parallels with the so called 'Praha Type' pottery found on sites in Bohemia, which suggests a common Slavic culture in north-west Germany and Czechoslovakia by the sixth century. This infiltration of north Germany was as influential on English history as was the dramatic Asiatic intrusions of the Huns which helped create it. While the activities of displaced Germanic tribes were of vital importance to the later Roman empire, 'the pressure of the Slavs was subtler and more insidious than the assault of German armies'.[46] Their effect on English history was as profound as that of the displaced Gothic tribes was on the empire.

The proto English also faced competition from the north. By the late fifth century, Danes from southern Sweden were drifting into the Baltic islands and northern Jutland. Continental Saxon sources knew these newcomers as 'Nordmanni' ('Northmen'). These

Northmen probably took the land which had been vacated by the Jutes.

Surrounded by these limitations to their growth the proto English moved westwards. It was a movement which took them from Angeln, Schleswig, Holstein, Mecklenburg and Jutland, through the melting pot of the terpen, to Britain. Thousands of ordinary men and women must have taken, quite literally, the advice given in the Old English poem, *The Husband's Message*, to get

> . . . into the boat and out to sea,
> sea gull's range; southwards from here,
> over the paths in the foam.

(B) THE BEGINNINGS OF ENGLAND

Between the years AD 400–600 the Roman diocese of Britannia was shattered. Waves of immigrants, from northern Germany, transformed it into the embryonic kingdoms of England.

How and why these immigrants came to Britain are basic questions. The answers are neither simple nor clear however, but a particularly persistent tradition has survived. According to this the first English arrived in the mid-fifth century. They came as mercenary troops at the invitation of the British governing authorities. A rebellion against these authorities led to a period of uncontrolled settlement. This was briefly checked, and then continued into the sixth century. The sources of this tradition, and their reliability, will need to be examined carefully. However, it must be admitted that the beginnings of relations between the British and German tribesmen clearly pre-dated the middle fifth century. Archaeological evidence makes this clear.

The Roman army had utilised German troops in a number of ways. The most noteworthy was in the role of auxiliary units. These units fulfilled a number of vital duties to complement the work of the legions. They provided cavalrymen, slingers, archers and general infantrymen.[47] The garrisons on Hadrian's Wall were comprised of auxiliaries. Some of these were of Germanic, or semi-Germanic origin. They included the following units:

I Frisiavonum (cohors quingenaria), from the river Scheldt area;

I Baetasiorum civium Romanorum (cohors quingenaria), from modern Holland;
I Ulpia Traiana Cugernorum civium Romanorum (cohors quingenaria), from North Germany.

In addition two units (stationed at Benwell, Chesters, Birrens, and at Burgh) had Rhineland connections.

Other types of unit found on the wall were the numeri (singular numerus). They were irregular troops. Usually recruited from non-citizens of the empire, they may have been comprised of four centuries per unit. Three units, who garrisoned forts on the wall, were of German origin. The three were called:

cuneus Frisionum Aballavensium;[48]
cuneus Frisiorum Ver;
numerus Hnaudifridi.

The latter two garrisoned Housesteads fort.

None of this points to an English presence. What it does do, however, is indicate a longstanding relationship between Britain and German tribesmen, via the offices of the Roman Army, although some of these units did come from areas already feeling Saxon influence (for example, the three Frisian numeri). In other words, whilst unprecedented German folk movement into Britain took place in the mid-fifth century, it would be far from correct to see this as the start of German interest in Britain.

Archaeological evidence has shown that the Roman administration was using German irregular troops to guard towns and roads from the mid-fourth century onwards. These mercenary troops used a type of Roman pottery, mass produced for German tastes. Produced on a wheel, and characteristically red or grey, it has been recognised in nine types on the basis of shape and decoration. In each type the bosses, dimples or free linear designs in the clay demonstrate a Germanic market in Britain. Although it appeared in the early third century it was most common from the mid fourth century onwards. This 'Romano Saxon' ware has been found at many sites on the east coast. These include Aldbrough (Humber), Ancaster (Lincolnshire), Bradwell-on-Sea (Essex), Brancaster (Norfolk), Burgh Castle (Norfolk), Caistor by Norwich (Norfolk), Colchester (Essex), Felixstowe (Suffolk), Great Casterton (Lincolnshire), Richborough (Kent) and the city of York.[49] Much of this area corresponds to the so-called 'Litoris Saxonici' (the Saxon Shore) with its forts to keep out Saxon pirate attacks and the longstanding threat of attacks by Picts from north of Hadrian's Wall.[50] The evidence for English mercenaries in this area clearly shows the established Roman policy of setting a thief to catch a thief. Indeed it is a matter of conjecture as to whether the 'Saxon Shore' gained its name from its enemy or its defenders — so definite is the evidence for the early English presence.

The pottery evidence not only demonstrates Roman industry supplying continental troops: there are a growing number of sites that have produced purely continental types of pottery, but found in a Romano British context. This indicates that English troops, with their Germanic culture, coexisted with the Roman society. Rough Saxon pottery, of a type found on the river Elbe, has been found along the Thames valley at Abingdon, Ham, Mitcham and Oxford. These Thames-side sites have produced a pottery type known as a faceted carinated bowl. It was handmade, rather than wheel thrown, and can be subdivided into three main types. Its significance lies in the fact that it was a type popular before the mid fifth century. It reveals a close link between Roman controlled German villages in Britain and the continental homelands. The Thames valley, however, was not the only area that contained carinated bowl-using communities. Others existed at West Stow (in Suffolk) and at Colchester, Heybridge and Mucking (in Essex). Some of the pottery from Mucking bears a striking resemblance to European examples from the terp at Feddersen Wierde. This evidence forces the earliest date for these communities back well before AD450.

The assembled clues show that characteristic Germanic handmade pottery was being produced in this country by, at the latest, the early fifth century. English cremation cemeteries, dating from before the cessation of Roman authority, were concentrated near Roman centres or on transport routes. Examples include the cemeteries discovered at the Ancaster Gap, Caistor by Norwich, Cambridge, Catterick (North Yorkshire), Brundall (Norfolk), Heworth (Durham), Kirton Lindsey (Lincolnshire), Malton (North Yorkshire), Markshall (Norfolk), Sancton (Humberside), West Keal (Lincolnshire) and York. Such cemeteries served sizeable English communities. These communities were placed at strategic points in the Roman administrative framework. This distribution was mostly in the east of England and north of the Thames. The pattern of sites is similar to that of sites showing a use of the Romano

Saxon ware. If both were used by German troops this is hardly surprising.

The European parallels to British finds cover the breadth of proto English territory. At Caistor a purely German type of cremation urn was very similar to Suebic fashions. Parallels also exist from fourth and fifth century contexts in Denmark, Holstein, Fünen, Norway and Schleswig. The geographical distribution is not the only noteworthy factor. The dating of some of the items is also striking. At Greetwell Roman villa (Lincolnshire) a pot was found similar to ones from eastern Holstein, made not later than AD350, and from Fyn in the fourth century generally. Pots of the type common on Fyn in the fourth century have also been unearthed at Sancton and at Caistor by Norwich and Wormegay in East Anglia. British sites have produced considerable ceramic material from the fourth century. Some of these are unstamped pieces from Anglian areas on the continent. Others are Saxon style large jugs. An example of this kind of item is the spout-handled urn found at Great Addington in Northamptonshire. Some of these fashions remind experts of second- and third-century items in northern Europe.

Some Anglian tribesmen may have been settled in East Anglia as early as the late third century. Some may have migrated from Frayde to Caistor by Norwich. Others seem to have moved from Fyn to Elkington in Lincolnshire. At Caistor the new defences, erected before AD300 may have been defended by Germanic troops. Myres asserted that 'Whatever the historical implications of these links with third century fashions may be, they cannot be ignored in any assessment of our earliest Anglian pottery.'[51] Clearly this line of argument goes even beyond that suggested for Romano Saxon pottery. If these claims have any merit then they suggest that English military *émigrés* were present in Britain over a century before the close of official imperial rule. However, coexistence does not imply that social intimacy always took place. That there is evidence for such intercourse is indisputable. At Winchester the last phase of use of the Roman cemetery was dominated by military levies with a south German origin; at Dorchester (Oxfordshire) military accommodation was provided in the town itself; the whole matter of the production of Romano Saxon pottery suggests that Roman workshops geared their production to meet the demands of a Germanic market in some areas. Nevertheless it would be misleading to assume that this was true of all the towns settled by the newcomers. Despite the argument for cultural intercourse there is also much material evidence that suggests that in the final phase of the Roman administration many sites saw English and Romano British coexisting *without* fusion, indeed with very few social contacts. Just what factors affected such relationships is not clear. Whatever they were they seem to have varied from area to area, with the general drift of lessening social ties in the decades around 410. It may have been that the size of the English population was an important factor. Where they become a dominant section of the population the mixing may have lessened. In such situations the newcomers would have possessed the social cohesion to develop their own peculiar culture whilst the natives may have had an incentive to keep themselves apart and avoid being 'swamped' by the barbarians.

The scenario outlined above would not be accepted by all historians and archaeologists. Among them there has developed something of a pro- and an anti-German party.This has become particularly noticeable over the question of the origins and users of Romano Saxon ware. Among the anti-German party this has been interpreted as purely Roman pottery but with decoration inspired by barbarian fashions. According to this school of thought, the earliest English pottery and settlement should be looked for in the decades after AD400 and not before. This party includes such diverse names as Michael Wood, Lesley and Roy Adkins, Sheppard Frere, Peter Salway, John Gillam, Stephen Johnson and Richard Reece. Frere went as far as to suggest that there were in essence, two forms of Romano Saxon ware in use. One type dated from the fourth century and was made by Romano Britons for Romano Britons. The other dated from the fifth century and was produced for an English clientele. Johnson has written that there is no real evidence for a Saxon presence in Britain before AD420. He has pointed to an absence of early Saxon cross bow brooches and early short arm brooches (*Stützarmfibeln*) in this country.[52]

Ranged against these are what we may term the pro-German party. These insist that the Roman coarse pottery decorated to suit Germanic taste, and found in the east Midlands and Saxon shore forts in the fourth century (possibly third century at Caistor next Yarmouth), is proof of an English presence, being served by the Roman market economy. The pro-German party includes Hurst, Hunter-Blair, Green and the prestigious J. N. L. Myres. The pro-German party rests much of its case on the geographical distribution of Romano Saxon ware. If one were wishing to place troops in a manner that would deter attacks from continental enemies, or Pictish marauders, then they would clearly be sited in areas that have shown a marked occurrence of Romano Saxon pottery.

The most important factor in the pro-German argument is that it does not rest exclusively on the evidence of Romano Saxon ware. Even if this were to be totally excluded by fresh research, this would not account for the evidence of early German pottery found in this country. Even if the outline date of the third century, for some items, is incorrect the evidence for fourth-century ware is very strong indeed. To this can be added those pieces which can be clearly dated from the first half of the fifth century. If the hypothesis is accepted then it comes to possess a logic of its own. The various waves of immigrants, from around 450 onwards, merely replaced earlier (if numerically smaller) groups. This is a persuasive answer to those that assume that 410 or 450 were clear-cut dates that began or ended historical eras.

> The notion that everything Saxon must necessarily be later than everything Roman, not only flies in the face of the available dating evidence but is plainly contrary to all historical probability.[53]

This does seem to be a fair conclusion to the argument.

Early English settlers did not only appear as a result of late Roman government policy. As order broke down, from the late fourth century onwards, private enterprise also played a part. Rich villa owners seem to have recruited mercenaries to guard their estates. Military belt buckles, showing German influence, have been discovered at a number of villas — Chedworth, Cupsham, Hotbury, Icklingham, North Wraxall, Lullingstone, Popham, Spoonley Wood, and West Dean. However, this evidence is ambiguous. The troops stationed at these villas may have been native levies. Of more consequence is the Saxon pottery found at Shakenoak villa and at Orton Hall farm, and the Anglian pot found at Greetwell. Germanic architecture was probably responsible for structures unearthed at Latimer villa and Rivenhall villa. These military *émigrés* may have been used as much to deter rebellious peasants as to fight pirates out for loot. The exact status of these settlers is no clearer than that of their predecessors. The earlier may have been 'laeti' (recruited from conquered tribes) or free men recruited into the auxiliary units of the Roman army. The latter may be covered by the term 'foederati' (first used in AD406) and implying tribesmen alloted land, in imperial territory, in return for military service. Both the earlier men and the latter 'treaty troops' could have been drawn from mixed ethnic backgrounds.

In the north of England, south German tribesmen may have been recruited. A fourth-century brooch found near Sancton was neither Angle nor Saxon. It is typical of another tribe — the Alemanni. We know that this tribe, under their ruler Fraomar, was settled in Britain in Roman times (AD372). Other Alemannic and Frankish remains have come from Driffield (Humberside). It is just possible that some folk memory of this stationing remains in the place name Almondsbury (West Yorkshire). It has usually been accepted that the name is derived from the old Norse 'Almannathing' ('Assembly of all the men'). However, an earlier form may have survived into the Viking period, when it was overlain by the new language.

The key point in this discussion is that these settlements long pre-dated the traditional time of English arrival. They clearly show a well-established Roman policy of using frontier tribes to confront their own kind. The policy of settling bodies of foederati, or treaty troops, is well evidenced from the early fifth century in Roman Europe. It built upon a number of precedents well-established over centuries. When Romano British gentlemen recruited groups of English warriors, or higher authorities recruited larger bodies of men after the official end of Roman authority in 410, they did nothing new. They would not have regarded themselves as innovators. Neither would they have considered their actions as unduly dangerous. Following a time-honoured policy they simply continued, in Britain, a well-tried Roman administrative ploy. The difference between conducting this policy in the fifth century and conducting it previously would not have been apparent to them. The difference was quite simply that the situation in Europe had changed. Land hunger in north Germany meant that the Angles, Saxons and their allies had been converted from pirates to settlers. The urge to move was felt by whole peasant communities, not just by warrior aristocrats out to reward their followers. In addition to this the resistance of the empire was crumbling. Land hunger combined with the real possibility of carving out a new home in rich Roman territory. It was against this background that British authorities acted after 410. They continued to play the old imperial game. However, unknown to them, the rules had been significantly changed. ·

In AD410 the Emperor Honorius wrote to the local tribal councils (civitates) of Britain. The crux of his letter was the statement that Britain must begin to look to its own defence. Honorius wrote to the civitates not to the senior administrator — the Vicarius (the Vicarius Britanniarum had previously been the deputy of the Praetorian Prefect of Gaul, the four provinces of Britain having made up a diocese of the Gallic prefecture). This may imply the lack of a central administration in Britain and its replacement by *ad hoc* local arrangements, based on the tribal areas. Each civitas was probably administered by executive officers (magistratus) and a council (ordo) as was the case with the 'chartered towns' of Roman Britain (despite the criticisms that have been raised against this tradition, as recorded by the historian Zosimus (*c*. 500), it seems best to assume that Honorius meant Britain and not Bruttium in Southern Italy. His text clearly indicted Britain by calling it Brettania). It is wrong to regard this as the Romans 'leaving Britain'. This would be incorrect for at least two reasons. Firstly, since AD383 Britain had rebelled twice, once under Magnus Maximus (the Macsen Wledig of the Welsh *Mabinogion*[54] poems), and a second time in AD406–7 when three usurpers — Marcus, Gratian and Constantine III — were elevated by the army in Britain. Both Magnus Maximus and Constantine III took large sections of the British army with them when they crossed to the continent, in pursuance of their imperial ambitions. The second reason is quite simply that the British urban classes and the villa aristocracy were profoundly Roman. There may indeed have been a pro-British and a pro-imperial faction in British political life after AD410 (one determined to rule independent of Rome, the other looking to an eventual reunification). What matters is that both were probably very similar in their social outlook and both had vested interests in the preservation of the status quo in Britain. Indeed the rebellion of Constantine III may well have arisen from a dissatisfaction with Roman inability to defend the province. It was more a British contribution to imperial defence than some form of Celtic separatism aimed at overthrowing the Roman way of life. Concerning the aftermath of 410 the Byzantine historian Zosimus wrote how the British 'fighting for themselves, freed the cities from the attacking barbarians'.

The historian, Procopius, writing with the aid of early-fifth-century sources, commented that: 'the Romans, in fact, were never able to recover Britain, but it remained . . . under tyrants'. By tyrants he was probably referring to rulers elevated from among the British governing classes, without regard to Rome and its emperor.

The tribal councils that took on the responsibility for defence were based on the Roman administrative centres: Calleva Atrebatum (Silchester, Hampshire); Corinium Dobunnorum (Cirencester, Gloucestershire); Durovernum Cantiacorum (Canterbury, Kent); Isca Dumnoniorum (Exeter, Devon); Isurium Brigantum (Aldbrough); Novomagus Regnensium (Chichester, West Sussex); Ratae Coritanorum (Leicester); Venta Belgarum (Winchester, Hampshire); Venta Icenorum (Caistor by Norwich); Venta Silurum (Caerwent, Gwent); and Viroconium Cornoviorum (Wroxeter, Shropshire).

To this list we may add a capital for the Catuvellauno tribe at Verulamium (St Albans, Hertfordshire) and two for the Durotriges at Durnovaria, or Durnonovaria (Dorchester, Dorset) and Lindinis (Ilchester, Somerset). A probable capital for the Parisi was at Petuaria (Brough on Humber, Humberside). The Colonia of Camulodunum (Colchester) probably served the Trinovantes. The Civitas Carvetiorum was possibly Carlisle (Cumberland) or Kirby Thore (Cumberland) and that of the Demetae was at Maridunum (Carmarthen, Dyfed).

Other major towns included Londinium (London), Eburacum (York), Glevum (Gloucester), Isca (Caerlion, Gwent), Deva (Chester, Cheshire), Lindum (Lincoln) and Aqua Sulis (Bath, Avon). From the third century Britain was divided into four provinces — Maxima Caesariensis (ruled from London), Britannia Prima (ruled from Cirencester), Flavia Caesariensis (ruled from Lincoln), and Britannia Secunda (ruled from York). These four provinces made up the Roman diocese of Britain.

It was the responsibility of the tribal authorities to fill the gap left by the regular Roman troops that had gone to the continent. There is every reason to believe that they did this by continuing to employ Germanic mercenaries. The English population on the east coast, and in the east Midlands, continued to rise significantly during the first half of the fifth century. This is the period when the type of English pottery known as 'stehende Bogen' became more complex in its style (the name means 'standing curves' and describes the high arch pattern worked into the side of the pot as grooves). This type has been found at Caistor by Yarmouth (Norfolk), Caistor by Norwich, Markshall, Cambridge, Dorchester on Thames, Leicester, Sancton, Thurmaston (Leicestershire) and Caistor on the

Wolds (Lincolnshire).[55] Such areas had a history of Roman siting of treaty troops. They lay on the eastern seaboard between Suffolk and Yorkshire and in the valley of the upper Thames. The later types show an extension of the distribution into the central Midlands and Northamptonshire. In addition there is evidence to suggest a wider distribution of the later type in the east Midlands. Overall it points to a continuity of policy, indeed an expansion of it.

An area where something of the type of policy aimed at can be demonstrated is at Silchester. The capital of the British Atrebates seems to have created some form of frontier on the south bank of the Thames. On the southern bank of the river the early English communities of Abingdon (Oxfordshire), Long Wittenham (Oxfordshire), Aston (Berkshire), Reading (Berkshire) and Wallingford (Oxfordshire) seem to have demarcated a frontier. This is confirmed by late Roman material found at Silchester and the absence of any early English material from the town. The cantonal Capital was the first major town on the road west of London. It was sited on a nodal point in the Roman road system. From it one road ran north east to Verulamium; one north to Alchester (Oxfordshire); one to the west that branched to Bath and Abonae (Sea Mills, Avon) and a second branch to Cirencester; one ran south west to Old Sarum (Wiltshire); one ran to Winchester; one ran to Chichester. Its 6–7.6 m high walls and its commanding position on the road network made it one of the most important sites in southern England. Its defences were further strengthened by an earthwork in the late fifth century or even early sixth century. An Ogham script memorial stone of the sixth century may indicate the use of Irish mercenaries in the town. It is highly likely that it adopted a conscious policy of restricting English access to the town and that the Thames was the northern boundary of its subject territory. Coins to be found in the town are so worn that they indicate a money economy that survived well into the fifth century.[56] The evidence of boundary ditches may imply more than the town's survival into the sixth century.[57] They may mean that Silchester played a strategic role in the defence of London.[58]

North of Silchester the excavated remains (AD410–50) show a predominance of cremation ritual and are sited close to Roman centres in East Anglia and the Midlands. However, south and east of the Thames, inhumation dominated in the early English cemeteries and the towns shunned too close a contact with the English immigrants. This may indicate two different settlement policies in two separate areas — divided by the Thames. It is possible that the treaty troops employed by the British of Silchester were intended to defend the area from the English settled further north. Here they may already have begun to swamp Romano British culture in and around East Anglia and on the rivers flowing into the Wash (see Figure 1.3).

Figure 1.3: Early English on the Upper Thames

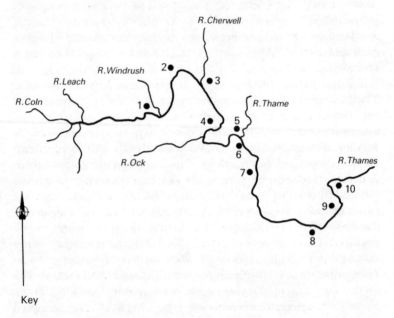

Key

● Sites with evidence of early Germanic Occupation

1.Brighthampton; 2.Cassington; 3.Oxford; 4.Abingdon;
5.Dorchester; 6.Long Wittenham; 7.Wallingford; 8.Reading Area;
9.Lower Shiplake; 10.Aston;

However, there is every likelihood that the Chilterns did not fall into English hands for over 160 years after AD410. This contention will be examined more closely in relation to the kingdom of Wessex. Suffice it to say, at this point, that although dark grey Romano Saxon ware has been found in the theatre-cum-rubbish dump, at Verulamium,[59] the city shows a remarkable absence of English material in any quantity. Apart from the English communities at Luton (Bedfordshire) and Stevenage (Hertfordshire) there is a real gap in early English settlement between the mid Thames and the upper Lea. Even the Luton and Stevenage sites seem to have had a very restricted, if continuous, occupation, arguing for tight British control over their development. Here, then, we have a situation reminiscent of Silchester. A sub-Roman centre kept itself free of close contact with the English and carefully settled and controlled those immigrants that did arrive in its territory. If the argument pursued later on in this study is correct, this policy may have been maintained, at Verulamium, until the battle of Bedcanford in AD571. For this period the wheat, barley, oats, beans and spelt produced on the fertile soils of the western Chilterns[60] may have maintained something of the decaying remnants of Romano British agriculture and the town economy.

If both these assertions are true and both Silchester and Verulamium maintained a vigorous defence of Romano British life until the sixth century then the analysis of why the Thames frontier was maintained (outlined above) must be false. If Verulamium only, or Silchester only, had survived then the analysis might stand up to criticism. However, the probable survival of both into the sixth century severely damages it. Why should Silchester maintain a fortified frontier when the Verulamium territory provided it with a buffer zone against the ambitions of the English of East Anglia and the Wash? One possible answer is that the Silchester English were not placed on the Thames to ward off other Germanic bands. They may well point to antagonism between the two British territories. Their presence may have been necessary to stop the development of some policy of hegemony based on Verulamium. This is at least as plausible an answer as to argue that they were intended to guard against an English menace that did not exist in the Chilterns area!

Whatever the truth was behind the siting of English colonists in the Thames valley in the first half of the fifth century, one thing can be asserted with confidence. Their presence could not prevent the eventual decay of the two British centres. The dislocation of trade, caused by the unsettled times, struck at the very heart of urban existence. The basis of the life of the cities was trade. As it fluctuated and declined so did urban life. Verulamium was eventually abandoned; the territory of the Atrebates did not survive into English administration — its area was later represented by two English regions that bore little resemblance to the former tribal territory.[61] By the summer of 1985 excavations (by the University of Reading) on the amphitheatre had still not found any recognisably early English material to fill the hiatus between the abandonment of the site, in late Roman times, and its reoccupation in the early Middle Ages.

The examples of Verulamium and Silchester nevertheless provide useful information concerning Britain in the period 410–450. They show that some form of provincial life based on urban centres continued. In AD428–9 Bishop Germanus of Auxerre travelled from Gaul to Britain to combat the spread of a heresy known as pelagianism. Constantius' *Life of Germanus* (written between AD470 and 490) describes how he preached in both urban and rural settings. It also records that on his visit to Verulamium he healed the blind daughter of an official. The man is described as having the power of a tribune. This reference, probably to a magistrate of the municipium, indicates a continuity of urban life, as outlined above. The title 'tribunus' was a loose one and could range in meaning from a military unit commander to an official with a government commission. The account also assumes that contact between the church in Gaul and that in Britain was being maintained. This is particularly significant when we recall that accounts of Germanus' life also indicate that he again visited Britain in the early to middle 440s (although it should be admitted that some historians consider the second visit to be a 'literary echo' of the first). However, both the English on the Thames and the *Life of Germanus* indicate that this society was under threat. On Germanus' visit he helped to organise resistance to a joint raid by Saxons and Picts. This bloodless victory, in which the raiders were panicked by the British shouting 'Alleluia' has been traditionally set at Maes Garmon, at Rhual, near Mold in Clywyd. However, it may easily have taken place in eastern England and have been 'transferred' to Wales by Welsh refugees who later fled English rule. For such a raid we do not have to hold the indigenous English population on the east coast responsible. It was probably a warrior band fresh from raids into Holland or Gaul, that was acting in concert with Pictish pirates. The last point that we may note from this examination of the territories north and south of the Thames is the possibility of English colonists playing a part in British power politics and internal rivalry. Its importance lies in the fact that one of the traditional accounts of the coming of the English describes their arrival as connected with divisions among the British. Since the traditions of a mid-fifth-century English arrival are so strong it is to that tradition that we now turn.

There are four key literary sources for the traditional account of the English in Britain: *The Ruin of Britain* by Gildas, *The History of the English Church and People* by Bede, the *Historia Brittonum* of Nennius and the *Anglo Saxon Chronicle*.[62] The work of the British churchman Gildas was written in the sixth century. (Dates for its writing vary within the decades AD530–50.) It was written as a denouncement of the state of Britain, politically, and ecclesiastically, in the sixth century. In it he also attempted to provide a historical framework as a base for this. This history of Britain, from its origins to Gildas' own day, has survived intact and is a rambling, often erroneous account. Gildas clearly drew on many sources, some of them fanciful and fabulous, others with some historical validity. Despite all his weaknesses his work is one of the oldest of our sources. The work of Gildas was drawn upon and tidied up by the English monk Bede. His book was completed *c.* 731 and used not only Gildas' book but English oral traditions. In this way he added details to the rather sparse account in *The Ruin of Britain* and interpreted some of the more ambiguous of the calculations of Gildas. A far different book is the *Historia Brittonum*, sometimes attributed to Gildas, sometimes to another British churchman, Nennius. The work is an ill-constructed collection of different traditions. In it the author attempted to tell the history of Britain from its founding by Brutus, a descendant of the Trojans(!), to the coming of the English. It has also had attached to it a series of Anglian genealogies that at some stage passed through Welsh hands, and a history of the British in the north. In one twelfth-century manuscript Nennius was made to excuse the poor construction of his work: 'Coacervavi,' he says, 'omne quod inveni.' ('I have made a heap of all that I have found.') It is, in short, not so much a source as a collection of sources! This leaves the *Anglo Saxon Chronicle*, which is an English account of the invasions. It exists in a number of versions which may be described as A,B,C,D,E and F). The major manuscripts for the migration and settlement periods are the Parker Chronicle, manuscript A (or more exactly Ā) ; the Laud Chronicle, manuscript E; and the Bilingual (English and Latin) Canterbury Chronicle, manuscript F. Occasionally material may be provided by folio 178 of the British Museum manuscript Cotton Tiberius A. iii (which is designated manuscript β and probably once constituted the missing genealogical preface of manuscript B) and the Abingdon Chronicles (manuscripts B and C). A later version — known as *Aethelweard's Chronicle* — was written, in Latin, in the ninth century and based on a lost copy of the *Anglo Saxon Chronicle*. The *Chronicle* was probably compiled on the basis of other chronicles and church records in the ninth century at the court of King Alfred of Wessex. There is every reason to believe that it contains genuine oral traditions dating from the fifth and sixth centuries. Despite its reliance on Bede, in key places concerning the invasions, it does seem to possess traditions obviously gleaned from other sources of its own. Its chronology, especially for the events up until AD600, is likely to be highly suspect in many areas. Indeed it would be short-sighted to imagine it to be a straightforward unbiased account: its sometimes clipped and sometimes censored entries, designed to please West Saxon patriotism and the genealogical interests of the royal house, need to be examined with care and occasionally with suspicion!

Having looked briefly at the nature of the evidence it is now necessary to examine what these sources tell us about the arrival of the English in Britain. It is important to remember that we should not expect a neat dovetailing of this evidence. The various traditions need to be fitted together with extreme care. We should not be afraid to admit areas where the traditions clash or where we cannot fully reconcile divergent opinions.

Gildas wrote that the British were plagued by marauding Picts (from north of Hadrian's Wall) and Scots (originally from Ireland, but who later settled in some numbers on the Mull of Kintyre and eventually gave their name to Scotland). Faced with these disasters the British appealed to Gaul for help. Their appeal was to the Roman consul Agitius (Agicius). This was not answered. The British continued to face problems — this time a famine! However, growing British resistance resulted in a temporary control of Pictish and Scottic raids. This was followed by a time of prosperity and then an epidemic of some kind. Only then does Gildas' work introduce us to 'the ferocious Saxons' (23.1). It recounts how the British council led by a proud tyrant ('superbus tyranus') brought Saxon mercenaries 'into the island like wolves into the fold, to beat back the peoples of the north' (23.1). The old Roman provincial council had been a politically impotent body comprised of delegates from the various civitates of the British provinces. This new council must also have been formed from the representatives of the now independent tribal administrations who had developed greater political ambitions. Some historians have gone so far as to suggest that the British attempted to establish a senatorial republic, but there is only tenuous evidence to support such a far-reaching conclusion. Whatever the exact structure of the government, its policy brought Saxon troops into Britain. These Saxons came in three ship-loads. These were settled 'on the east side of the island' (23.4) and were later reinforced by more settlers from Germany ('the lair of the barbarian lioness'). This situation continued until a revolt broke out over the question of payment — the mercenaries claiming they were not being paid enough. Gildas painted a dramatic picture of this revolt. He wrote of cities that were destroyed, British inhabitants either killed, enslaved or forced to flee overseas '. . .singing a psalm that took the place of a shanty "you have given us like sheep for eating and scattered us among the heathen" ' (25.1). This disaster was followed by a British rally under a leader named Ambrosius Aurelianus and a drawn-out war in which one of the later British victories was the siege of Badon Hill.[63]

Bede's account is very similar to that of Gildas and he clearly based it on *The Ruin of Britain*. However, it does have significant differences. Bede altered the name of Gildas' consul from Agitius to Aëtius. He also gave names to the leaders of the English. He identified them as the brothers Hengest and Horsa. He also gave a breakdown of the tribes that invaded Britain (examined in Chapter 1 above), their origins and which English kingdoms arose from which tribes. He implied that they were not only Saxons but included other tribes as well.[64] He also gave a date for the invasions (lacking in the account of Gildas). Bede dated the English arrival as being in the seven-year reign of Martian and Valentinian which Bede began at 449 (actually 450). He also gave a name to the tyrant. Bede named him as Vortigern. In the chronological summary appended to *The History of the English Church and People* (Book 5, Chapter 24) Bede again dated the coming of the English to the joint reign of Mar(t)ian and Valentinian. This is the period 450–7. However, elsewhere (Book 5, Chapter 23; Book 5, Chapter 24) he calculated the arrival of the English as 446–7. This may have been an attempt to connect his tradition with the only datable item in Gildas' account — the third consulship of Agitius (Aëtius) beginning in 446. However Bede's work seems to telescope Gildas' account of famine, British recovery and plague down to one year! We may feel that Bede, in an enthusiasm to base his chronology on Gildas, sacrificed a more persuasive chronology in the tradition that he had inherited, independently of Gildas.

To these two accounts can be added that of the *Historia Brittonum* of Nennius. There are two sources of evidence that can be gleaned from this collection of material. The first is from a chronological computation at the head of a set of Easter Annals (probably themselves lifted from a series of tables used to calculate the date of Easter and to which had been added noteworthy historic events). However we evaluate Easter Annals the references are intriguing. Having corrected some obvious errors in the calculations we are left with Vortigern beginning to rule in 425 and bringing Saxons into Britain in 428. This clearly clashes badly with either of the dates offered by Bede and what chronological content there is in Gildas.

Within the *Historia Brittonum* there are other traditions which have been recorded, however they are not of equal historical validity and may have drawn on a number of sources. In these traditions it was recorded that Vortigern granted Thanet to three shiploads of German mercenaries who came at a time when there was civil strife in Britain. The account alludes to some threat from the Romans and from Ambrosius.[65] It may be that Vortigern feared a Roman re-occupation as well as some kind of internal challenge to his power. This may indicate that Vortigern was not the unchallenged head of a British state. Indeed the British council of Gildas may not, in fact, have represented a descendant of the old provincial council as has been assumed so far. It may merely have consisted of those notables who backed Vortigern or any other dominant figure who represented their interests. The feared Roman invasion is hard to identify accurately. It may have been part of the power politics of Aëtius, who held Gaul with a large army of Huns. This may indicate a date about 430 — which would be quite appropriate. (There is no real evidence to support the view advanced by some scholars that a Roman administration was re-established in the 420s or even until as late as 442.) The English leaders were named by Nennius (as in Bede's work) as Hengest and Hors(a). This arrival was given a date in the late 470s. However, this is contradicted in the same passage, in the same manuscript, and should be discounted as a serious calculation. After this error follows an account of the work of Germanus. The account then returns to the Saxons: 'After the Saxons had continued some time in the island of Tenet [Thanet] . . .' they were reinforced from Germany. Vortigern married the daughter of Hengest (recorded variously as Renwein, Renwen, Roawen and as Rowen in the twelfth-century manuscripts of Geoffrey of

Monmouth[66] and as Alis Ronwen in the Welsh *Triad* poems).[67] The kingdom of Ceint (Kent) was given to the English. More mercenaries arrived from Germany to fight the Picts. The new arrivals were commanded by Hengest's son Octha (or Ochta) and Ebissa (either a son or nephew of Hengest). This is followed by more traditions of Germanus, in opposition to Vortigern, and fabulous tales of castle building in Snowdonia and 'a boy born without a father' whose name is revealed as Ambrosius (son of the Ambrosius mentioned earlier in the text?). At last the account returns to the Saxons, now engaged in a revolt against Vortigern's son, Vortimer and grandson Guorthemer, having agitated for more supplies and payment. Yet more Saxons arrived from Germany; the British council was massacred by the Saxons (under the pretence of ratifying a treaty) and Essex, Sussex and Middlesex were ceded to the mercenaries. Shortly after this, Vortigern is said to have died, either as an exile or by being swallowed by the earth! (The *Historia Brittonum* contains *both* accounts!) The kingdom of Kent then passed from Hengest to his son Octha and after this the campaigns of Arthur are outlined by reference to twelve battles, in which he held back the English advance, culminating in the British victory at Badon.

The *Anglo Saxon Chronicle* dates the coming of Hengest and Horsa to the seven-year reign of Mauricius and Valentinian. (Mauricius is from manuscript A of the *Chronicle*. In manuscript E and manuscript F the form Marcian is preserved.) This probably arose from the same Kentish tradition that Bede drew upon. Although both manuscripts A and E go on to quote extensively from Bede there is evidence that they also possessed a source independent of Bede. This source enabled the compilers of the *Chronicle* to construct a more detailed account of the English campaign in Kent than can be lifted from Bede.

Lastly there are two Gaullish chroniclers of uncertain reliability who recorded events in Britain for 440 and 441. According to these Gallic sources Britain 'passed into the power of the Saxons' in these two years. (Some historians consider this entry to be a ninth-century gloss, but this has not been proved.)

Having examined the material the first impression is that the material cannot be reconciled. In short we may summarise it as follows:

1. The Easter Annals date the arrival of the Saxons to AD 428.

2. The Gaullish chronicles date the capture of Britain by the Saxons to AD 440–1.
3. Gildas' work gives a likely date after AD 446 for the arrival, then rebellion, of the Saxons.
4. Bede's work gives two dates, AD 446–7 and AD 450–7, as the date of the Saxon arrival.
5. The *Anglo Saxon Chronicle* gives a date AD 449 (450–57).
6. The *Historia Brittonum* gives a rambling account in which the arrival of the Saxons, in Vortigern's reign, is separated from their revolt by a large section of the narrative (and by time?). Its dates cannot be relied on.

The ground can be cleared a little if we discount Bede's date of 446 as an artificial attempt to begin his chronology from the appeal to Agitius (Aëtius). It can be cleared further if we assume that the 'proud tyrant' of *The Ruin of Britain* is not the Vortigern of the Easter Annals chronological computation. If this is correct then Bede's identification of the proud tyrant was false and a combination of two traditions, of two different comings, of different Saxons at different times. This mis-identification could have influenced the compilers of the *Anglo Saxon Chronicle*. Also the naming in the *Historia Brittonum* of the two leaders of the Saxons who arrived in Vortigern's reign may have arisen from a similar confusion of events. If this is accepted then the rambling account of Nennius does not clash with the chronology being established here. Hengest and Horsa would not have led the original band. It was their subsequent conduct in Britain that overshadowed and eclipsed previous English leaders. This would account for the fact that they appear as the first English colonists in Bede's account and the *Chronicle*. They were first, not in the sense that they had no antecedents in Britain, but in the sense that they led a revolt against the British authorities and initiated a period of uncontrolled English settlement. This would account for the way Gildas described the Saxon arrival as if there was no precedent for it in Roman or sub-Roman military policy. The reason for this misleading attitude is clear. The failure of the policy had, for Gildas, overshadowed and discredited all previous policy. It was to the immediate architects of the failure that Gildas turned his anger — the British leaders and the Saxons who revolted. It was of course an understandable action on Gildas' part. It simplified a complex and ambiguous situation. Any other approach would have necessitated a total reappraisal of

Roman and sub-Roman policy. This would not have suited Gildas' purpose. He was primarily lamenting the passing of legitimate Roman rule and condemning the rule of illegitimate tyrants. That the Saxon revolt took place under the latter was, to Gildas, a sign of divine judgement on their rule. It would hardly have suited Gildas' purpose to have traced the roots of such a policy back into the imperial epoch. However understandable this outlook, it muddies the water considerably for those wishing to discover how and when the English arrived in Britain. The problem was compounded by the fact that later English writers were similarly content to keep this simplified structure as a framework for their accounts. Like Gildas they were struck by the fact that a new era had dawned in the mid fifth century, with a successful English revolt. In addition to this they wrote for ruling dynasties who traced their ancestry to warriors who arrived in Britain at the start of this new era. These dynasties could have found no use in acknowledging the fact that they were preceded by generations of English colonists and perhaps even rival noble families. These preceding settlers were 'buried' under traditions of noble houses that began in the English revolt and no earlier. These earlier Englishmen have left no voice in chronicles, poems or genealogies (all subject to the censorship of later rulers). They bear mute testimony to the fact that history is, more often than not, written by the winners not by the losers.

If we accept all that has been presented so far we may well agree with the following summary of events concerning the coming of the English: 'In AD428 at the invitation of Vortigern, to an unknown area; in 440 AD, in circumstances wholly unknown; and to Kent in about 450 AD'[68] (450–7) at the invitation of a proud tyrant and led by Hengest and Horsa.

The confusion of Vortigern and the proud tyrant may be explained if we accept that 'Vortigern' was a title rather than a personal name.[69] The word Vortigern (Vertigernus or Uurtigerno in Bede, Wyrtgeorn in Old English) was derived from Vertifernus or 'over lord', 'high lord'. It probably originated as a title but by the first half of the fifth century it could be found in the personal form Foirtchernn in the Irish *Book of Armagh* and in Scottish sources as Foirtgirn. However, it may have retained something of the form of a title. This is supported by the fact that Gildas' phrase 'proud tyrant' may have paraphrased, in Latin, a title (Vortigern) in British. As we have seen, the dates of Gildas' proud tyrant clash with that of Vortigern.[70] Nevertheless Gildas' record echoes the meaning of the latter's name. If indeed it was a title not a name, it would explain the confusion in Bede's writing and elsewhere. In which case we should talk of Vortigern I and Vortigern II (proud tyrant). It is instructive that in the *Historia Brittonum* the writer suggested that Vortigern (Vortigern I) was descended from 'Paulmerion who built Gloiuda, a great city upon the banks of the River Severn and in British is called Cair Gloui, in Saxon Gleucester' (Gloucester). Whatever the historicity of this genealogy it places Vortigern's origins in the rich villa country of the Cotswolds. There is also other evidence to connect him with Powys. Together these clues may indicate that he had a considerable power base in the Severn valley and the Cotswolds. They may also imply connections with the royalty of the Cornovii or the Dobunni. In short, a fitting background to a man titled 'over lord'.

After this discussion it is now time to turn to the English themselves — to Hengest and Horsa, leaders of the Germanic revolt. As befits the period the very historicity of these men has not gone unquestioned. Their names, Hengest (stallion) and Horsa (horse/mare) sound suspiciously unreal. It has been argued that they were purely mythological characters. Like Woden they served only a symbolic purpose. They represented some kind of pagan horse cult[71] and are no more vital to an understanding of English history than Romulus and Remus are to Roman history. Bede explained (2.5) that 'the kings of the Kentish folk are commonly known as Oiscings' after Oisc (or Aesc), Hengest's son. The term 'Oiscings' means the 'sons/descendants of Oisc'. Some historians have argued that this was the case because Hengest had no historic role in the founding of Kent, otherwise the kings of Kent would have been known as Hengestings. Further proof for this view, it is claimed, can be found in Bede's account of the death of Horsa (1.15) who '. . .was subsequently killed in battle against the Britons and was buried in east Kent, where a monument bearing his name still stands'. As long ago as 1936[72] it was considered that the origin of Horsa might be traced to the remains of a Roman inscription (for example, 'cohors' obliterated except for '. . .hors') that gave rise to the legend of Horsa — the inscription having been assumed to represent his tombstone. However, even if this was the origin of the story recounted by Bede, it does not prove Horsa to be a figment of the imagination. Indeed the whole argument can be stood on its head. It is equally logical to argue that if Horsa was a historic figure then that in itself might have led Kentish people to associate an inscription with him, if it seemed to resemble his name. Thus a historical figure might prompt a legend about that figure. All this of course is based on the assumption that Horsa was not commemorated by some kind of inscription. It is possible that sub-Roman practices were adopted by the newcomers and that this led to some kind of marker to a grave, supplied by indigenous stonemasons.

The argument against the historicity of Hengest does not stand up to scrutiny. That later Kentish kings called themselves after his son does not mean that the line did not originate in Hengest. The kings of East Anglia were known as the 'Wuffings', but Wuffa was not the first of the line to rule in Britain. According to a genealogical tradition, preserved in the *Historia Brittonum*, that honour went to Wuffa's father Wehha but this fact did not give rise to a 'Wehhingas' ('the descendants of Wehha'). This is a direct parallel with Kent. However, no one suggests that Wehha was a mythical figure who was ignored by later historical monarchs! The reasons behind these omissions may be that the first rulers did not truly consolidate the kingdom. Perhaps it was the next in line who made the situation stable and gave his name to the dynasty. Similarly the assertion that Hengest represented a horse cult does not take examination well. In the *Dictionary of English Place Names*[73] Ekwall noted, under the entry *Hengest*,[74] 'often difficult to distinguish from the *personal name* Hengest'. He went on to suggest the following meaning for the place name, Hinxton (Cambridgeshire) 'perhaps Hengestinga-Tun "the tun (homestead/village) of Hengest's people"'.[75] There is no suggestion that this was the Hengest of Kent but the example serves to show that nouns could easily become personal names in the migration period. There is nothing improbable about Hengest's name being an example of such a process. Additional support for this assertion is provided by the incident retold in *Beowulf*, lines 1068–1159, and the scrap of poetry known as the *Finnsburg Fragment*.[76] According to the compiler of this story Hnaef the 'half Dane' visited his sister Hildeburgh the wife of Finn, the king of the Frisians (also called Jutes in this story). The Frisians attacked the Danes by night and killed Hnaef. The surviving Danes, led by a warrior called Hengest, forced a compromise situation in which Finn accepted the Danes as his followers on equal terms with the Frisians. Finn was bound to give '. . .honour to the Danes of Hengest's party, providing rings and prizes from the hoard, plated with gold, treating them identically in the drinking hall as when he chose to cheer his own Frisians'.[77] The following winter many of the

Danes left for Denmark, others for 'Friesland'. (Line 1126 — presumably to the mixed Saxon, Jutish settlements on the coast.) Hengest remained at Finn's stronghold. However, with the spring the feud burst out again. Finn died at the hands of the Danes. Hengest took Hildeburgh home to Denmark.

The Hengest of the Beowulf story and the *Finnsburg Fragment* may or may not have been the Hengest who settled in Kent. There is every likelihood that they may have been identical. However, whether they were one and the same is not the issue. The main point of the story is that Hengest, or at least the name, has historic validity. If they were the same then Hengest of Kent is shown to be active elsewhere in Europe. If they were different then we have two examples of a man named Hengest. This clearly must present a problem to those who argue that the very name is indicative of mythological origins. If we accept Hengest as a historical figure it is a fair assumption that his brother's name — Horsa — was a nickname. It could clearly have been a play on the more famous brother's name. In this way we have two mercenary leaders named 'Stallion' and 'Mare' without recourse to a strained mythological interpretation. Their relationship (as recorded in the available sources) seems to have initiated the type of joint kingship so characteristic of Kent in the seventh century. Some historians have considered this to have been a projection backwards (into the fifth century) of a seventh- and eighth-century view. Dr B. A. F. Yorke has gone so far as to say that 'A common feature of foundation legends is not so much to illuminate the past but to explain or justify the present by projecting its conditions back into an earlier era.[78] Whilst this may be true, in some instances, it is surely not necessary to take it as a general rule. The later pattern of rule could just as easily have been based on earlier precedents.

Whatever the exact date of the arrival of Hengest and Horsa there is every reason to think it took place in the decade AD 450–60. The eventual revolt should then be placed in the 450s and 460s. There is corroborative evidence for a dislocation of British life in the 460s and 470s. In AD 455 the British church altered the dating of Easter in line with continental practices. However, when another alteration took place, on the continent, some 30 years later, it was not reflected in Britain. Clearly something had happened in the south east of Britain to sever contact with Gaul. Another factor may have been Frankish expansion. Prior to the 460s many English colonies were established in Gaul. It was after all the next logical move in their drift along the channel coast from their original homeland in the Ems Weser region. However, from the 460s to the 480s the growth of Frankish power cut off this route. In this period the only route left for the expanding Saxons and their allies lay over the North Sea and English Channel to Britain. In this way Hengest and Horsa were merely the vanguard of a succession of new colonists. The success of this colonisation rested on the crippling blow dealt to British authority by the Germanic revolt in the decades after AD 450. This of course brings us back to the settlement in Kent.

The exact racial origins of the troops employed by Vortigern II (proud tyrant) have caused some controversy. Bede (Book 1, Chapter 15) maintained that the people of Kent originated from Jutish settlers but the situation was clearly not as simple as this. A little earlier Bede wrote that it was the Angles or Saxons who came to Britain at Vortigern's invitation. At this stage he made no reference to the Jutes. Coupled with this we have a total absence of any reference to the Jutish name in Kent. There is better evidence for a Jutish nation in southern Hampshire, opposite the Isle of Wight. In addition the Hengest of the poetry was placed in the company of Danes and the Frisians were referred to as Jutes! We could hardly hope for a more complex situation. Perhaps some sense can be made of this if we recall the Jutish racial confusion examined earlier. We may be left with chiefs who were of Jutish origin when the term had become virtually meaningless. This may explain why the Frisians were referred to as Jutes by the *Beowulf* poet. Generations of inter-tribal mingling may have broken down rigid tribal divisions. It may also be instructive that Hnaef was referred to as the Half Dane — implying mixed racial origins. Also, if we accept an original Jutish home in Jutland, close contacts between Jutes and Danes might be expected. This would explain Hengest's role in Hnaef's comitatus. In a similar way other bands of Jutes may have maintained close contact with migrating Saxons and groups of Angles. This would account for the apparent ambiguities of Bede. The impression of a racial mixture in the fight at Finnsburgh is complete when we recall that among Hengest's warriors the poet named a certain Sigeferth Chief of the Secgan. Thus, if we accept Hengest, in *Beowulf*, as the Kentish chief, we have a picture of Danes, half Danes, Jutes and Secgs versus Frisians and Jutes. No better picture could be painted of the so-called 'Michgruppe' (mixed culture) that was so characteristic of the Saxon homelands in the Elbe Weser region in the fourth century and that came, in the fifth century, to be true of large areas of the North Sea coast. The ceramic remains of the earliest Kentish settlers (and other early settlers in Essex, Middlesex and Surrey) point to an original home in Jutland but also to Frisian contacts. Pottery from Canterbury, Bekesbourne, Bifrons, Deal, Eastry, Faversham, Guildown, Hanwell, Hollingbourne, Howletts, Lyme, Mitcham, Mucking, Northfleet, Orpington, Riseley, Jarre in Thanet, Westbere and Wingham have parallels in Danish sites from Drengsted Galsted and Trawlborg, in the centre, and Knude Rubjerg and Voerbjerg in the extreme north of the peninsular.[79] There are also parallels to be found in Schleswig and in Saxon dominated settlements at Feddersen Wierde, Beetgum, Ezinge and Hoogebeintum. Lastly small cruciform brooches of an early date and found in Kent are reminiscent of Danish types and provide more evidence of the Jutish origin of the original Kentish people.

Hengest the Jutish chieftain led a mixed Saxon/Jutish band of warriors into Kent to defend the south east of England from Roman reoccupation. The literary statements concerning the deployment of mercenaries echoes Aëtius' use of Alans against the Huns in the 440s.[80] The widespread deployment of treaty troops in Kent had no fourth-century precedent (unlike Caistor by Norwich, for example) and can only be understood in terms of closing off the route from Gaul. The original commitment of treaty troops was a small one. Both Gildas' and Nennius' accounts agree on three shiploads. Nennius, however, added the phrase 'exiled from Germany' to explain the availability of the forces. Nennius placed their original settlement in Thanet. He made a poor attempt to link the name Thanet (Old Welsh 'bright island' or 'fire island') with a British name Ruimm or Roihin ('bond') having assumed (wrongly) that Thanet was related to the Old English for 'thong'. Despite this false etymology the ceramic discoveries at Sarre support his location of the treaty troops. In the fifth century Thanet was a large island separated from the mainland of Kent by the Wantsum Channel, in places some 594 metres broad.[81] It was an ideal place to contain the initial force.

Nennius' account makes it clear that the arrival of Hengest and Horsa was only the beginning of a large-scale folk movement. The *Historia Brittonum* outlines the arrival of 16 and then 40 extra ships. Whatever the exact size of the new influx the implications are clear to the student of the period. The original commitment was drastically increased (according to Nennius' figures by almost 1800 per cent!). The result of this expansion was the ceding to the English of Kent (apparently without the Kentish King Guoyrancgonus being consulted!). Nennius gave the origin of these reinforcements as Scythia! This can be dismissed as an obvious error and must have been a mistaken reference to the northern world generally. This interpretation is strengthened by the later inference that Hengest was in contact with the rulers of the Angles. This incidentally is the only reference in the *Historia Brittonum*, to the homeland of the troops, universally referred to in the book as 'Saxons'. The *Anglo Saxon Chronicle*, under 499 (manuscripts A and E) and 488 (manuscript F), also refers to reinforcements from Angeln. The meaning may be that Hengest sent messages to Jutish communities living among the Angles. Alternatively the use of 'Angle' in the *Chronicle* may be a deliberate attempt to purge the account of all references to the Jutes. It was only at this point that the writer referred to the English fighting the 'Scots and the people who dwell in the north near the wall . . .' (Picts). Gildas wrote of Saxon colonies on 'the east side of the island'. This ambiguous term must cloak a general redeployment of English troops along the eastern coast. This has left evidence, in the form of pottery, in Yorkshire, Lincolnshire and East Anglia. In these areas pure Anglian and Anglo-Frisian pottery point to the arrival of newcomers from the continent in the decades after AD450. This Anglo Frisian pottery — a smooth well-made type, characteristic of the Saxon dominated terpen — has been found at Hough on the Hill and Sleaford (Lincolnshire) as well as at Northfleet and Sarre (Kent). In Norfolk examples have been found at Caistor by Norwich and North Elmham, although this area also continued to attract a direct immigration from Anglian Schleswig which would dominate English settlement north of the Wash by the end of the fifth century. In these areas the newcomers must have reinforced existing English colonies of long standing.

The English who allegedly spearheaded the assault on Pictland were led, according to Nennius, by Octha and Ebissa (both sons of Hengest in one manuscript, though Ebissa was made a nephew of Hengest by the writer of another manuscript). Traditionally they were supposed to have led a raid as far as the Orkneys and settled beyond the 'Frenessic Sea'. This latter point may have been a reference to a northerly outpost of English settlers. The phrase Frenessic Sea appears in one manuscript in the form 'Mare Frenessicum' but in another as 'Mare Fresicum'. This may have the meaning of 'Frisian Sea'. If so it is hard to locate other than on the eastern seaboard. However, the second form may be a reference to the northern shore of the Firth of Forth, around Culross in Fife. This coastline was described by a churchman in the *Life of Kentigirn*, as 'Litus Fresicum'. If this identification is correct then a force of mercenaries must have been settled on the land between the coast and the Ochil Hills. However, the settlement may have been on the southern shore of the Firth of Forth. It is of interest that within five miles of the sea, south of Northberwick, are Tyninghame and Whittinghame (Lothian). Both are examples of the archaic English place name type that ends in '-ingham', or 'village of the people of "X"' — a type characteristic of the colonisation phase of English history. They probably represent some sixth-century offshoot from the Kingdom of Bernicia, some 50 miles to the south. However, it may be that the 'people of the River Tyne' at Tyninghame and the 'people of Hwita' at Whittinghame represent an earlier colonisation related to Octha and Ebissa's campaigns in the north.

As a result of these troop dispositions the English came to dominate the east coast. There is a possibility that this period also saw the settling (or perhaps reinforcing of earlier settlers in some instances) of groups at Cambridge, Colchester, Dorchester, Dunstable, Kempston, Luton and Sandy. These controlled traffic along the Icknield Way and through East Anglia, in order to guard the rich lands along the Thames and in the south Midlands.[82]

When the revolt came it was centred on the original focus of settlement — the south east. This is not to say that it did not lead to uprisings elsewhere. The *Historia Brittonum* records a garbled tradition that an English chief named Soemil 'first separated Deira from Bernicia' in the mid fifth century. As it stands the entry does not make sense. The English Kingdom of Bernicia was not founded until the 540s. In the fifth century there was nothing to separate the English Kingdom of Deira from — except British rule. The tradition, meaningless as it stands, may preserve some dim folk memory of a revolt by the Anglian treaty troops of Yorkshire against the British. Such an uprising could have been a counterpart to the revolt in Kent.

The *Anglo Saxon Chronicle* and the *Historia Brittonum* give a graphic account of the war in Kent. Before we examine the campaign it is necessary to seek clarification concerning two of the combatants — Oisc[83] and Octha. From an overview of the sources there seems to be no problem with these two characters. They were the sons of Hengest. However, on re-examining the evidence it is not so simple. The *Chronicle* never refers to Octha, only to Hengest, Horsa and Oisc (or Aesc). It was Oisc who succeeded Hengest in AD488 according to the *Chronicle*. However, Nennius did not refer to Oisc but only to Hengest's son Octha who 'after the death of his father Hengest came. . .to the Kingdom of Kent, and from him proceeded all the kings of the province . . .' As if this were not confusing enough, Bede (Book 2, Chapter 5) made Octha the son of Oisc (also called Oeric), the son of Hengest. To compound this the genealogy known as *Cotton Vespasian B6, fol. 108 foll.* gives the order — Hengest, father of Ocga (Octha) father of Oese (Oisc). It is little wonder that, in desperation, a translator of the *Chronicle of Aethelweard* assumed that Ochta (Octha) was one and the same as Ese (Oisc)! To add to this a number of historians have maintained that Oisc was referred to by later Welsh poets.[84] The only character who fits the description is 'Osla Big Knife'. He can be found in the poems *How Culhwch Won Olwen*, and *The Dream of Rhonabwy*. However, the character of Osla Big Knife has been identified by Jeffrey Gantz as 'Octha son of Hengest?'[85] There are two possible solutions to the problem:

1. Oisc and Octha may have been the same person. A tradition of a campaign in the north followed by one in Kent may have caused the false equation: two campaigns equal two men.[86] This confusion may be reflected in Bede's work and in *Cotton Vespasian*, as well as in later Welsh poetry.

2. Oisc and Octha may have been two separate people — the sons of Hengest. According to the *Chronicle* (which omits Octha) Oisc reigned for 24 years after AD488 (manuscript A) which would take us to AD512 (manuscript E gives a reign of 34 years but this is probably too long). After AD512 a king named Eormenric is said to have reigned until AD563 — a total of 53 years. This is a considerable reign, and though not without parallel, (the next Kentish monarch — Ethelbert — ruled for some 53 years) it might be more credible were it shorter. It would be shorter if we assumed the existence of a king Octha, who ruled for a short period after AD512. This would agree with Bede. We would then have to assume a confusion of *order* in *Cotton Vespasian* but not in *persons*.

Neither of these two solutions is totally satisfactory. The first does not explain why such a confusion of names could have occurred in Bede's book, given his Kentish contacts, or in *Cotton Vespasian*. The second does not explain Octha's omission from the *Chronicle* and may rest on too stringent a concern for chronology when this is perhaps the weakest point of the *Chronicle* (that is, if the *Chronicle*'s dates bear no resemblance to reality then Oisc's reign could have begun much later than AD488 and there would then be no need to seek another, unmentioned reign to fill the possible gap between the end of Oisc's reign and the start of Eormenric's!).

In conclusion it must be admitted that no completely plausible answer to the problem can be found. Despite the drawbacks it is best to conclude that Oisc and Octha were two separate people — the sons of Hengest, and that Oisc succeeded Hengest and was himself assisted and eventually succeeded by his brother — Octha. This accords with the sequence in Bede and the personages of *Cotton Vespasian*, without actually contradicting Nennius or the *Chronicle*. The root of Bede's misconception of the relationship between Oisc and Octha may have been in a king list that placed Octha after Oisc. It would have been easy for such a sequence to have been remembered with the usual English formula 'Octha, Oiscing, Oisc, Hengesting . . .' ('Octha, son of Oisc, Oisc, son of Hengest') and so transform a king list into a genealogy. It is clearly something of this kind that led to Bede's account. The confusion of *Cotton Vespasian* (which reads 'Iurmenric (Eormenric) O. . .Oese Ocging, Ocga Hengesting'[87] makes the whole sequence suspect. Indeed the omission of a name after that of Eormenric (Iurmenric in this manuscript) may indicate some problem in the transmission of this material. The omission from the *Chronicle* of Octha may simply reflect a faulty tradition or the fact that his reign was not successful in military terms. The whole problem of artificial family relationships was not confined to the genealogical scribes of Kent. In Mercia King Penda was described as the father of a west Midlands prince named Merewalh.[88] There is evidence, however, that Merewalh represented a separate dynasty of a people who were annexed by Mercia. The family relationship here may simply indicate an annexation. Similarly, in late-sixth-century Wessex the scribes of several princes constructed quite impractical genealogies. These clearly smoothed over some tangled problem of legitimacy. If such examples as these could occur, it is hardly surprising that it happened, as in Kent, when the two men were related.

The campaigns fought by Hengest, Horsa and Oisc were recorded by Nennius and by the ninth-century writers of the *Chronicle*. According to Nennius the British were commanded by Guorthemer, the grandson of Vortigern (Vortigern II, proud tyrant). The campaigns had four major engagements. Firstly, the Saxons were driven back to Thanet and besieged there. Secondly (having been reinforced), the Saxons again menaced the British and a battle was fought on the river Derwent (Vatican manuscript). This river's name is identical with that of the River Darent in Kent. Thirdly, a battle was fought at a river crossing called Episford, in English, and Set Thirgabail, in British. Here Horsus (Horsa) was killed as was Catigirn, a son of Vortigern. Lastly a battle was fought 'near the stone on the shore of the Gallic Sea, where the Saxons being defeated, fled to their ships'. Later the 'Barbarians became firmly incorporated and were assisted by foreign pagans . . .' (Vatican manuscript) The last battle was probably at, or near, Richborough.

The *Anglo Saxon Chronicle* contains three battles under the years AD455, AD456 (AD457 in manuscript A) and AD465. The first was fought at Aegaeles Threp. This can be safely identified as Aylesford in Kent. It was obviously Nennius' battle of Set Thirgabail. At this battle Horsa died, and 'Hengest succeeded to the kingdom and Aesc his son' (manuscript A). Two alternatives exist as to the casualties at this battle. *Chronicle* manuscript A gives 4,000 British killed and *Chronicle* manuscript E, a more credible, four companies. The second battle was that of Crecganford (or Crayford). This seems to correspond with the second battle in Nennius' list. Crayford is on the confluence of the rivers Cray and Darent. The chronicler claimed that the British fled to London as a result of this battle. The third battle fought at Wippedsfleot probably corresponds to Guorthemer's last battle, on the shore of the Gallic Sea. The site may well have been near the Wantsum Channel. Whether this was on its northern outlet at Reculver or its southern, at Richborough, cannot be said with certainty. However, the reference to the Gallic Sea may point to the latter. It is of interest to note that the Old English word 'fleot' has 'the usual meaning — an estuary, a tidal stream, a creek or inlet, especially one on a tidal river'.[89] It can also mean a stream. The tidal element makes the Wantsum Channel a prime candidate for the site of this battle. The English account claims that twelve British nobles were killed here.

It is striking how the two accounts agree and clearly both preserve traditions of the campaign, as remembered by the English *and* the British. The major difference is the ordering of the battles. On consideration the English sequence is probably the most accurate. Its association of Hengest 'succeeding to the kingdom' and the battle of Aylesford is significant. It clearly implies a break with British authority and would characterise the first major English offensive (the *Chronicle* having omitted the inglorious siege of Thanet!). Moreover the order — Aylesford, Crayford — makes strategic sense. It would imply an attempt to encircle Rochester, followed by an advance on London along the Roman road. An advance halted at Crayford — the Roman Noviomagus — only ten miles short of London.[90]

The *Chronicle* account (as preserved in existing manuscripts) does not refer to any expulsion from England, although it records no battles between AD465 and AD473 which is suspicious! One manuscript of the *Historia Brittonum* states that Hengest was expelled for five years. A continental tradition recorded by Gerbrandus of Leiden (died 1504) claims that Hengest founded Leiden, on the Dutch coast. However, we are back on firmer ground when we say that the later *Chronicle* entries testify to a resurgence of English power in Kent. The entry for 473 reads: 'In this year Hengest and Aesc [Oisc] fought against the Welsh[91] and captured innumerable spoils and the Welsh fled from the English like fire.' (manuscript A)

The *Chronicle* (version F) makes the last line more explanatory by rendering it 'as one flies from fire'. The manuscript E of the *Chronicle* mangles the drama of it with a form that reads 'as fast as possible'. It is likely that the A version represents the most ancient form and was originally a line from a battle poem.

The *Historia Brittonum* source adds one last piece of information. It has a tale of how the British came to sign a peace treaty with the English and were treacherously murdered by the Saxons. In this British source the compiler of the story actually recorded the English words used by Hengest to signal the start of the massacre — 'Nimmath tha saxas'. The result was the loss of Essex, Sussex and Middlesex to the English. The intriguing aspect to the story is that it has a direct continental parallel. Widukind of Corvey wrote a similar account of actions by Saxons, who came from Britain to Cuxhaven in the first half of the sixth century. According to his story the immigrants treacherously slaughtered the notables of Thuringia, in a way reminiscent of the Kentish massacre. Perhaps the Saxon immigrants remembered something of what had happened in Kent, or perhaps they unknowingly imitated the tactic of Hengest.

Whatever the details of the revolt it opened the floodgates to a period of uncontrolled English settlement. With the exception of Saltburn on the North Yorkshire coast the revolt north of the Humber did not lead to a land seizure. Elsewhere the picture was very different. The pottery excavated, known as Buckelurnen Groups 1–4, may provide evidence as to the extent of the land seizure. This type, reminiscent of both the traditional Saxon and Angle homelands, probably represents the funerals of new immigrants into Britain. Its distribution may represent their expansion. The old areas of East and Middle Anglia, around the Wash, received a great influx of immigrants. The situation was similar on the upper Thames. New settlers spread into Warwickshire, Hertfordshire (Stevenage, Hertford) and the lower Thames valley. (Northfleet, Kent; Feering, Essex; Great Stambridge, Essex.) These new settlers were not committed to the old distribution, related as it was to Roman towns and roads. While old centres expanded (Cambridge, Caistor by Norwich, Heworth, Linford, Markshall, Mucking, Sancton, Thurmaston) many new ones sprang up with no relationship to the old Roman administration.

It is significant that within 30 years of Hengest's revolt the *Chronicle* records settlers in Sussex and Hampshire. The diocese of Britain was crumbling.

(C) THE BRITISH RECOVERY

There is evidence that the British succeeded in halting the English land seizure by a determined resistance. This did not involve an expulsion of the German mercenaries. What it did succeed in doing was to slow the English advance and reverse it in *some* places. This recovery has been linked to the names of two British leaders — Ambrosius and Arthur. The latter was a chieftain who led a heroic resistance around AD500 but later died in inter-Celtic conflict.

Gildas wrote:

> After a time, when the cruel plunderers had gone home, God gave strength to the survivors. Wretched people fled to them . . . their leader was Ambrosius Aurelianus, a gentleman who,

perhaps alone of the Romans had survived the shock of this notable storm: certainly his parents, who had worn the purple, were slain in it . . .under him our people regained their strength and challenged the victors to battle. The Lord assented and the battle went their way.

From then on victory went now to our countrymen, now to their enemies: so that in this people the Lord could make trial (as he tends to) of His latter day Israel to see whether it loves Him or not. This lasted right up till the year of the siege of Badon Hill. That was the year of my birth; as I know, one month of the forty-fourth year since then has already passed.[92]

Gildas did not mention Arthur (credited with the victory of Badon by Nennius and the Easter Annals) but he was aware of a British resurgence that has left marks on both literary and archaeological sources. The results of this recovery need to be assessed very carefully. Once they are considered, however, they are highly persuasive.

In the ninth century the ecclesiastic Rudolf of Fulda recorded a tradition that Saxons had landed at Hadeln, near Cuxhaven in the 530s. These Saxons had been then used by the Frankish King Theoderic who was at that time engaged in a war with the tribesmen of Thuringia. The oral tradition, referred to by Widukind of Corvey concerning a slaughter of Thuringian nobles by Saxons, can be demonstrated to have arisen from the same phenomenon of reverse migration to the continent. Ceramic material on the continent may also support this idea of a 'backwash'. Several types of characteristic English pottery (and cruciform brooches) have been discovered in the cemeteries of Mittelfranken and Wurtemburg in central and southern Germany. Some of the pottery dates from after AD550. Clearly these regions received infusions of newcomers who kept the style alive. Such newcomers preserved fashions that differed from the indigenous tribes of the area. The newcomers must have come direct from England and not been absorbed by their new neighbours. Other similar finds have been discovered at Remagen and at Wormsbollwerk. As the great expert on English pottery J. N. L. Myres has noted, this type of evidence (and the presence of stamped chevron pots at Wehden)

may reflect a backwash of Saxon folk to the continent in the generation that followed the successful British resistance to the invaders that culminated at Mons Badonicus (Badon Hill) between 490 and 516.[93]

Whatever the exact cause of the movement the phenomenon is intriguing. It is difficult to avoid the conclusion that its cause was a British resistance movement. The only other possibility is that the population reached an unacceptable density in those English areas on the east coast, from Kent to Yorkshire. However, this begs an obvious question. If the numbers were too high in these areas why was the excess population not removed by a fresh wave of colonisation in Britain? The obvious answer is that political and military conditions did not favour such a policy of an expanding frontier. It is possible that some of the great dykes that dominate the south-western approaches to East Anglia were actually dug by the English in order to mark a fixed frontier. Such an enterprise might have been prompted by the British resurgence in the early sixth century.

If we accept the idea that the English were forced to accept a postponement of further military adventures we might well ask if there is any evidence to support this contention in English literary sources. The *Anglo Saxon Chronicle* may provide some tentative clues to the perceptive reader. The Dark Age compiler of the *Chronicle* could find no tradition of Kentish activity from 473 to 568 except the accession of Oisc in 488. For Sussex the picture must have been bleaker. After campaigns in 477, 485 and 491 no king of Sussex was mentioned by the chronicler until Ethelwald, in 661. For Wessex the traditions that have survived are more confused. Battles that took place in 495, 501, 508, 514, 519, 527 and 530 were known to the chronicler. However, after 514 no battle led the chronicler to claim a victory for Cerdic, the ruler of the royal house of the Gewisse (as the West Saxon family was known). The exception being that of Wihtgarasburh on the Isle of Wight. This lack of military expansionism may be underlined by the fact that between 530 and 552 the folk tradition was so sparse that only the following accounts survived, to be recorded later:

534   Cerdic died. Cynric became king. Isle of Wight given to two men (Stuf, Wihtgar)
538   Eclipse of the sun on February 16
540   Eclipse of the sun on June 20
547   An entry about Northumberland

Even accepting the flexible chronology of these entries there is a fair degree of agreement between the English literary sources and the continental ceramic evidence. From *c*.500 the English advance was halted or slowed down and a backwash to the continent occurred. This is in accordance with much of the account in Gildas. Indeed, to be fair to him, he did not actually claim that Badon was the only, or the last, conflict between the British and the English. Therefore the minor battles on the Solent, mentioned by the chronicler, do not clash with the British account of events. We might also add that what seemed important to the English of south Hampshire might have appeared more as frontier incidents to the British authorities. A south coast version of 'Braves off the reservation'!

So far we have considered the viability of the idea of containment of the English; some areas of early English occupation, however, may have actually been evacuated in the early sixth century. If such an evacuation did take place it should be possible to find gaps in occupation and sequence in some settlements and cemeteries. For a start, this cannot be found in the great cremation cemeteries on the east coast. In the primary foci of English settlement a complete sequence of pottery fashions can be demonstrated as existing from the early fifth century (or earlier) right through to the mid seventh century. For gaps we need to look to the periphery of the English settlement. In Wiltshire a gap exists between the material left by the users of the early cemetery at Bassett Down and the later ones at Rodmead Down, Roundway, Purton and Alvediston.[94]

In Kent the dominance of the users of Jutish and Anglo Frisian pottery, and early cruciform brooches, ended in the early sixth century. In Sussex gaps occur between the users of the early cemeteries at Alfriston and High Down and the later users (later sixth century/early seventh century) of the cemeteries at Hassocks, Moulscombe, Pagham, Saddlescombe and Glynde. On the upper Thames there is evidence that, while the settlements survived, links with East Anglia and the Cambridge region were severed in the early sixth century. Developments in pottery that occurred in these latter areas were not reflected on the upper Thames or in Bedfordshire in a way that might be expected. It is also likely that English colonists left eastern Essex, Hertfordshire, east Suffolk and much of Buckinghamshire. In the region about Verulamium those that continued were tightly controlled and prevented from expanding.

On the lower Thames about London (in Surrey, north Kent and Middlesex) some settlements were not eclipsed. At Croydon,

Guildown, Ham, Mitcham, Shepperton and Walton Bridge continuity has been proven by study of the ceramic sequence. A similar pattern has emerged concerning the early-sixth-century settlements along the Warwickshire Avon at Baginton, Bidford and Stratford. Why these people were unaffected is not clear. They may have had some treaty relationship with their British neighbours. They may even have been in the employment of British authorities. It is impossible to tell. What is clear is that the English advance was halted for a generation.

Notes

1. See the work of Paul the Deacon (*c.* AD790), *Historia Langobardorum*, 4.22.

2. See the ecclesiastical *Life of Alcuin* (*c.* 820s).

3. See Asser's *Life of King Alfred*.

4. This title was used by Offa of Mercia as early as 774

5. E. Ekwall, *Concise Oxford English Dictionary of English Place Names* (Oxford, 1960), 4th edn, p. 167.

6. Despite the reticence of L. and J. Laing in *Anglo Saxon England* (London, 1979), p. 26.

7. Bede, *A History of the English Church and People*, 1.15. All subsequent quotes from Bede are from the translation by L. Sherley-Price in the Penguin Classics series (Harmondsworth, 1968), revised edn.

8. See Procopius, *The Gothic War*. For more information on Procopius and his ideas about Britain see E. A. Thompson, 'Procopius on Brittia and Britannia', *Classical Quarterly*, 30(1980), pp. 498–507.

9. Other sources describe these as Suevi, Swabians, Swaefe. In Roman times the name was not used consistently. Caesar used it of tribes near the Rhine, Tacitus of tribes in north and north west Germany.

10. Tacitus, *The Germania*, 38.

11. This group included the following: Semnones, Langobardi, Reudigni, Aviones, Anglii, Varini, Eudoses, Suardones, Nuithones and Hermunduri.

12. Tacitus, *Germania*, 38.

13. The tribal name may have been derived from the old Germanic word 'angul' or 'fish hook', a name inspired by the shape of the Jutland peninsular.

14. Prof. P. V. Glob, *The Bog People* (London, 1969), pp. 67–8 and photograph on p. 62.

15. Boelkilde, Hjortspring, Undelev.

16. Tacitus, *Germania*, 38.

17. Glob, *Bog People*, p. 117.

18. Tacitus *Germania*, 6.

19. Ibid., 7.

20. Ibid., 13.

21. Ibid., 14.

22. Other general names used among the Germans were 'Franks' ('spearmen'), 'Alemanni' ('men of all kinds'). For the origin of 'Saxon' see the *Shorter Oxford English Dictionary on Historical Principles* (Oxford, 1973), vol. 2.

23. Sidonius was a Gallo Roman aristocrat in the Auvergne. He was later city prefect of Rome and about 470 he became Bishop of Clermont.

24. Orosius was a theologian and a historian. He wrote a world history and also engaged in a debate with the heretic Pelagius in 415.

25. H. Schutz, *The Prehistory of Germanic Europe* (Yale, 1983) p. 316.

26. M. Alexander, *The Earliest English Poems* (Harmondsworth, 1977) 2nd edn, pp. 38–42. The majority of poems quoted in this study are from this excellent translation. Occasionally other translations are quoted (and this is noted) or my own arrangement used.

27. See R. H. Hodgkin, *History of the Anglo Saxons* (Oxford, 1952), vol. 1, for general comments.

28. Bede's comment that Angeln was left depopulated is supported by archaeological work. This has revealed that the major cemeteries went out of use towards the end of the fifth century. See J. Morris, *The Age of Arthur* (London, 1973), p. 106.

29. In Bede's work the name appears as 'Iutae'; in Old English it may have appeared as 'Iotas' or 'Eotas'.

30. R. G. Collingwood and J. N. L. Myres, *Roman Britain and the English Settlements* (Oxford, 1937) 2nd edn, p. 345.

31. Theudebert reigned c. 534–48.

32. D. J. V. Fisher, *The Anglo Saxon Age, c. 400–1042* (London, 1973), p. 26.

33. Sir Frank Stenton, *Anglo Saxon England* (Oxford, 1971), 3rd edn, p. 14.

34. Venantius Fortunatus, *Carmina*, 9 January 1973.

35. Procopius, *Gothic War*, 4.20.

36. See the entry for 'Jute' in the *Shorter Oxford English Dictionary on Historical Principles*, vol. 1.

37. Schutz, *Germanic Europe*, p. 315.

38. The Germanic troops in Kent preferred the title of 'Cantware' or 'dwellers in Kent'.

39. This interpretation would agree with Bede's basic account while allowing for a greater degree of complexity. More evidence in favour of Bede's general geography can be found in King Alfred's preface to a translation of Orosius in which Alfred wrote that the original homes of the English were on the islands off Jutland.

40. Collingwood and Myres, *Roman Britain*, p. 344.

41. J. M. Roberts, *The Pelican History of the World* (Harmondsworth, 1980), p. 287.

42. See the general account by F. Dvornik in *The Slavs in European History and Civilisation* (New York, 1962).

43. F. Dvornik, *The Slavs: Their Early History and Civilisation* (Boston, 1956), p. 33.

44. Ibid., p. 32.

45. This group later appeared in continental Saxon writings as the 'Obroditi'.

46. Morris, *Age of Arthur*, p. 279.

47. The units were designated as: 'alae' (cavalry) or 'cohortes' (infantry). A unit made up of ten centuries was called a 'milliary', one of six (the usual auxiliary number), a 'quingenaria'.

48. A 'cuneus' was a unit of irregular cavalry.

49. Sub-Type 'F' of Romano Saxon ware has also been found at Abingdon, Cambridge, Elkington, Heworth, Hoxne, Illington, Kettering, Loveden Hill, North Luffenham, Oxford, Thetford.

50. S. Johnson, *Late Roman Fortifications* (London, 1983), Chapter 8, examines coastal defences. See also S. Johnson, *Later Roman Britain* (London, 1980). This has maps of the channel defences in Britain and on the continent (map 13, p. 98; map 14, p. 106; map 16, p. 113) and maps of defences in west and northern Britain (map 15, p. 109).

51. J. N. L. Myres, *A Corpus of Anglo Saxon Pottery of the Pagan Period*

(Cambridge, 1977), vol. 1, p. 41.

52. S. Frere, *Britannia* (London, 1978), revised edn, p. 375; Johnson *Later Roman Britain*, pp. 176–7 and pp. 171–4. P. Salway in *Roman Britain* (Oxford, 1984), pp. 386–8, rejected the notion that German troops left evidence in the form of belt buckles. However, the pro-German case rests on much more than this.

53. Myres. *A Corpus of Anglo Saxon Pottery*, p. 125.

54. *The Mabinogion.* The translation quoted in this study is by J. Gantz in the Penguin Classics series (Harmondsworth, 1976).

55. J. N. L. Myres. *Anglo Saxon Pottery and the Settlement of England* (Oxford, 1969), map 3, opposite p. 44.

56. J. Wacher, *The Towns of Roman Britain* (Leicester, 1975), p. 276.

57. S. Frere, *Britannia* p. 422. He noted that fifth-century metalwork, glass, Irish Ogham script (sixth century?) and boundary ditches point to '. . .a stage of agreement or equilibrium between the invaders and the Britons. . .which may have extended into the sixth century'.

58. Wacher, *Towns of Roman Britain*, pp. 276–7. See also Johnson *Later Roman Britain*, map 17, p. 199, for an outline of the defences of Silchester.

59. I am grateful to the administrators of the Verulamium Museum, St. Albans, for allowing me to examine these sherds and for furnishing me with information regarding 'military' belt buckles recovered from the same site.

60. See the work by Dr K. Branigan, *Town and Country — Verulamium and the Roman Chilterns* (Buckingham, 1973).

61. J. Haslam, *Anglo Saxon Towns in Southern Britain* (Chichester, 1984), p. 55.

62. An excellent examination of most of these sources can be found in L. Alcock, *Arthur's Britain* (Harmondsworth, 1971), Chapter 2.

63. Quotations from Gildas are from *The Ruin of Britain and Other Works* (London, 1978), edited and translated by M. Winterbottom.

64. Bede *A History of the English Church*, 1.13. It is of interest to note that Agitius (probably the Roman general Aegidius) was not a consul but was military commander in Gaul 457–62. Aëtius was consul for the third time from 446.

65. In the chronological computations at the head of the annals Ambrosius is described as fighting a man named Vitolinus in the 430s. According to one tradition Vitolinus was the father of Vortigern.

66. Quotations from Geoffrey of Monmouth are from *The History of the Kings of Britain* (Harmondsworth, 1966) and translated by L. Thorpe as one of the Penguin Classics. This quote is from p. 159.

67. Quotations from the Welsh Triads are from *The Triads of Britain* (London, 1977), translated by W. Probert from the Welsh compilation of Iolo Morganwg. In this case from pp. 27–8.

68. Alcock, *Arthur's Britain*, p. 109.

69. Morris, *Age of Arthur*, thought that his personal name was Vitalinus and that 'Vortigern' was a title used by one man only. D. Dumville, 'Sub Roman Britain: History and Legend', *History*, 62 (1977), thought that Vortigern and the 'superbus tyranus' were one and the same man.

70. It should be noted that an association of Vortigern with St Germanus does not easily fit a date in the 450s when the 'proud tyrant', of Gildas, ruled.

71. P. H. Sawyer, *Roman Britain to Norman England* (London, 1978), p. 13. See also J. E. Turville Petre, 'Hengist and Horsa', *Saga Book of the Viking Society*, 14, part 4 (1956–7). On the continent similar work has been carried out by J. de Vries.

72. Collingwood and Myres, *Roman Britain*, p. 358, note 1.

73. Ekwall *Concise Oxford Dictionary*.

74. Ibid., p. 234.

75. Ibid., p. 241.

76. The majority of quotations from *Beowulf* are from M. Alexander's translation

(Harmondsworth, 1973) in the Penguin Classics series. Occasionally other translations are quoted or my own arrangements used. These quotes are from pp. 84–7 and
pp. 153–5.

77. *Beowulf*, lines 1090–4.

78. Dr B. A. E. Yorke, 'Joint Kingship in Kent, c. 560–785' *Archaeologia
Cantiana*, 99 (1983), pp. 1–19.

79. Myres *Anglo Saxon Pottery*, pp. 95–6 and map 7.

80. P. Salway, *Roman Britain*, pp. 476–7.

81. D. Hill, *An Atlas of Anglo Saxon England* (Oxford, 1981), p. 14.

82. Morris, *Age of Arthur*, p. 60.

83. Although the chronicler used the form 'Aesc' this author has followed Bede
and used the form 'Oisc'.

84. Collingwood and Myres, *Roman Britain*, p. 381. Morris, *Age of Arthur*, p. 113.

85. *Mabinogion* (Harmondsworth 1976), p. 114.

86. At least one scholar (J. Morris) implied this.

87. From the king list in the manuscript *Cotton MS Vespasian B6, fol. 108 foll.* of
the ninth century.

88. This reference can be found in the tenth-century *Liber Vitae of Hyde Abbey*.

89. Ekwall, *Concise Oxford Dictionary*, p. 182.

90. A. L. Rivet and C. Smith, *The Place Names of Roman Britain* (London, 1979),
p. 161.

91. The British were called the 'Welisc', an Old English word meaning 'foreigner'.

92. *The Ruin of Britain*, (London, 1978), pp. 27–8.

93. Myres *A Corpus of Anglo Saxon Pottery*, p. 52.

94. V. Evison, *The Fifth Century Invasions South of the Thames* (London, 1965),
p. 86.

2 ROMANS AND THE ENGLISH

For many years students of the so-called Dark Ages assumed that Romano British institutions vanished in the face of the Germanic invasions and land seizures. It was thought that the loss of the old social order was accompanied by the imposition of an entirely new pattern of settlement and land tenure. Where the new settlement pattern coincided with the old a ready explanation was to hand. Scholars assumed that this occurred because long deserted Roman sites were reoccupied in the middle or late Old English period. This reoccupation, it was thought, was due to similar needs for commercial centres in a trading economy. In other words, as an English market economy began to develop it looked to the same places that had assisted the growth and maintenance of the Roman economy. The resulting towns were therefore the product of coincidence rather than of continuity. This seemed to be a reasonable opinion based on the assumption that in Britain the break with the Roman past had been complete.

With regard to settlement patterns in rural areas a very similar hypothesis was worked out. Here it was assumed that the break-up of the old villa system led to the total decline of Roman administrative arrangements in the countryside. It was replaced by a different (and English) pattern of scattered nucleated villages. The fact that no villa could be shown to have had continuous occupation from Roman to English times clearly helped to reinforce this idea. The difference in rural settlement patterns was largely explained by the assumption that the invaders possessed a different farming technology to their predecessors. For a long time it was an 'article of faith' that the English possessed heavier ploughs and because of this were able to bring the heavier valley soils under cultivation. As a result of this idea it was thought that the ancient farming settlements on the chalk uplands (with their lighter soils) were replaced by a valleyward shift as a result of the English invasions. K. Feiling's opinion that a study of Britain, in the immediate post Roman period, would find that '. . .essentially ploughing methods and field tenures. . .are all new and by origin Teutonic' is an example of this generalisation. In his opinion this was part of a change which 'made an undoubted revolution' and involved the replacement of '. . .an old scheme of agriculture by a new'.[1] This 'undoubted revolution', it was thought, involved the clearance of woodland and virgin forest and the cultivation of valley land. This picture of dramatic change was made complete by the 'painting in' of British flight, or else slaughter, at the hands of the English. Such an impression of emigration or genocide was firmly rooted in the primary literary sources and only furthered the hypothesis of almost total discontinuity.

The picture of what happened at the dawn of English history has changed and is changing. Archaeological work, conducted since the Second World War, has altered our appreciation of the relationship between the English and the Romano British. Our concepts of how the newcomers interacted with the established towns and rural settlements have undergone something of an intellectual revolution. The 'Myth of Celtic survival' (or perhaps one should say 'non survival') has also been radically altered. As a result of this our outlook is now radically different to what it was 40 years ago. We now think differently about the fate of Roman culture; we now think differently about the fate of the British culture which (with its roots in the earlier Latin culture) replaced that of the imperial society before itself falling before the weight of English immigration and force of arms, over a number of generations. The new picture is not complete but it is emerging. Evidence has come to light which encourages us to doubt the generalised idea of total discontinuity. This does not mean, however, that continuity is now accepted in all cases. What it does mean is that current opinion stresses the possibility of continuity as opposed to the 'undoubted revolution' and discontinuity. This emerging picture is not without complexity or controversy. The English conquest of Britain was a piecemeal affair. It did not conform to some national tactical plan of operations,[2] neither was it achieved in one generation or even in one century, nor did the newcomers share a common social status or *modus operandi*. In some places they arrived as employees of the imperial system and were part of government policy with regard to policing; in other places they came as peasant ploughmen unfamiliar with Roman institutions; in yet others they came in the warband of a chief intent on carving out a kingdom for himself. For each the motive was different — regular pay and job security, land to farm, booty to share and a population to exploit. Uniformity should not be expected and certainly will not be found. Each group had a different social relationship with existing social structures and population. Each relationship matured and altered over time. It differed due to the standing of the immigrants and the developing state of British institutions after the end of Roman rule. It changed as the numbers of English men and women increased and as later immigrants found in Britain a little 'home from home' as opposed to a place of minority cultural and political status in an alien society. That which was true of the first Germanic auxiliaries on Hadrian's Wall was not true of the later treaty troops at Caistor by Norwich. That which was true of them was not true of Hengest and those who took part in the Germanic revolt of the mid fifth century. Lastly that which was true of the pioneering Hengest was not true of the well-rooted English monarchs of the sixth and seventh centuries. And at any time that which was true of an English aristocrat might not have been true of an English peasant ploughman and his family. Despite all of this a pattern is emerging. However, as we examine this pattern all that has just been considered should be kept at the back of our minds. The pattern may make more sense if we think of it in terms of English relationships with Roman urban life and then with Roman rural life. Later it will be necessary to consider how this relationship developed as the process of English conquest matured.

Continuity and Town Life

In an earlier chapter we accepted that the available evidence points to the likelihood of a Germanic military presence in this country from at least the fourth century AD. This acceptance must force us to remodel the old expectations regarding town life at the close of the Roman era. Large numbers of German troops must have been familiar with the functions and facilities of towns and cities. We have already considered examples of towns where Romano Saxon pottery and early English ceramic types suggest that some of the earliest English arrived as the result of late Roman government policy decisions. In addition to this it is now clear that many towns were fortified, or refortified, in the late fourth century. External towers were constructed, artillery was probably deployed on projecting bastions and ditches were deepened or altered. These 'improved' towns were able to defend themselves from a full-scale assault. These statements are not an attempt, however, to imply that they had to withstand some vast siege, with hordes of English at their gates! What they do imply is that such towns need not have been sacked by sporadic English raids. They could have withstood the fairly casual attacks of robber bands. Such towns may have been garrisoned by a local militia force, by troops of the regular army or by Germanic mercenaries. What is clear is that by the fifth century many towns were capable of defending themselves and many performed this task with the aid of English troops. The evidence does not seem to support the strong views expressed by Malcolm Todd who considered that '. . .the use of barbarian settlers as urban garrisons is so unlikely as to be absurd'.[3] Whilst he was describing the situation, as he saw it, before 410 there are persuasive reasons for thinking that German troops *were* deployed by both late Roman and post Roman authorities.

The presence of urban garrisons has left impressions on the archaeological evidence. At the Kent site of Canterbury sunken huts of the fifth century were built along the line of a Roman street (albeit set back some 10 m from it); at Dorchester on Thames there is good reason for thinking that military units may have used the timber-framed buildings and sunken feature huts discovered there and the inhabitants of these buildings may have been the same as those who used the early English cemetery just outside the walls; at the Hampshire site of Winchester the Lankhills cemetery indicates a high degree of fusion between the native population and the defending English troops; the relationship was much less intimate at Caistor by Norwich and Colchester but even at these places the military settlement was clearly created with regard to the towns. To these examples may be added those discussed earlier in this study.

When the major revolt came in the 450s, or 460s, it is tempting to ask what may have happened to these towns? Despite the economic decay, which they must have suffered, they may still have been important administrative centres within their regions. It is not too improbable to wonder whether

> With the collapse and the decay of urban life and institutions, political authority seems to have passed naturally into the hands of those who exercised military power and were no longer paid to wield it in the interests of their employers.[4]

Such a process would have facilitated the growth of English settlements from the remnants of Roman towns. It is a fairly logical assumption and one for which there is a mounting pile of evidence.

This evidence needs to be examined.

At York the Roman fortress continued to be occupied into late Old English times and an English royal residence may have been sited here in the late sixth century. The survival of the city would help explain why it became an episcopal centre in the 620s. The example of Canterbury has already been discussed but it should also be noted that the first Christian missionaries found that the Roman church was still in use in the 590s and that the English kings of Kent used the city as a royal centre. Similar evidence has been unearthed in London. Here there is reason to believe that an English royal residence was erected in the Roman fort at Cripplegate. The siting of later English administrative centres and courts in Roman administrative areas is worthy of note. At Winchester a later palace probably occupied the site of the Roman basilica (an administrative building) and at Gloucester a similar palace — at Kingsholm — was placed within the old legionary fortress of Glevum. The area was also used for a fifth-century burial. The *Anglo Saxon Chronicle* account assumes that this city was 'captured' by the English in the 570s (by Ceawlin, king of the West Saxons, after the battle of Dyrham in 577). However, in reality, there may well have been an English presence in the decaying city since the fifth century.

None of the evidence suggests the unhampered growth of towns in the period of the English migrations. At some sites (for example, the Roman city of Viroconium or Wroxeter (Shropshire) and that at Verulamium) the centre of settlement shifted to another site. At other sites (for example, the city of Calleva, or Silchester) the political fluctuations of the fifth and sixth centuries finally ended its existence as a going concern. Nevertheless at a number of places (for example, Bath, Canterbury, Cirencester, Gloucester, Lincoln, Verulamium) there is literary evidence that the occupation did not end due to the end of Roman rule and the troubled times. This is likely to be true of many other towns and cities. However, the continued occupation must have been on a considerably reduced scale. The loss of large parts of the Roman street plan at Canterbury, London and Winchester points to the decay of land holdings within these centres. Similarly although Roman walls continued to dictate the city boundaries at Chester, Chichester, Colchester, Exeter, Gloucester, Lincoln, Rochester and York for generations, this does not mean that the internal ordering of these towns survived from the Roman period. Nevertheless the evidence does suggest that in a large number of places occupation was continuous, or if broken then re-established at a very early date. This of course begs an obvious question — if a market economy collapsed what manner of occupation could have existed at such centres? This is a fair question and the answer must surely be that it must have been in one, or more, of the following forms:

1. The occupation may have been a very limited one and based on a site associated with traditional authority and administration. This would fit those examples where Roman government buildings were used by the newcomers. In these cases the new rulers may have used the old sites in order to give their rule an aura of respectability and legitimacy. Like a certain Gothic chieftain they might have stated that 'I hope to go down in posterity as the restorer of Rome since it is not possible that I should be its supplanter.' It was this type of mentality that caused Odovacer (the Germanic commander who deposed the last official emperor of the western empire — Romulus Augustulus — in 476) to accept the authority of the eastern Roman emperor and accept the high imperial title of 'patrician'. It is interesting to note that many of those who worked the revolution that ended the Roman empire were themselves highly conservative. They believed in authority and tribute and the benefits of organised rule but they wanted 'a piece of the action' for themselves! The type of occupation that this would have entailed may have been no more than that of a ruler and his family and his warband.

2. The occupation of a site might have been assisted by the continued use of a Christian church or shrine. This is difficult to prove categorically but some experts believe that this might have been the case concerning some of the churches at Canterbury (St Martins and possibly Christchurch), London (St Brides, St Martin in the fields, St Andrews, Holborn) and York (St Mary, Bishophill Junior). Other Roman sites became English episcopal centres. These include Dorchester .on Thames, Felixstowe (Kent), Rochester, Winchester and Worcester. To this list should also be added those examples already mentioned — Canterbury, London, York and Leicester. Each of these cities achieved episcopal status by the 680s at the latest. Six of them achieved it by as early as the 630s. This may hint at some degree of continuity in the sanctity of sites from the Roman to the English periods.

3. There is a strong possibility that towns may have suffered

serious decay *before* the coming of the English in force. The classic period of Roman town life may have ended as early as the third century AD. If this view is correct (and it is a controversial one) then it may lead us to assume that towns had declined in their importance before the fifth century and the end of Roman rule. This would leave us with

> . . . a period dominated by the villa and the village, estate, parish and village from about 250–750 and then the emergence of England proper. Instead of asserting that all our changes were made by hyperactive Saxon settlers in between 450 and 550 . . .[5]

This implies that towns did not go through a severe change of character in the migration period, but had already achieved some degree of role stabilisation. The role which they had assumed was probably that of administrative centres for rural estates. They had in all probability become 'enlarged administrative villages', rather than urban centres with all the trade and manufacturing specialisation, and population density inherent in the definition of a 'large town'. This may have been particularly true of the minor towns with their close links with the agricultural communities. However, even larger towns (whose economic base had declined) may have become more self sufficient and have taken to administering the surrounding estates from within the transformed urban community (enlarged administrative village). The 'urban villa' (once considered by many scholars a contradiction in terms) has now become increasingly recognised and may have been an essential unit in the functioning of the reduced urban role from the fourth century onwards. Nothing makes better sense than rich landlords retiring to the relative security of the local towns and running their estates from there. Indeed the concept of the 'urban villa' and the enlarged administrative village goes far beyond the picture of a mere absentee landlord. These concepts offer a radically different alternative. They envisage an ex-urban community that fully integrated itself into the rural economy. Far from merely exploiting its rural hinterland it became part and parcel of the administration of that hinterland. It exchanged the role of market for that of market *and* estate managing centre. From being an economic superstructure raised over a rural substructure it settled into and became substantially absorbed by its base. Archaeological work in the future may find more evidence of late Roman towns actually performing some of the functions of a farmstead writ large. At Gatcombe, near Bath, a fortified farming centre has been discovered covering some 6.5 hectares. It was surrounded by walls which were 4.5 m thick. When first recognised it was thought to be a small town. It was built sometime in the third or fourth centuries AD. It may represent the next stage on in the process that produced the enlarged administrative village. The settlement at Gatcombe had evolved away from the functions of a town whilst preserving a degree of defence unknown in the case of any other villa in this country (such examples, however, are far from rare on the continent). Other 'Gatcombes' may await discovery but we already have ample evidence from conventional towns: Barton Farm was a prosperous fourth-century farmhouse situated *inside* the walls of Roman Corinium (Cirencester); suburban villas were constructed directly adjacent to the Roman town of Magnis (Kenchester, in Hereford and Worcestershire); at Verulamium a corn drying oven was constructed inside the town in the fifth century; many towns, even before their transformation, may have owned large areas of land beyond their walls and let it out to tenants. It is likely that all of these examples illustrate stages in the transformation of town functions in late Roman Britain. The Germanic tribesmen who first encountered towns in the fourth or fifth centuries would have met centres that possessed a *raison d'être* that could survive the end of Roman rule and the eclipse of British authority in the period after 450. They would *not* have entered centres whose functions were redundant or about to become so. A town that had such a viable role in 410 might have kept it until 600 or later. Despite periodic contractions it would have achieved a *modus vivendi* that could survive in the face of adversity.

It is clear that not all settlements survived to become English towns. Despite this the three major factors, that have just been outlined, would help to explain some of the key mechanisms at work which could have assisted continuity. In some towns all three factors may have been at work, at others two or perhaps only one. What these arguments do show, however, is that there are now both practical and theoretical reasons for doubting the old verdict on continuity as applied to town life at least. Dr Reece, who has advanced the radical theory regarding the early date for urban decline, has not accepted the idea of German mercenaries as a major fact of life in the fourth century. However, in the advance from his work (as proposed by this author) it is thought highly likely that English troops did take part in the defence and eventual control of these towns. Such towns would have been the obvious places to deploy troops intended to guard the surrounding estates. Indeed given the mood of social unrest in other parts of the empire from the fourth century onwards (for example, the discontented peasants, or 'bacaudae', in Gaul) it would have been a wise move for villa owners and estate managers to employ military detachments in order to protect their investments from peasant rebellions as well as from raids by Picts, Scots and English pirates.

Having examined the evidence it does not seem too unjustifiable to assume that in a number of cases walled towns (and even some unwalled settlements) experienced either continuity of occupation or at most a minimum of dislocation and occupational discontinuity. Variations in the pattern may have been due to the degree of importance of various towns within the Roman administrative framework. Their inherent functions may have dictated their continuity or discontinuity more than the effects of barbarian land seizures.[6]

Continuity and Rural Life

The line of the argument, adopted above, points to the question of continuity in rural areas. This rural, agricultural base was the persistent substructure that gave rise to the development and continuation of towns both in their classical sense (as market centres, foci of local political and fiscal administration, centres of economic diversification) and in the more radical sense (as rural administrative centres appended to the villa estates). The fate of the countryside is crucial to any understanding of the relationship between the conquerors and the conquered.

The question of what is actually meant by continuity must be clarified. It could be considered as one, or more, of the following:

1. Continued use of a Roman villa building.
2. Continued use of the field system of a villa.

3. Continued use of previously cultivated land (regardless of the previous field pattern).
4. Continued use of the settlements of villa employees and attendant labourers, tenants and peasant farmers.
5. Continued use of the estate boundaries of a villa estate.

Faced with this whole issue it could be immediately objected that all such possibilities are spurious given the different agricultural techniques employed by the new Teutonic farmers. To this assertion it can now be argued that it is very doubtful whether the newcomers did in fact possess superior methods or equipment. At Chalton Down (Hampshire) an English village flourished in the sixth and seventh centuries. It was sited on a spot which, according to the old theory, should have been reserved for a British village. Archaeological work has shown that its five hectare site was surrounded by so-called 'Celtic fields' normally associated with non-English settlements and farming technology. The example of Chalton Down has caused a number of experts to consider whether other English sites await discovery on the chalk downland of southern England. It has also prompted the thought that many villages in valleys (traditionally classed as 'typically English') were the result of settlement shifts in a later period of English history and were not a product of the migration period. The earlier villages in many cases may have been on the chalk uplands in a number of areas. To this may be added the evidence that suggests a valleyward shift in the late Roman times.[7] This would mean that even when English villages were founded in the fifth and sixth centuries they may have superseded earlier Romano British ones. In short, the theory of an advanced technology has begun to crumble. In addition the so-called 'three field system' that has long been associated with the early English is now thought to be the product of later developments. This system was once quoted to show the difference between Romano British and English farming methods. This idea was based on the work of an older generation of historians at the end of the nineteenth century (for example, Meitzen) and in the early twentieth century (for example, H. L. Gray). This theory is now no longer held with any degree of confidence. As a result of all this new work, much less is now known about the agricultural practices of the early English than was once thought. This is both frustrating and at the same time liberating. It frees the student of the period from the old stereotypes but does not furnish him or her with enough material to produce a new model. This is perhaps a little too negative. There is sufficient material available to suggest that the English immigrants were, in most cases, drawn towards already cultivated land. Not enough is yet known to create watertight stereotypes. This may be because these were not valid at any time. The available evidence now deserves to be considered in some detail.

Despite all that has been written so far there is no conclusive evidence that any villa passed intact into English hands. This is not to say that they were unfamiliar with the villa way of life. A number of villas have produced material that can only have been used by Germanic immigrants. At Greetwell villa, in Lincolnshire, a small plain biconical pot may have been deposited there by an immigrant from eastern Holstein, or the Baltic island of Fyn, around AD350.[8] In Oxfordshire, at Shakenoak villa, pottery of Saxon type has been found from the same context as late Roman pottery. At Orton Hall Farm, near Peterborough, sites 'H' and 'L' on the dig produced early English material from a Romano British site.[9] At Latimer villa two buildings were erected on the edge of the villa courtyard (one was possibly used as a granary). The construction of one is reminiscent of cruck-built types found on the continent at Wijster and in Westphalia. At Rivenhall villa a barn was converted, in the fifth century, into an English hall. This later site seems to demonstrate peaceful continuity, at least in terms of the outbuildings of the villa.[10] More contentious evidence is provided by the so-called 'military belt buckles' found in the villas at Barnsley, Chedworth, Clipshall, Holbury, Icklingham, Lullingstone, Popham, North Wraxall, Spoonley Wood and West Dean. These have traditionally been identified as belonging to Germanic troops employed to guard the villas. Much of the work on these buckles has been associated with the name of Sonia Chadwick Hawkes who conducted research on them in the 1960s. These buckles have also been recovered from 14 Roman towns. More recently, however, the emphasis, regarding these specific items, has shifted. Similar buckles have been discovered in purely Roman sites along the rivers Danube and Rhine. These examples were probably produced at imperial ordnance works in the period 340–80. This has caused a number of experts to revise their earlier appreciation of these buckles as indicating Germanic populations. However, despite this, similar buckles have been found in clearly English situations at Long Wittenham, Mucking and Reading.[11] These may indicate that at least *some* of these 'chip carved' buckles were worn by English troops. These examples illustrate something of a juxtaposition of Teutonic and British cultures but there is no proof that in any of these examples it gave rise to the continued use of a villa. Although some Cotswolds properties may have had lifespans that stretched into the sixth century none of them appears to have survived beyond this. If continuity is measured by the survival of a villa then the picture is not an encouraging one. Having said this it should be admitted that merely superimposing one site upon another does not necessarily show continuity. Indeed if the remains of successive villages, or settlements, are not on the same site this may point towards continuity of a kind. It might mean that both sites were in use together. In fact some forms of continuity mitigate against a building being taken on as a dwelling by newcomers. The use of villa buildings for burials, as at Shakenoak and the Lincoln-shire villa of Denton, show physical juxtapositioning but not the use of a building for its original purpose. In both these cases the buildings were used as some kind of memorial. A similar burial took place in a deserted Roman bath house at Furfooz in Belgium.[12] Architectural 'fossils', used in this way, hardly constitute the kind of continuity of occupation that we are looking for.

Many explanations have been offered as to why the English did not take over villas and use them as farm houses. Although a fear of ghosts may have played a part it is much more likely that the villa buildings were simply not suited to English culture or tastes. Their size and layout were not Teutonic and without the kind of infras-tructure present in their heyday probably became very unattractive in a short period of time. Plaster would have peeled, roof slates would have fallen and in winter the buildings stood large and cold without their hypercaust systems to centrally heat them. Their abandonment was no doubt as much due to this as to changes in systems of land tenure etc.[13] The place of residence was surely much less important than the land itself. Continuity might have occurred around a villa without being part of the whole villa system or involving the use of the villa itself:

> The continuation of rural life based on the villas is something rather different from the continuation of the villa system, if by this we mean the whole economic framework of which the villa formed a part.[14]

The decline of the villa residences must have been accelerated by the probable transfer of their role to the towns and villages and the removal of their owners or managers. Even when occupation continued for a while it was not of a kind that arrested the process of physical decay. At Tarrant Hinton villa the wood ash remains of fires were found on the floors of two rooms and in a corridor. At Keynsham villa, between Bristol and Bath, 4–6 cm of dirt was allowed to build up over the floors and a hearth was constructed with reused Pennant Stone tiles, over an ornate tessellated pavement. Whilst some villas fell to violent attack the majority simply succumbed to wind and rain and fell down. At Spoonley Wood villa, near Cheltenham, this author found that the floors of the ruined building are still strewn with the roofing tiles, deposited there when the roof collapsed. In some instances squatters inhabited the ruins of villas. These may have been lower class ex-workers on the estates or the impoverished descendants of the original owners, or managers, of the estates. We lack the necessary evidence to say more about these squatters. It may be romantic to picture '. . .an Anglian warband cooking in an abandoned villa'[15] but in most cases we lack the material evidence which is needed to make such a precise identification.

Whether or not the incoming English used the existing Romano British field systems is difficult to say. It is not helped by a number of factors. There is still no general agreement, for example, as to the exact nature of the layout of fields in the fifth century (prior to the English migrations). Just how the so-called 'Celtic fields' related to the 'Roman long fields' is not always clear.[16] In addition to this, many of the Roman field systems, which have been studied, are on marginal land. Now, early English fields are likely to underlie land which has been ploughed for the past one thousand years. Such intensive cultivation may have destroyed evidence concerning previous layouts of fields. Therefore, if English fields, of the period under study, were placed over earlier fields it is probable that the clues have been irretrievably lost. This means that of the first two definitions of rural continuity (listed above) neither has so far provided us with solid proof. However, before the matter of field systems is left there is one point worth raising which, whilst relevant to the discussion regarding field layout, is pertinent to much of the discussion relating to Roman buildings and later occupants. The loss of material evidence, noted already, may not be confined to the area of fields. It is possible that excavation techniques traditionally used to uncover Roman sites (for example, 'box digging' and 'exploratory trenches') may have destroyed the much shallower remains of flimsy wooden buildings of Teutonic type. Philip Barker, Staff Tutor in Archaeology at the University of Birmingham, has written that

> Excavations may be misleading in that, either by taking too small a sample of the site in boxes or trenches, or by digging too intensively, especially in the upper levels, whole periods of the site's occupation have been lost, ignored or distorted.[17]

Traces of wooden buildings may only appear by means of a more careful removal of whole layers of soil, combined with the recording of finds in their respective layers. This will give a clearer picture of the chronology of site occupation. Clearly this whole problem is central to the discussion of site continuity in the post Roman period. It may mean that sites that did experience continuity have not been recorded as such. This negative evidence, however, cannot be quantified and in consequence cannot be used to prove a point one way or the other. It should though be remembered when the proponents of discontinuity quote these sites as corroborative evidence.

The researcher and student of the period is on much firmer ground when considering whether English farmers used previously cultivated land — regardless of its field layout. It is highly possible that Romano British farms were worked until they and their surrounding area passed into English hands. Even if the land was abandoned it would have taken a long period of time to turn into wasteland. Firstly it would have reverted to rough grassland. Then the grassland would have developed into thickening scrub. The colonisation of this scrubland by Oak, Ash, Birch, Hazel and Hawthorn would have eventually converted the area into light woodland. This whole process might take a total of 50 years. By the time that mature trees had become established the loss of light would have led to the dying back of bushy vegetation and the drying out of the ground. At all of these stages it would have been easier to reclaim this old cultivated land than to tackle the primary forests with their stands of Oak, Alder, Elm and Lime. Romano British farmland, even if abandoned, must have appeared attractive to the early settlers and their families. To this it can be added that the siting of villas on the best land would have made them prime sites for continued cultivation. Whilst many later Old English villages were sited in different places to those used in Roman times this is not so true of many early ones. A number may illustrate a close relationship to older sites (for example, the communities at Barnsley Park, Mucking, Shakenoak, West Stow and Winchester). Suffice it to say that any shrewd English farmer would have seen the benefits of taking over already cultivated land and turning it to his own use.[18]

If the English did take over villa land they may have established control over the British villages that once served the villa estates. We now know that the countryside of Roman Britain was one in which there were many nucleated villages. The old orthodoxy that it was made up of villas, farmsteads and hamlets only, has been exploded for some 20 years now.[19] Many of these villages were probably made up of tenants of the local villa. Other villagers may have been free farmers, detached from the villa system. Yet others may have leased land from a local town. The size of this latter group must have been increased as towns took on more of the economic functions of the villa. In these cases the first and third forms of land tenure would have been combined. (Some villages may have been occupied by agricultural labourers tied to the local villa estate.) Many of these villagers farmed the gravel terraces and their villages have been studied in the southern fenlands of East Anglia, in Somerset and along the river gravels of the upper Thames.[20] Although the villas declined there is increasing evidence that suggests that these villages did not. They have left evidence of their continued existence in the form of handmade 'grass tempered pottery'. This type of pot was produced in the fifth and sixth centuries and was a domestic response to the collapse of the large-scale Roman pottery industry. Grass tempered pottery has been discovered in the villa fields of Barnsley Park villa. This may indicate that a subservient native settlement, situated on the edge of the arable fields, survived the decay of the villa. There is no reason to suppose that it did not continue into the 570s when the region passed into the control of Ceawlin, king of the West Saxons. Other potsherds, of this type, have been discovered at Kingscote, Uley and at Cirencester. At Frocester villa sherds were found within the villa building and over 100 sherds were discovered in the courtyard. At Spoonley Wood villa the villa fields have so far produced only mica impregnated sherds of coarse grey, wheel-thrown, Romano British pottery.[21] Whilst this may have been used into the fifth century it was not found in datable contexts. In this, as in other examples, the evidence may be yet awaiting discovery.[22] These examples indicate continued use of the villa fields by British farmers, particularly in the region around Cirencester. However, the continued use of estates and villages should not be thought of as unique to the Cotswolds. There is no reason to make such an assumption.

The nucleated village has often been quoted as a typical English type. The line of argument pursued so far may indicate that this is an over-simplified view of its origins. The pattern that has come to be identified as Teutonic may, in reality, have been superimposed on an older and well-established set-up. This is particularly likely given the assumption that the land farmed by the occupiers of such villages would have been very attractive to the Germanic newcomers. It is also relevant that a number of 'English' villages occur where Roman roads cross rivers (Bourton on the Water (Gloucestershire) is an example of this as is the village of Bidford on Avon[23] in Warwickshire). A number of these were built over Romano British villages. These villages were probably not deserted when the English arrived. This pattern of 'English ford villages' being based on an earlier pattern may be more widespread than was once thought. The transfer of authority in an area may have been more important than a transfer of the actual farming community. In many areas the fifth and sixth centuries may merely have seen an alteration of the land-owning class. Those who worked on the land may have remained fairly immobile. Over time their language and culture would have been submerged under the rising tide of English colonisation. Many English villages sited close to old Roman villas may originally have been Celtic in racial composition. Such a peasantry would have passed from the hands of one landlord to another. As Lewis Carroll remarked in *Alice Through the Looking Glass*, 'The question is "who is to be the master?" that's all.'

The possibility that English nobles took over the role of British landlords raises the question of whether entire estates passed into Germanic hands.[24] This happened in a number of well-documented cases on the continent, despite the decay of the local villa.[25] Some historians have suggested that specialised Roman legal terms can be seen to underlie later English land charters and that some of these later documents describe Roman concepts of land tenure. A Roman framework for later land holdings has been suggested for areas as far removed as western Yorkshire and East Anglia. It is possible that when English kings confirmed charters or made land grants (such as that of King Ethelred (675–704) to the nunnery at Withington in Gloucestershire) they were referring to estates of Roman origin. This point has been raised by a number of distinguished experts such as Professor W. G. Hoskins who claimed that the stereotype differences between British and English estates may fail in reality.[26] The point has been pushed further by the claim that Brixworth, Great Dodington, Latimer, Longeville, Orton and Rivenhall villas show a degree of estate/area continuity. At Maxey villa the continuity may have been more short-lived.[27] On the basis of this premiss it is possible to construct a series of models which describe possible relationships between a 'new' English village and a Roman villa. These models have then been applied to reality in such a way as to suggest that such relationships are not only hypothetical but can be demonstrated in the field.[28] However, the more cautious scholar might add that even if such relationships did exist the models cannot prove that modern parish boundaries overlie old villa estate boundaries. Therefore whilst the 'estate continuity models' seem to be supported by evidence, regarding parish boundaries, at Barnsley, Bramdean (Hampshire) and Chart Sutton (Surrey), even this does not prove the point categorically. Despite these slight reservations the recent research in this field has produced significant results.

The theory of estate transference is an attractive one. It offers a coherent explanation as to why many later English estate boundaries followed the courses that they did. It appears to offer an area in which hypothetical models can be applied directly to real situations. This in itself has made it attractive to a new generation of historians who have benefited from practices used in the social sciences. Having said all of this the crunch comes when very recent research has seemed to undermine the validity of this approach as applied to this particular area. In a statistical survey of pagan English burial sites and their relationship to parish boundaries, Ann Goodier was forced to conclude that 'It is unlikely that pre existing land units dictated the boundaries of Anglo Saxon estates . . .' In her survey Goodier found a 'lack of correlation of boundaries and fifth century burials but of sixth and especially seventh century dead buried on boundaries of land units.'[29] The present author confirmed something of this thesis in research at the pagan English cemetery at Castle Acre in Norfolk in 1985. Here sherds of grooved cremation urn pottery could be noted in the ploughshare right up against the boundary hedge of Castle Acre parish. According to Goodier's thesis such cremations were probably of sixth-century date and this may be confirmed with regard to some pieces from the Castle Acre site, although others from this cemetery were clearly from the fifth century.

These ideas seem flatly to contradict the work of experts such as D. J. Bonney who suggested that parishes in the vicinity of the east Wansdyke were based on ones earlier than, or contemporary with, that earthwork.[30] This led P. J. Fowler to assert that 'The Wansdyke evidence is crucial, and whatever the date of that earthwork . . . it crossed an area already divided up into economically viable land units, best envisaged as Roman estates.'[31] As a result of Goodier's work it is now difficult to accept the Wansdyke evidence as being generally applicable. It is possible that it and some of the other examples cited were and are atypical. Some may even be illusionary. This does not rule out continuity of settlement but it does raise severe problems concerning the general acceptance that Roman estate boundaries survived into the sixth and seventh centuries. As with so many other areas of this study, proposals have been met by counter proposals and the simple has become more complex. With careful thought, however, it is possible to reconcile something of the two positions. This can be done by assuming that in the period AD450–600 estate boundaries were in a state of flux. According to this assumption English boundaries could have been based on British ones that had themselves developed from Roman ones and were still developing in the fifth and sixth centuries. This may be a tenable position if two premises are accepted: the first is the assumption that landholdings, even in Roman times, were not unitary. They were liable to division or consolidation over time. Alteration could have been built into the system in a large number of areas. Secondly, the period from 350 onwards saw considerable developments in the life of the rural community. This may have led to an increasing fluidity in the layout of land and in estate boundaries. With the loss of the more centralised control provided by a local villa (able to keep a close eye on immediate farming practices) such processes of change may well have been accelerated. This explanation would help explain why sixth- and seventh-century English burials were placed on estate boundaries and fifth-century ones were not. By the sixth century the new (English) aristocrats may have arrested the tendency of peasant farmers to redistribute land. In the fifth century the English would have only been a minority in many areas and lacked the political authority to control local land arrangements or peasant private enterprise. This would have meant that these primary immigrants and settlers lived (and were buried) in an extremely fluid rural situation. This would explain why their burials (often at the edge of land units) when excavated do not seem to square with modern boundaries that in reality sprang from sixth- and seventh-century antecedents. The evidence for the Wansdyke would then not be a problem. Assuming a date for its construction in the late sixth or early seventh centuries (a contention discussed in a later chapter) it would have been built when flexible rural boundaries were becoming less plastic. In this way it may have crossed estate boundaries that were British but had themselves experienced a degree of evolution from Roman originals. The question of whether peasant communities are likely to have assisted in the redistribution of land is a well-attested one. The researcher need only refer to large-scale land redistribution in Russia in 1917 or, more appropriately, in the prefecture of Gaul towards the end of the Roman administration.

The evidence has been examined and the least that can be said is that the case for overall discontinuity is no longer a viable one. New evidence suggests that it is an inadequate explanation of events. However, it would be wrong to put another simplistic conclusion in its place. The clues point towards continuity in a number of areas although as we have seen, some are more persuasive than others. It is likely that German troops guarded at least some villas. It is also clear that such troops were used in the towns. Compatibility of agricultural techniques meant that the early English were able to establish their communities close to Romano British settlements. Government policy, both in the late Roman and post Roman periods, assisted in this juxtapositioning. Following the revolts of the mid-fifth century, English villages were still probably sited with reference to the position of well-cultivated land and British villages once dependent on the now defunct villa system. In many areas this simply involved a change of landlords, in other places the land may have been temporarily abandoned. As this process continued into the sixth century the apparent relationship with the old Roman system became much less distinct. The orientation towards Roman administrative foci was swamped by new immigrants who sought out land on their own terms. However, this very land constituted the strongest link with the Roman past. Its use mitigates against an assumption of too sharp a break between the new and the old culture.

In conclusion the picture that emerges is quite a complex one. It has and had great regional differences. It differed from the south, with its relatively dense English population, to the north, where the English must have constituted a tiny minority for many generations. Although even here the old subjugation of the rural population to the army in the military zone, south of Hadrian's Wall, must have made them particularly susceptible to the control exercised by the new English military aristocracy that established itself by the end of the sixth century in Northumberland. Overall though it is reasonable to assume a fair degree of contact between conquered and conquerors. It is neither necessary nor prudent to assume that the arrival of the English worked a revolution on the landscape and practices of rural Britain.

If Roman institutions did not vanish in a maelstrom of barbarian attacks it is only to be expected that something of the old society may have survived in the form of place names. This should be differentiated from the Celtic contribution to English place names. This will be dealt with later and is a different type of evidence. The presence of Celtic place name elements in English place names demonstrates a British presence in English territory. This is vitally important but it does not prove contact between the English and the earlier Latin culture. By the time that the Old British, or Early Welsh, place name elements were adopted by the newcomers the former Roman culture had passed away in most respects. The Celtic elements came later on the chronological scale than the Latin ones and at a time when Roman civilisation was fractured, decayed and no longer relevant in its own right.[32] What is at issue at this juncture is whether this civilisation was still, to some degree, vibrant into the mid- to late-fifth century and whether it had an impact on the coining of English place names.

A number of scholars have rejected the likelihood of any real contact between the English and Latin speakers. According to this school of thought it was mostly the non-Latin speakers' pronunciations of river and place names that survived to give rise to names based on Welsh forms but found outside of Wales. Due to this it has been argued that only five Latin place names survived into the English period. They were Cataracta which became Catterick; Calcaria which became the Kaelcacaestir mentioned by Bede (Book 4, Chapter 23); Spinae which became Speen in Berkshire; the element 'colonia' that survived in the place names of Colchester and Lincoln. Indeed it has been proved that the English name of

London is derived not from the Roman Londinium but from the Old British form Londonion. Despite the strengths of these arguments there *is* evidence to suggest that the situation may not have been so clear cut in reality. In some areas Latin may have enjoyed a short-lived influence on some of the Germanic immigrants. This is particularly likely if, as we have concluded, such people were in this country before the beginning of the fifth century.

A striking example of what is meant by this is provided by the place name element 'wic'. It is derived from the Latin word 'vicus' which may have been a reference to Roman farmsteads or units of local administration. It was adopted by the English and over time gained a number of meanings. It came to mean 'dwelling place' or 'quarters'. In some areas it came to mean 'dairy farm' and in other places 'quarters around a saltworks'.[33] The meaning of 'quarter of a town' is not unknown either. Its use was extended to cover 'hamlet' or 'village' and when combined with the English word 'ham' (as Wicham, Wickham, etc.) it may have meant 'village near a wic or vicus'. This mass of possible definitions may support A. H. Smith's comment that, taken over time, 'its exact meaning is obscure'.[34] Of all these uses the one which concerns this study is that of 'wicham'. There is reason to think that this was the earliest English use of the element. The reason for this assumption is that there is now a lot of evidence which suggests that 'ham' was used in the earliest period of English settlement following the migration from the continent. This period of settlement followed hard on the initial immigration phase. In these cases of the use of wic it may have arisen because early English agriculturalists were familiar with the remnants of Roman agriculture and speech. Only this would help explain why they took Roman farms as points of reference when coining names for their communities. It suggests geographical juxtapositioning when both were functioning. A number of these places were manors when the Domesday Book was compiled in 1086: Wickham, near Welford (Berkshire), Wickham Hall near Farnham (Essex), Wycomb near Scalford (Leicestershire), Wykeham near Nettleton (Lincolnshire), Wykham near Banbury (Oxfordshire). This may be an indication of their antiquity as centres of old land units and offers mute testimony in favour of what has been suggested so far in this section.[35] In fact of all the major examples of this place name, three-quarters were sited within one mile of a Roman road and half were close to Roman agricultural sites[36] or small towns.[37]

More contentious is the matter of the origins of those place names

called Eccles or the like. It is not known precisely when this place
name element entered the English vocabulary. Its meaning is
'church' and it was originally derived from the Latin word 'ecclesia'.
This probably gave rise to the Old British word 'ecles', the Primitive
Welsh 'egles', the Old Welsh 'eccluys' and finally the Welsh word
'eglwys'. It is likely that the word was loaned to the English from the
Old British or Primitive Welsh (which were themselves derived
from the Latin). For this reason this word will be cited later as an
example not of Latin survival but of the survival of native Celtic/
British culture. However, it is possible that some of the examples of
Eccles to be found in the south east of England may have been
borrowed from Latin speakers. Eccles near Attleborough
(Norfolk), Eccles near Hickling (Norfolk) and Eccles near
Rochester (Kent) may have their origins in the period before
AD500.The Kentish example is situated one mile from the course of
a Roman road and in the Darenth Medway region where there is a
high rate of survival of Roman place names. This may indicate that
a Latin enclave survived in this area, despite an expanding English
population, from the mid fifth century onwards. It has even been
speculated (by M. Henig in his study of religious practices in Roman
Britain) that Eccles (Kent) may have been the site of a villa
church.[38] These churches may have been recognised by the first
English troops and their positions preserved in place names.

What was true of the Eccles places may have also been true of
those places that preserve use of the element 'camp'. It can be found
in a number of examples including: Addiscombe (in the Greater
London area), Balcombe (Kent), Barcombe (Sussex), Campsey
(Suffolk), Epscombe (Hertfordshire), Hanscombe (Bedfordshire),
Maplescombe (Kent), Ruscombe (Berkshire), Sacombe (Hertfordshire), Shudy Camps (Cambridgeshire) and Swanscombe (Kent),
etc.[39] The word was borrowed from the Latin 'campus' or 'field'.
This borrowing seems to have been confined to speakers of Old
English, Old Frisian and Old Low German. In west Hanover the
word came to mean: 'A large area of arable land in the
neighbourhood of the farm house'.[40] In Old English (where over
time it has been confused with the word 'combe' or 'narrow valley')
it had the more general meaning of an 'enclosed piece of land of any
kind' (arable, pasture or woodland). The place name specialist
Margaret Gelling, explored the possibility that it might have had the
rather more specific meaning of uncultivated land around a town or
villa which, when broken in by English farmers, assumed the more

general meaning of 'enclosure'.[41] Such land on the outskirts of towns, or on the edges of villa estates, may have constituted the kind of land given to the earliest English rural military *émigrés* in return for military service. Three of the examples cited — Addiscombe, Campsey and Shudy Camps — are close to place names derived from a wicham original. The confinement of the use of this element to the south-eastern part of England may be further proof that it was borrowed by the earliest English troops deployed alongside Latin speakers. This dating framework is the most persuasive one as the element fell into disuse at an early period.[42] This observation by A. H. Smith in the 1950s fits in well with what has been considered so far. As Roman institutions decayed, so did the use of the word camp. Picked up by the early German settlers it soon fossilised and was no longer used as a 'living' name-forming word.

In addition to the major examples quoted above there are ones that may repay consideration. They include the uses of the elements 'funta', 'port', 'corte', 'faefer' and 'croh'. Funta was probably borrowed from the Primitive Welsh 'funton' which was itself derived from the Latin word 'fontana'.[43] In this case it is not an example of a loan word direct from the Latin. By the time that it was adopted as an English word for 'a spring', Latin had given way to Old British or Primitive Welsh. The writers of the *Introduction to the Survey of English Place Names* went as far as insisting that it could '. . .hardly be a loan direct from Latin'. This conclusion was later followed by the place name specialist Eilert Ekwall.[44] Nevertheless the distribution of this place name *is* highly suggestive. Of some 15 examples the geographical distribution is limited to southern counties from Essex to Warwickshire and especially in Hampshire and Wiltshire. This may suggest that its earliest use was in those areas with the most pronounced Latin culture. In these areas it is quite possible that English and Latin speakers lived side by side in the early fifth century. It is phonetically possible that the word could have been borrowed direct from the Latin.[45] The use of the word may then have arisen from those places where Romano British farmers had channelled or organised water resources. This was probably the case as the English had their own word for a spring — 'wiella'. The adoption of another word would only make sense if that other word signified something subtly different. It is revealing that in a number of places (for example, Bedfont, in the old county of Middlesex, etc.) the word funta was combined with the Old English word 'byden', meaning 'a vessel', 'a tub', 'a butt'. This may indicate that funta, in these contexts, meant a Roman water trough or irrigation channel. These may still have been functioning when the word passed on to English lips.

Having looked at the example of funta it now remains to examine briefly the remaining possibilities. The word 'port' was often used in the Old English period to mean 'a harbour'. This is because it ultimately derived from the Latin word 'portus' or 'harbour'. This word underlay the name 'Portus Adurni', the name of the Saxon Shore fort which the English came to call Porteceaster or Portchester (Hampshire). There is reason to suppose that some coastal sites were known by this name in Roman times. English coastal travellers would then have borrowed these names from Latin speech. Examples may include Portishead (Avon), Portland (Dorset), Portlemouth (Devon), Portsmouth (Hampshire) and Portslade (Sussex). Should future research reveal Roman harbour installations, or a harbour settlement, at these places it will be corroborative evidence for the ideas discussed so far.

The uncertainty over the port place names extends to that which contains the word 'cort(e)'. Found in the case of Dovercourt (Essex) it had the meaning of 'a short plot of ground, a piece of land cut off'[46] and may have been related to the Latin word for 'an enclosed yard'.[47] The word 'faefer', found in Faversham (Kent), may have been a loan word from the Latin for 'metal working centre'. It is interesting to note that Faversham was the English centre of such work in the late pagan period (late sixth/early seventh centuries). The area was noted for its production of the so-called 'Kentish disc brooches'. The element 'croh' in Croydon, in south London, may be an example of a loan word from the Latin for the Autumnal Crocus flower. English mercenaries definitely operated in the Croydon area and may have picked up this word before it faded in favour of the more common name Saffron.

The place name examples that have been offered for consideration are a mixed bunch. Some are rather speculative whilst others (wicham, camp, and possibly those derived from eccles) are more solid and form firmer evidence. It is difficult to ignore, however, the conclusions to which they point. Taken all round — the weaker evidence with the stronger — they offer supportive evidence to what has been advanced earlier in this chapter on the basis of archaeological discoveries. This simply reinforces the necessity of adopting a multi-disciplinary approach to historical research.

Having accepted the premiss that English and Latin cultures

experienced a degree of mixing it now remains to see what evidence there is for the survival of a British population in English areas once the conquest was relatively complete. This takes us beyond the initial stage of English settlement and on to a time when the colonisation process was maturing. It takes us on into a period when, for the native population, the Latin culture and Roman ways had declined in favour of a native Celtic/British culture. Such a culture obviously developed and survived in Wales where it was the heir of the earlier way of life. It is just possible that some compilations of Welsh documents may show that Roman land units were still in vogue in south-eastern Wales as late as the 550s and perhaps even later![48] A similar culture survived in Cornwall and parts of the north of England for a long period of time. None of this is surprising. These were areas where the English conquest either never really took place or was long delayed. In these areas a Celtic culture was free to evolve. A more intriguing question is whether such a survival occurred in those areas that became England?

The Myth of Celtic Survival

Both British and English propagandists have left us with a very negative picture of English treatment of the native population. The 'fire and the sword' images of the surviving literature might make us despair of finding any Celtic survival in English territory. This has become one of the dominant myths to come out of this period of history. It is in essence a 'culture myth'. Used in this way the word myth does not mean 'lie' or 'untruth'. The words are not synonymous. Rather, the word myth means 'an understanding of the cultural past'. It is a vehicle by which opinions can be expressed and the significance of events portrayed. It has much in common with the word legend. Both contain a kernel of reality overlain with impressions and elaborations. Many of them constructed long after the events that they purport to describe. Such myths do explain something genuine in the social order. However, much more importantly they present the social order as we perceive it or would like to see it. Culture myths interpret prevailing ideas about society. Consequently, if a culture myth is not the same as a lie it is not the same as the truth either!

Curiously enough both British and English writers subscribed to a very similar mythology regarding the treatment of the native British by their new masters. For those who have read the words of Gildas the picture seems to be one of unrelieved gloom. Gildas contrasted the ordered legitimacy of imperial rule with the British tyrants who competed for power in the sixth century. Gildas used the word 'tyrants' precisely. In his opinion their origins and actions lacked legitimacy. In a similar way he contrasted the peace of Roman times with the lot of those British people who fell into the hands of the German barbarians. He wrote how '. . .they were fated to be slaves for ever. . .' Others were forced to hide in '. . .the high hills, steep, menacing and fortified'. The towns were left '. . .deserted, in ruins and unkempt'.[49] According to Gildas many of those who could not escape were slaughtered. Reading his work it is easy to get an impression of largely depopulated Britain. To be fair to Gildas clearly there was a kernel of truth to his account. Many Britons did flee abroad. *Great* Britain is called this to differentiate it from Little Britain or Brittany. Many Britons must have fled to Wales, Cumbria or the Dumnonian peninsular of Devon and Cornwall. However, much more than this motivated Gildas as he wrote. He believed that God was punishing the Romano British for their sins. To him they were a Dark Age Israel scattered for their iniquities. He went so far as to describe the chaos caused by the fifth-century English revolt as 'just punishment for the crimes. . .' of the British. His second concern was to portray the English as depraved as was possible. Gildas often reserved semi-zoological terms for them. They were 'wolves', a 'pack of cubs', 'dogs', a 'virulent plant'.[50] From these standpoints he carefully constructed a picture of systematic genocide and flight. It was the foundation for the British culture myth concerning Celtic survival.

The English interpretation of events led to similar conclusions. According to the *Anglo Saxon Chronicle* entry for 473, the Welsh 'fled from the English as from fire'! Other traditions tell how the South Saxon king Aelle slaughtered all the occupants of the Roman fort of Anderida in Sussex. This is the language of flight or extermination. West Saxon sources offer a similar viewpoint. In the entry for 530 the *Chronicle* account describes the campaign of the West Saxon ruler Cynric on the Isle of Wight. It is likely that by the 530s the island was largely depopulated. Much of the Hampshire mainland had been occupied by the warbands of the royal house of the West Saxons (the Gewisse). This must have prompted those who lived on the island to flee to the British-held territories in Dorset, to the west of the great forest of Selwood. This is surely the explanation behind the original English account of the campaign. The chronicler was at pains to record that Cynric '. . . ofslogan fea men' ('. . . slew a few men'). The event was recorded in *Aethel-weard's Chronicle* with the words 'paucos Brittanos' ('few Britons'). This was not enough for the makers of the English myth. Later the word 'fea' ('few'), in the text, was altered to read 'feala' ('many'). Only a substantial massacre was fitting for a noble son of the West Saxon royal house. It is a revealing, if shocking, glimpse into an entire mentality. It is consistent with the themes of Old English heroic poetry. A man's virtue was measured by his martial capabilities. Martial capabilities were measured by slaughter. It had a grim logic all of its own. Extermination was not a matter over which the English myth makers fought shy. In this way the classic picture of the English conquest was born. It was history from the stylised viewpoint of the warrior aristocrat. It was not so much colonisation as 'fire and the sword'. With the conversion from paganism this heroic theme was overlain by another one. This second theme had echoes of Gildas about it and strands of it can still be found woven into Bede's account of English history. This second theme was that the English were agents of God's anger on the British. It could almost have been written by Gildas! Bede compared Ethelfrith, the genocidal English king of Bernicia and Northumbria, with Saul the Old Testament king of Israel. After the battle of Chester (607), where the British of Wales were destroyed, Bede concluded that the English had 'made a great slaughter of the faithless Britons' who by divine fiat had suffered 'the punishment of temporal destruction'. It was an interpretation which Gildas would have approved of. With it the two mythologies can be seen to join. From both British and English sources the Myth of Celtic Survival (or rather non-survival) was complete. The literary sources combined against objective reporting. As a wise man once wrote — truth is the first casualty of warfare.

Until comparatively recently historians had a large measure of faith in these dominant mythologies. The fire and the sword imagery of English poetry and of Gildas had won many converts. It went hand in hand with the received orthodoxy concerning the total change wrought by the English on the landscape of Britain. In 1926 G. M. Trevelyan in his *History of England* wrote of English warriors: '. . . storming the earthwork camps and stone girt cities, burning the towns and villas, slaughtering and driving away the Romanized Britons . . .' These warriors were accompanied by others '. . . of the agricultural population to take up new homes in the ground so roughly cleared'.

Works such as those of J. Beddoe (*The Races of Britain*, 1885), W. Z. Ripley (*Races of Europe*, 1899) and H. J. Fleure (*Races of England and Wales*, 1923) attempted to show the absence of Celtic survivors by reference to the appearance of nigrescence in the British population. Such racial studies only served to buttress the ideas of a generation of scholars here represented by Trevelyan. These ideas were encouraged by the striking paucity of archaeological evidence for the survival of a British culture in English areas. Whilst this is still a serious problem other evidence has emerged which challenges the dominant myths. Although it is true that only some 20 words have survived from British into English there is other evidence which suggests a fairly high survival rate for the Celtic population, albeit under English masters.

The study of Old English personal names has proved to be very revealing. Cerdic, founder of the dynasty of the West Saxons bore a British name. It implies that dynastic unions were possible with British families. It is not a unique piece of evidence. The name of Caedwalla (a later king of Wessex) was of British origin. He had a brother called Mul. That is 'mule', or the half-breed. Caedbaed, an English king of the kingdom of Lindsey, bore a British name. Other English nobles had part of their name formed from the element 'walh' or 'wealh'. This was the English word which eventually gave rise to the modern national proper name 'Welsh' and 'Wales'. It meant 'foreigner' and eventually 'serf' or 'slave'. An interesting example of the use of the word in its earliest form can be found in the earliest English poem *Widsith* where the phrase 'Rome Welsh' (line 69) was used as a description of imperial citizens. The word also occurs in the more familiar guise of Walnut. This means 'foreign nut'! Amazingly this word was used as a name by a number of English royal persons! Cenwealh, a seventh-century king of Wessex bore an example of such a name as did Ethelwealh a king of Sussex. A particularly noteworthy use of it was made by a seventh-century English dynasty in the west Midlands. Here one of the members was named Merewalh. He was an English king, of probable Angle stock, but his name meant 'famous Welshman'! Other Englishmen are known from charters and genealogies who carried such names as Wealhheard, Wealhhere and Wealhhun. A number of place names contain it in its genitive singular and imply the use of it in men's names. Some place names witness to the use of otherwise unrecorded hypocoristic (pet name) forms such as W(e)alca and W(e)alaca. All of this presupposes a great deal of cultural mixing between the two communities. It does not agree with the images of flight or extermination. It makes one wonder if these images are as outworn and discredited as the practice of measuring so-called racial stereotypes by reference to the incidence of nigrescence in a modern population.

There are a number of reasons why it is now less than fashionable to accept the idea of an English 'Final Solution'. Since we have already started to look at place name evidence it is in this area that the enquiry begins. Place names that purport to demonstrate Celtic survival can be divided into three classes:

Class 1: Those place names that contain a racial description which indicates Celtic inhabitants at that place.

Class 2: Those place names formed from an element which is ultimately Celtic in origin.

Class 3: Those place names that demonstrate Celtic linguistic survival to a late date in an otherwise English area.

Class 1

The first class of names includes those place names that contain 'Walh', 'Cumbra' or 'Brettas'. We have already examined the use of Walh. When used in its genitive singular it usually represents a personal name. Otherwise its use means quite simply 'the Welsh'. There is some debate as to whether its use in place names should be regarded as indicative of a village of Welshmen or a village of serfs.[51] Even if only some of these names were coined as a reference to Welshmen it is still revealing.[52] However, current opinion is now coming down on the side of those who have assumed that the usual Dark Age meaning was 'Welshmen' rather than 'serf'.[53] The other problem with this particular element lies in correctly identifying it in a place name. All too often it can be confused with other Old English words such as 'wald' ('wood land'), 'wall' ('wall') or 'walu' ('ridge of earth or stone'). A Middle English spelling with 'Wale-' is usually needed in order to confirm it as a proper name. The second proper name of interest is that of Cumbra. Unlike Walh this has no ambiguity about it. It was an English borrowing from the proper name used by the British themselves. It may have come into use as a politer way of addressing British people when the form Walh was becoming associated with servitude.[54] This of itself would indicate a desire to conduct relations with the British in a fairly diplomatic way. The third form — Brettas — is more commonly found in the north of England. It has often been accepted as a Viking word which described people of Celtic origin who migrated with them into Cumberland, Derbyshire, Lancashire and Yorkshire. If this was the case then these examples are not relevant to this discussion. There is the long shot that these names, however, represent British communities who survived as distinct entities into the Viking period.[55] Listed below are fairly comprehensive lists of the main examples of the place names in Class 1.

Walh/Wealh (plural, Walas/Wealas)[56]

Kings Walden (Hertfordshire)
Saffron Walden (Essex)
Saint Paul's Walden
   (Hertfordshire)
Walbrook (Middlesex)
Walburn (North Yorkshire)
Walcot, or Wawcott (Berkshire)
Walcot (Lincolnshire)
Walcot (Lincolnshire)
Walcot (Lincolnshire)
Walcot (Northamptonshire)
Walcot (Oxfordshire)
Walcot (Shropshire)
Walcot (Shropshire)
Walcot (Warwickshire)
Walcot (Wiltshire)
Walcot Lodge (Northampton-
   shire)
Walcote (Leicestershire)
Walcott (Hereford/
   Worcestershire)
Walcott (Norfolk)
Walden (North Yorkshire)
Wales (South Yorkshire)
Waleswood (South Yorkshire)
Walford (Hereford/
   Worcestershire)
Wallabrook (Devon)
Walla, or Western Wella

Brook (Devon)
Wallasey (Cheshire)
Wallington (Berkshire)
Wallington (Surrey)
Walmer (Kent)
Walpole (Suffolk)
Walsall (Staffordshire)
Walsham le Willows (Suffolk)
Walsham North (Norfolk)
Walsham South (Norfolk)
Walsworth (Gloucestershire)
Walton (Derbyshire)
Walton (Kent)
Walton Ulnes (Lancashire)
Walton (Suffolk)
Walton (Staffordshire)
Walton (Sussex)
Walton (West Yorkshire)
Walton (West Yorkshire)
Walton Hall (Lancashire)
Walton Inferior (Cheshire)
Walton le Dale (Lancashire)
Walton on Naze (Essex)
Walton on Thames (Surrey)
Walton on the Hill (Lancashire)
Walton on the Wolds (Leicester-
   shire)
Walton Superior (Cheshire)
Walton upon Trent (Derbyshire)

Walworth (Durham)
Walworth (Surrey)

Extinct examples of this form:

Walfords (Essex)[57]
Walterhall (Essex)[58]
Weala Brucge (Berkshire)[59]
Wealas Huthe (Surrey)[60]
Waledich (Wiltshire)[61]

Cumbra

Comberbach (Cheshire)
Comberford (Staffordshire)
Combermere (Cheshire)
Combermere (Cheshire)
Comberton (Cambridgeshire)
Comberton (Hereford/
  Worcestershire)

Comberwood (Gloucestershire)
Cumberland (regional and
  county name)
Cumberworth (Lincolnshire)
Cummersdale (Cumberland)

Brettas

Birkby (Cumberland)
Birkby (Cumberland)
Birkby (Lancashire)
Birkby (North Yorkshire)
Bretargh Holt (Lancashire)
Bretby (Derbyshire)

An extinct example of this form:

Brettegate (once in the city of
  York)

Class 2

The second class of names is made up of those place names that have preserved a Welsh or Old British element. These show the survival of the native language after the English conquest. Indeed although we have seen that Latin speech, and its influence, cannot be ignored, it must be admitted that it was Celtic speech (Old British, Primitive Welsh) which transmitted its traditions regarding place names in the majority of cases. It is only fair to add that many of these are topographical names, describing natural features. These seem to be the most conservative type of place name.

   To help the researcher some examples of the Class 2 names are given below. This list would not claim to be anything like exhaustive.

Bre. A Welsh/Cornish word meaning a hill. It was probably derived from the British word 'briga' or the late British word 'brega'. It can be found in a number of place names including Bredon (Hereford/ Worcestershire) and Clumber (Nottinghamshire), etc.

Brocc. This is probably from the British word 'brocco' or 'badger' and has survived in the country name for this animal (Brock the badger). It is not easy to separate it from the Old English word 'brocc' or 'broc' from which we get the modern English word 'brook'. It may have been this similarity that caused the early colonists to use the word, as it resembled one in their own language.

Combe. This element has its roots in the Welsh word 'cwm' which probably developed from the Old British word 'Kumba', meaning a 'deep valley'. As it was similar to the Old English word 'cumb' — 'basin', 'bowl', it was easily accepted by the early English as it was similar both in sound and meaning.

Eccles. This element has already been discussed with regard to the survival of Latin speech. However, the most likely origin of most names containing eccles is in the Primitive Welsh language. Unfortunately the element can also be confused with other — English — words. It can be confused with the words 'aclaes' or 'oak pasture' and with a hypothetical English personal name 'Eccel' (or 'Ecel'). However, where 'church' was the original meaning this offers proof of the survival of Celtic institutions into the English period. The following is a fairly comprehensive list of place names containing eccles.

Ecchinswell (Hampshire)
Eccles (Kent)
Eccles (Lancashire)
Eccles (Norfolk)
Eccles (Norfolk)
Ecclesbourne, river (Derbyshire)
Ecclesbourneglen, river (Sussex)
Ecclesfield (South Yorkshire)
Eccleshall (Staffordshire)
Eccleshall (Warwickshire)
Eccleshill (Lancashire)
Eccleshouse (Derbyshire)
Eccleshouse (Derbyshire)
Eccleston (Cheshire)
Eccleston (Lancashire)
Eccleston (Lancashire)

Eccleston, Great (Lancashire)
Eccleston, Little (Lancashire)
Eccleswall (Hereford/Worcester-shire)
Exhall (Warwickshire)
Exhall (Warwickshire)

Extinct examples of this form of name:

Ecclesbroc, river (Hereford/Worcestershire)[62]
Eclesbroc, river (Kent)[63]
Ecelesburna, river (Hampshire)[64]
Ecelesbeorh (Berkshire)[65]
Eclesbroc, river (Surrey)[66]
Eclescumb (Somerset)[67]

Penn. From the Old Welsh 'penn' and the probable Old British 'penno', this had the meaning of 'a height, a hill'[68] Some examples seem to indicate a very early borrowing of this element from the Old British language. Examples of this can be found in Kent, Surrey and Sussex.

Pill. From the Old Welsh word for 'a tidal creek' this element has survived in the names Huntspill (Somerset), Pylle (Somerset) and Walpole (Norfolk).

Other topographical names that have preserved Celtic elements are rivers and stream names. These become progressively more Celtic the further one goes towards the west of England[69] The clear inference from this is that as the English moved westwards they must have met more and more Celtic speakers. As a result of this even the names of relatively minor rivers and streams were preserved. The names of larger rivers survived even in those areas of the earliest English settlement. This was clearly because they were key landmarks. The largest of them (for example, the Thames and Severn) must have been known throughout the northern parts of Europe. These then are less significant. The real importance lies in the increasing intensity of Celtic names mentioned earlier and outlined in the 1950s by K. Jackson in the influential book *Language and History in Early Britain* (and noted above). It is an interesting fact that the Celtic river name survival rating for the eastern part of Yorkshire and Humberside is strikingly low. This may represent the presence of foederati in this area at an early period with an attendant disruption of the native way of life. Perhaps the most famous Celtic river name to survive nationally was that of the ubiquitous 'Avon'. Rooted in the Celtic word for 'river' it may actually have been a river name in its own right. In areas that remained Celtic (for example, Wales) it developed into the modern Welsh word 'afon'.

Class 3

This last class of names highlights the linguistic survival of pockets of the Old British language into a comparatively late period. This can be proved from these names because they demonstrate that Primitive Welsh was being spoken in these areas due to the nature of the words used and the fact that they reveal linguistic developments that can be dated with a fair degree of certainty. This means that in these places Old British freely developed into Primitive Welsh. An example of this type is Pensax (Hereford/Worcestershire). It means 'hill of the Saxons'. Not only does it illustrate a time when the English were a minority in the area but it also follows the grammatical form — noun first — which was characteristic of Welsh speech from the sixth century onwards. Similar linguistic considerations suggest that Welsh language speakers were at Lichfield (Staffordshire) until the 670s and at Hints (Staffordshire) until at least the second half of the sixth century. This latter example despite the presence of English villages along the Warwickshire Avon, at Baginton, Bidford and Stratford from at least AD500. As a matter of interest there are a number of other examples which, like that of Pensax, indicate an English minority in a Celtic area. One is that of Nansawsen in Cornwall. Others such as Pennersax and Glensaxon are in Southern Scotland. These three examples, however, probably date from the seventh or eighth centuries and do not possess the linguistic significance of Pensax.

These names serve to illustrate something of the clues that have survived the passage of time. As one looks through the ancient sources other examples of survival also come to mind. The regional names of the English kingdoms, or administrative units, of Bernicia, Craven, Deira, Kent, Kesteven, Leeds and Lindsey were all derived from Celtic forms. Berkshire may be another example with possible origins in a British forest name — 'Bearruc'. With regard to those from north of the river Humber the reason for this is clear. For many generations the English in this area were a ruling minority in a largely Celtic population. It is hardly surprising therefore that so many Celtic names were adopted. Such actions may be assumed to have arisen from shrewd English *realpolitik*. It belongs in the same category as the use of the name Merewalh in Shropshire. In both cases a gesture was made to a largely alien population by a small ruling class of military aristocrats.

Having taken all of this evidence into consideration there are still far fewer surviving Celtic place names than might be expected. If the case for Celtic survival were based on place name evidence alone then it would be a less than comprehensive one. Even the place names which contain a racial description may imply that those so described were a minority in the area and stood out as such. In consequence we *must* look elsewhere for other, supportive, evidence. However, before the field of place name study is left there is one consideration that should not be ignored even if it is somewhat avant-garde.

It is possible that some English place names contain unrecognised

Celtic, or even Latin, elements. This could have happened if garbled British words became assimilated to phonetically similar English adjectives, nouns, personal names and verbs. In short any English place name forming element may conceal a Celtic one or even a Roman one. There is some evidence to support this idea. In the example of York the Romano British name 'Eboracum' became associated with the Old English word for a boar — 'eofor'. Because of this Eboracum became Eoforwic and then Iorvik under Scandanavian influence in the Viking period. From this it eventually developed into York. Had no pre-English form been recorded then a purely English origin might now be ascribed to York. A similar process may have taken place in the formation of the place name Gloucester. Here the Romano British form 'Glevum' became Gloucester through an association with the Old English word 'gleaw' or 'wise', 'prudent'. At Salisbury in Wiltshire a similar process occurred. Bede recounted how the town of Rochester gained its name from the personal name of an English chieftain — 'Hrof'.[70] However, it is much more likely that the name was derived from the Romano British 'Durobrivis' and that Bede's etymology is a red herring. It seems that for some reason this Roman name became associated with the English word for 'roof' (or 'hrof'). These well-documented examples should give any researcher pause for thought. It may be that the process outlined in these cases was a much more widespread one than anyone has hitherto realised. This would serve to undermine much of the basis of place name study as for many place names no records of forms exist from before the early Middle Ages. By this time any Romano British name (except in the case of large or important centres) would have been lost. Etymologies based on these early and 'reliable' forms may be actually almost worthless. It is true that they will be faithful representations of English place name forming elements. However, these elements may simply have been used because they sounded like an original Latin or British one. In other words these etymologies will not represent the true name, or antiquity, of the example in question. It is not intended that this verdict should be levelled at all English place names but it must be asked — how is it possible to tell whether or not this scenario applies to a place name under discussion? If the scenario is correct then it would help explain the large number of otherwise unrecorded personal names that are quoted in order to explain the roots of many English place names. Many of these are claimed as side forms, derivations of known names or pet names based on known names. These abound in studies of English place names and in well regarded etymological dictionaries in order to explain the origins of a large number of place names. Many of them are undoubtedly genuine. Others, however, may represent an incomplete assimilation of a Latin or British original to a known English personal name.

The present author developed these ideas whilst preparing a paper on the place names of east Dorset for the publication of the Poole Museum Society.[71] Although Dorset cannot have been colonised until well into the seventh century and must have preserved a fairly vibrant Celtic society, only some 1 per cent of the place names in the county are of proven Celtic origin according to the orthodox methods of etymological research. It was suspicion about the low nature of this figure that led to the hypothesis outlined above. The ideas that have been elucidated above would help to reconcile low ratings such as these with the evidence that is being slowly uncovered by other disciplines. It is at this point that these other clues should be introduced and examined. The linguistic evidence is important but other corroboratory evidence can also be produced despite the ravages that time has worked on all forms of the evidence.

As the English expanded north and west in the sixth century there is every likelihood that they greatly increased their Celtic subjects. In both Wessex and Northumberland the orbits of English power were extended by military victories that smashed or crippled the infrastructures of Celtic government but surely not of the under-lying society. Whilst such victories opened up huge tracts of land to the invaders it took a number of generations before they could fully occupy these areas. On the frontiers of such English states there was the added danger of Celtic resurgence backed by still independent Celtic kingdoms. The sheer size of the new areas coupled with the threat and the reality of Celtic revanchism must raise real questions about how meaningful the English 'occupations' were in the first two or three generations. In these areas — far from the foci of primary settlement — English 'occupation' may have been nothing more than claimed authority for a long period of time. In short, if the English settlement in the east rested upon a fairly abundant Teutonic population that of the extreme north and west rested on the power politics of kings and force of arms. The lack of their compatriots would have made it both necessary and desirable to use native labour to support the wealth and comfort that was the desire of a king and his comitatus. Exploitation lay at the heart of German warrior society. In the absence of large numbers of their own kind (albeit of a lower class) to rule and exploit, the Celtic population offered a large pool of experienced (if unwilling) cultivators. To be blunt, an English aristocrat was not prepared by his socialisation and outlook to get his hands dirty in ploughing because he had been so unfortunate as to end up in a frontier area with a dirth of English peasants and so short-sighted as to have massacred the alternative labour market. The obviousness of this desire for slaves led M. M. Postan (in *The Medieval Economy and Society*, Chapter 1, 'Roman Heritage') to assume that

> On these purely a priori grounds we cannot take it for granted that the Anglo Saxon conquerors were so perversely destructive and so indifferent to purely economic considerations as to expel or to exterminate the Romano British manpower throughout the 150 years of their military progress towards the west.

This has come to be the growing opinion of scholars in the 1970s and 1980s and there is no reason to think that it will alter as we look into the twenty-first century of the Christian era.

In areas such as those outlined above a real cultural interaction could have taken place and there is good evidence for believing that it did. Nowhere is this more apparent than in the field of Hiberno Saxon art. This art form was the result of combined English and Irish influences. It implies that enough native Celtic influence survived in order to act as a communication medium between the English and Celtic culture abroad. There are a number of items that illustrate this phenomenon. The *Book of Durrow* was probably written in the second half of the seventh century. It was probably written in Northumberland although its art work has close parallels with Irish styles. Although it is English its six decorative 'carpet pages' contain themes reminiscent of Celtic art. An even better example of this artistic synthesis is provided by the *Durham Gospel Fragment A.II.10*. This incomplete fragment of an illuminated manuscript dates from the middle of the seventh century. It exhibits the spiral form of decoration so characteristic of La Tene Celtic art. This form of decoration can clearly be seen in the spiral knots executed in blue, red and yellow on the colophon at the end of Mark's Gospel. In the example from this Gospel the spirals take the form of trumpet shapes. This spiraliform ornament was a central

theme in Hiberno Saxon art. It can be found on the carpet pages of
the *Lindisfarne Gospels* (written *c*. 690) and in the *Lichfield
Gospels*. The last example — also called the *St Chad Gospels* — has
complex spiral patterns on the left hand side of the opening page of
Luke's Gospel and on the complex initials 'X', 'P', and 'I'. Here the
patterns are in the main loop of the letter 'P' and form an external
decoration to the letter 'X'.

It is highly significant that the majority of these art forms were
produced in the north since they embodied '. . .a national style
common to Ireland and Northumberland'.[72] This latter kingdom
was an area where, as we have seen, the extent of English influence
was suspect. The classic La Tene techniques of using spirals might
have been reintroduced into Britain in the late sixth/early seventh
centuries, following an eclipse of its influence during the period of
the initial English migrations. However, it is just as possible that
when the style resurfaced, in English contexts, it represented the
work of a British sub-culture who had kept the traditions alive.
These art forms then became incorporated into the repertoire of
Germanic artists. As Ian Findlay put it: 'There must have been an
area where Irish traditions mixed continuously with Saxon. . .and
this area could only have been Northumberland . . .'[73] The
operative word in this analysis is 'continuously'. The art form may
represent an unbroken thread of Celtic culture. When this style
spread from Northumberland, in the early seventh century, it was in
the form of a finely integrated artistic concept. It was not merely the
result of one culture being superimposed upon another. Instead it
surely rose out of a sharing of experiences based on several generations of social intercourse between the two peoples.

The argument outlined above can be extended. If we accept the
idea that a Celtic population helped transmit ideas to their new
masters in Northumberland then it is possible that this may have
happened elsewhere. By the time of the conversion to Christianity
in the late sixth and early seventh centuries it is likely that a common
Celtic culture — using spiral patterns — had developed in north
west England, Northumbria, Ireland, southern Scotland, Wales
and the south west of England.[74] There may even have been Celtic
enclaves in English areas which not only existed but actually
conducted themselves according to thoroughly Celtic customs. In
other words their survival was not at the expense of their culture —
in the short run at least. St Chad is said to have met Celtic speakers
in the fens of East Anglia as late as the seventh century. In many of

these areas the Christian church enjoyed a great influence (definitely so in those western areas that were the last to experience the influx of Teutons). In 'enemy occupied territory' craftsmen of Celtic stock must have continued to look to the west of Britain for developments in their native art forms which could be added to their own improvisations. From the fifth century onwards even in the areas of primary settlement they may well have been inclined to collaborate with Germanic master craftsmen. In fact, 'it would be reasonable to assume that the taste for spiral ornament was already present in the English mind before the conversion.'[75]

An early example of such ornamentation can be found in the treasure unearthed from the English boat burial at Sutton Hoo in Suffolk. Experts still debate the exact date that this hoard was put together although the latest numismatic evidence available to the British Museum has led scholars to go for a date in the 620s as the most plausible. Among its treasures are a number of objects of Celtic manufacture, or which were inspired by Celtic themes. The most obvious Celtic objects are three 'hanging bowls' made of tinned bronze. The three circular panels attached to each bowl along with five inlaid plaques, or escutcheons, exhibit the spiral peltas and trumpet-like terminals used later in the decorations on the *Durham Fragment A.II.10*, the *Lindisfarne Gospels* and the manuscript from Lichfield.

Some 150 hanging bowls have been found in this country. There is a consensus that they originated in Northumberland, western Britain and southern Scotland. They were produced in a Celtic milieu and were influenced by Christian tastes. It is of interest to note that the largest hanging bowl discovered at Sutton Hoo may well have been manufactured according to Christian specifications. Many such bowls, found in English contexts, were crudely patched in antiquity or simply allowed to wear through. As obvious relics of plunder or irregular trade they resemble poorly maintained antiques. The East Anglian examples do not belong in this category. Damage that did occur was repaired by an English craftsman. A silver patch decorated with birds (eagles?) heads, executed in the Germanic art form known as Style II, reveal a conscious effort to preserve the bowl. Similarly a decorative boar's head had its eyes filled with garnets.In this way an English metalsmith or jeweller replaced the lost enamel originals. (The boar's head is adjacent to an enamelled circular escutcheon that has millefiori glass insets.)

A number of items in the boat grave are decorated with millefiori work (that is multicoloured glass set in enamel). On the hanging bowl this work is purely Celtic. On other items it appears for the first time in Germanic jewellery! A metal worker used it on the magnificent purse lid, on the curved clasps and on the pyramidical mounts from the suspension strap of the sword. It implies the fusion of two traditions in order to produce spectacular jewellery. Even the cloisonne (enamel and wire) work of the gold shoulder clasps seems to foreshadow the patterns to be found later on the carpet pages of the *Book of Durrow* and other Hiberno Saxon Gospel books of the seventh and eighth centuries.

So far we have talked primarily of Hiberno Saxon art. The discussion began with the examination of Irish styles to be found in English work. The argument was then extended by postulating a British sub-culture in Northumbria which assisted in the transmission of this style. It was then noted that contributions to the development of this art form may have come from the west and south west of Britain as well as from Ireland. The Sutton Hoo evidence helps to take the discussion one stage further. It shows a well-rooted fusion of cultures in an area where the English had been well-established for generations.It shows the care taken by English craftsmen to work within a framework created by Celtic artists and to draw on the reservoir of their knowledge in the creation of new pieces. All this took place at the turn of the sixth/seventh centuries in a kingdom where Teutons had dominated the society since the middle of the fifth century and had been present in numbers since the fourth century at least. The conclusion to be drawn from this is that which appears in the authoritative British Museum handbook to the Sutton Hoo treasure:

> We recognise a clear instance not merely of juxtaposition, but of creative fusion between the two traditions, Celtic and Anglo Saxon. The jewellery already shows, in the first half of the seventh century, a Hiberno Saxon, or more properly a Celto Saxon aspect.[76]

Whilst Irish traditions were responsible for a great input of ideas it would be short-sighted to think that Ireland was the only source of such material. Much of it was native to this country and to the substantial Celtic population which was not massacred by the English.

The law code of Ine (a seventh century king of Wessex) referred to a British population which enjoyed established legal rights. He fixed compensations for the taking of a British person's life (eg. 50 shillings for that of a slave, 600 shillings for the life of a substantial landowner and other sums for grades in between). This indicates that some Britons held land in their own right, others lived in servitude. It has been estimated that in late seventh century Sussex there were perhaps 20,000 slaves. Some of these may have been English. Even in the earliest period English farmers probably soon found themselves under the authority of local landowners of their own race. Few English men can have been truly free and independent; many must have either rented land or owed services in labour or kind to their 'superiors'. In such a situation it must have been possible for a number to descend the social scale into slavery. Nevertheless the number of slaves in Sussex (and in Kent) does seem very high and it is likely that many were Celts who had not preserved their independence. This situation may have been similar in other, less well documented, English kingdoms and would indicate that even in the south the British population was not only recognisable but large.

Celtic survival has left many odd clues. All the clues have to be put together, not just those that are the darlings of individual academic disciplines. Too often the compartmentalisation of research does not do justice to a need for comprehensive study, let alone the complexities of human nature. A strange relic of Celtic survival could be found in the Lake District until as late as the early twentieth century. Cumbrian shepherds preserved peculiar systems of counting their sheep. These systems dated from ancient originals. A number of variants of these number systems existed for the hills around Borrowdale, the Coniston valley, Eskdale and Kirkby Lonsdale. The words used for '1', '5', and '10' are given below together with their equivalents in Old Welsh, Cornish and Old Breton. These particular numbers have been chosen as the systems seem to have revolved around the practice of counting in fives.

	Coniston	Borrowdale	Eskdale	Kirkby Lonsdale	Old Welsh	Cornish	Old Breton
1.	yan (yen?)	yan (yen?)	yaena	yaan	un	un/onan	unan
5.	pimp	pimp	pimp	mimp	pimp	pymp	pemp
10.	dick	dick	dec	dik	dec	dek	dek

It is clear that these Lake District number systems preserved lost Celtic originals. This might appear hardly surprising in an area as

remote as Cumberland. It experienced a late English settlement
(outside the datelines of this book) and can hardly have appeared a
very attractive area to English farmers. On its high fells the
indigenous people must have had a great chance of surviving with
aspects of their culture. Its area name of Cumberland aptly illustrates this. Some may argue that the survival of the number systems
is no more surprising than the survival of the Cornish language until
the eighteenth century in the south western peninsular of England.
Indeed Cornwall preserved its own royal house until the tenth
century when its last ruling king seems to have been named Huwal.
What is far more exciting is the discovery that a similar counting
system survived in Norfolk of all places! Here the numbers for '1',
'5' and '10' were:

1 — yan,   5 — pimp,   10 — dik

Its similarities to the Lake District systems is obvious. In addition to
these its variants for the numbers '3' (tethera), '6' (sethera), '7'
(lethera) and '8' (hovera) are identical to some Cumbrian variants.
Others of its numbers show some differences. However, they are
always variations on a common theme. The Norfolk system needs to
be considered alongside the archaeological evidence discussed in
relation to the Suffolk site of Sutton Hoo.

At an earlier point in this chapter it was noted that a dirth of
archaeological evidence has not helped the search for Celtic survival
in English areas. In many places the end of Roman occupation
seems to have signalled the end of all occupation. Many sites seem
to have little to say about lifestyles after the close of Roman rule.
The absence of pottery fragments and other clues has led many
experts to conclude that Celtic inhabitants became extinct. The
clues examined above show that this conclusion just will not do.
However they do not erase the major problems that arise out of the
seeming absence of evidence on many sites. A number of answers to
this problem can be constructed.

1. With the collapse of the great Romano British pottery
   industry, by the end of the fourth century, the native British
   would have been forced to use their existing pottery until it
   broke beyond use. This, when found on a site, would be
   impossible to date. A piece of black burnished ware, found for
   example at Keynsham villa, may be dated according to its

construction but no one can conclusively say when it was finally discarded (as opposed to when it was made). When the last pottery ran out platters of wood or of leather may have been used.

2. British villagers may have adopted a hybrid Celto English existence of the type which produced the jewellery at Sutton Hoo. Decorated quoit brooches found in Kent may well have been made under Celtic influence. This would help explain other items found in Kentish graves. Some were clearly Roman antiques. Others are far more ambiguous. The two bronze bracelets found in the inhumation cemetery at Chatham Lines between 1779 and 1782 were made with expanded ends of Celtic type. They may imply either a Celtic craftsman at work in the area or the funeral of someone of mixed race. This may be true of the so-called 'Roman' objects discovered in the English cemeteries at Cliffe at Hoo, Crundle, Dover (site 1), Kingston, Priory Hill, Sarre and Worth. The example at Worth is remarkable. Here there is every likelihood that a hybrid culture emerged. The 'notch and groove motif' found on some of the English cruciform brooches may have been borrowed from Roman forms and 'underlines the extraordinary degree to which they [German craftsmen] were dependent on provincial Roman ornament for a wide range of ideas and techniques'.[77] This may also help to explain the ornaments worn by the young girl, inhumed in grave 11 at Holywell Row, near Mildenhall in Suffolk. Around her waist she wore decorative copies of Roman latch lifter keys. This whole discussion raises questions about some, at least, of the Romano British objects found in English contexts in so many places. When we see museum labels that allege that such objects found their way to their last resting places 'From a Raid' — such as the Romano British brooches found at Bidford on Avon — we may at least question whether this is the universal answer.[78] There may be a less dramatic but just as plausible an explanation by reference to hybrid cultures.

3. The third option is that the Romano British may have almost fully assimilated with the early English. It is likely that option 2 was in fact a stage on the way towards this third option. It is now thought likely that the Romano British cemeteries at Kelvedon and Colchester, in Essex, were used well into the English period and that the natives simply adopted the styles

of the newcomers but remained where they had always lived. Many British villagers may have adopted a form of English culture and have benefited from the emergence of English markets and the consumption of basically English goods. They might have adapted themselves out of existence as earlier the Jutes had done. The growth of trade between the two peoples would help explain something of the nature of pottery types produced in Somerset and Avon in the fifth, sixth and seventh centuries. While this area preserved facets of Roman life until the late seventh century it was also influenced by English styles long before the English conquered the areas south of the river Avon. Some of the handmade pottery found in Somerset and classified as 'pre Saxon' may need redefining. Some of it resembles handmade English pottery of the pagan period. In Somerset and in Gloucestershire such grass tempered ware has been found in post Roman contexts; in Wiltshire the contexts have been variously described as post Roman and early English; in Berkshire it has been found in culturally English settlements and the same type of pot has been unearthed, from mid-late Old English sites at Chedder Palace (in Somerset). At the most it is evidence of assimilated cultures. At the least it is 'evidence of exchange by trade or gift across. . .an ill defined or non existent cultural or political frontier'.[79] That many people did not recognise cultural divisions can be seen in the cruciform stamped pot (of English type) found in the British cemetery at Cannington (Somerset) and by pots found at Camerton (Avon), Congresbury (Avon) and Evercreech (Somerset). An English silver belt buckle was found beneath the resurfaced south west gate of Cadbury hillfort in Somerset. Other English metal work has been discovered at the Welsh sites of Dinas Powys (South Glamorgan) and Dinorben (Clwyd). At Publow (Avon) the place name records the burial mound of an English warrior (no later than the early seventh century and probably much before this) in this area that must have been predominantly Celtic well into the seventh century.

These three options go a long way towards answering those who criticise an acceptance that British people continued to thrive despite 'gaps' in the archaeological records. Taken together with the other clues they help to redress the balance made so uneven by the one-sided literary traditions. Fire and the sword may dominate the poetry but coexistence was more the reality. Coexistence — even if it meant that the Celts were eventually forced down the social scale to become the serfs (wealhs in Wessex, laets in Kent) who in time were to serve their Germanic masters. When they reached this level they probably found themselves next to poor Englishmen who enjoyed no better fate but this lies outside of the scope of this study.

Notes

1. K. Feiling, *A History of England* (London, 1950), p. 26.
2. Despite the opinions offered by V. Evison, *The Fifth Century Invasions South of the Thames* (London, 1965).
3. M. Todd's views have been outlined in *Roman Britain 55 B.C.–400 A.D.* (London, 1981), pp. 247–8.
4. M.Biddle, 'Towns' in D. Wilson (ed.), *The Archaeology of Anglo Saxon England* (Cambridge, 1976), Chapter 3, particularly p. 105.
5. Dr R. Reece, 'Town and Country: the End of Roman Britain', *World Archaeology*, 12 (1980–1), pp. 77–92.
6. Biddle, 'Towns', p. 112.
7. P. Salway, *Roman Britain* (Oxford, 1984), pp. 622–3, discussed the possibility that Roman farmers extended their agriculture onto land '. . . worked extensively in later ages'. See also J. Wacher, *Roman Britain* (London 1978), pp. 107–9.
8. J. N. L. Myres, *A Corpus of Anglo Saxon Pottery of the Pagan Period* (Cambridge, 1977) vol.1, p. 3; *Anglo Saxon Pottery and the Settlement of England* (Oxford, 1969), p. 76, and Figure 6.
9. See comments by Dr MacKreth in M. Todd (ed.), *Studies in the Romano British Villa* (Leicester, 1978), p. 209.
10. P. Salway *Roman Britain*, p. 611.
11. In the cases at Long Wittenham and Reading in association with Saxon-type urns of the early-mid fifth century. For the traditional view see S. Chadwick Hawkes's article in *Medieval Archaeology*, 5 (1965),pp. 1–70.
12. The Shakenoak example is more complex as on that site ditches of the sixth to eighth centuries were dug into an extensive Roman settlement implying a considerable use of the site.
13. L. and J. Laing, *Anglo Saxon England* (London, 1979), p. 40.
14. J. Percival, *The Roman Villa* (London, 1976), p. 171.
15. Feiling, *History of England*, p. 121.
16. Wacher (1978) *Roman Britain*, p. 108.
17. L. Alcock, *Arthur's Britain* (Harmondsworth, 1971), pp. 152–3. See also P. Barker, *Techniques of Archaeological Excavation* (London, 1982), 2nd edn, p. 24.
18. A. L. F. Rivet, *The Roman Villa in Britain* (London, 1969), p. 216.
19. S. Hallam, 'Villages in Roman Britain: Some Evidence', *Antiquaries Journal*, 44 (1964), p. 19 ff.
20. See the work of D. Benson and D. Miles in *The Upper Thames Valley* (Oxford, 1974).
21. Found by this author during a study of the villa fields in the spring of 1985.
22. According to the director of Chedworth villa (in conversation with the author) the nineteenth-century excavators probably dumped large amounts of evidence in

the bank on which the director's house is built.

23. At Bidford early English settlers may have travelled from Middle Anglia.

24. Not a new idea: see H. P. R. Finberg, *Roman and Saxon Withington: a Study in Continuity* (Leicester, 1959).

25. M. M. Postan, *The Cambridge Economic History of Europe, I: the Agrarian Life of the Middle Ages* 2nd edn, (Cambridge, 1966).

26. W. G. Hoskins, *The Making of the English Landscape* (London, 1970).

27. For a general view of this see C. Taylor, *Village and Farmstead* (London, 1983).

28. P. J. Fowler, 'Agriculture and Rural Settlement' in D. Wilson (ed.), *The Archaeology of Anglo Saxon England* (Cambridge, 1976), pp. 40–2.

29. A. Goodier, 'The Formation of Boundaries in Anglo Saxon England. A Statistical Survey', *Medieval Archaeology*, 28 (1984), pp. 1–21.

30. D. J. Bonney, 'Early Boundaries in Wessex' in P. J. Fowler (ed.), *Archaeology and the Landscape* (London, 1972), pp. 168–86.

31. Fowler in Wilson (ed.), *Anglo Saxon England*, p. 39.

32. Even on this issue it would be wrong to be too dogmatic. It has been shown that in Somerset 'recognisable facets of the Roman occupation . . . may well be defined for perhaps three centuries after the collapse of Roman central administration. V. Evison, H. Hodges and J. Hurst, *Medieval Pottery from Excavations* (London, 1974),p. 98.

33. *English Place Name Society* (EPNS), vol 1, part 2 (Cambridge, 1925), pp. 64–5.

34. A. H. Smith, *English Place Name Elements*, EPNS, vol. 25 and 26 (Cambridge, 1956), part 2, p. 263.

35. A full list of sites along with other evidence for Latin survival in place names can be found in M. Gelling, *Signposts to the Past* (London, 1978).

36. For example, Wycomb (Gloucestershire).

37. For example, Wickham Market (Suffolk).

38. M. Henig, *Religion in Roman Britain* (London, 1984), p. 227.

39. Smith, *English Place Name Elements*, part 1, pp. 79–80.

40. *EPNS*, vol. 1., part 2, p. 14.

41. Gelling, *Signposts*, p.77.

42. Smith, *English Place Name Elements*, noted under the entry 'Wicham'

43. E. Ekwall *Concise Oxford Dictionary of English Place Names* (Oxford, 1960), p. 190.

44. *EPNS* vol. 1, part 1, A. Mawer and F. M. Stenton (eds), (Cambridge, 1925), p. 19.

45. Gelling, *Signposts*, p. 86. For a distribution map of this and other Roman place name elements see S. Johnson, *Later Roman Britain*, map 20, p. 288.

46. Smith, *English Place Name Elements*, part 1, p. 108.

47. E. Ekwall, 'The Celtic Element', *Introduction to the Survey of English Place Names. EPNS*, vol. 1, part 1, p. 20.

48. W. Davies, *An Early Welsh Microcosm: the Llandaff Charters* (Aberystwyth, 1978), and W. Davies, *The Llandaff Charters* (Aberystwyth, 1979).

49. Gildas, 'The Ruin of Britain' in *The Ruin of Britain and Other Works* (London, 1978), edited and translated by N. Winterbottom, 25 (the last quotation of the three is from 26).

50. Ibid., 23.2–4.

51. Smith, *English Place Name Elements*, part 2, pp. 242–4.

52. *EPNS*, vol. 1, part 1, (Cambridge, 1925), p. 18 comments that names containing 'Wal' may indicate that Britons were exceptions in a largely English population.

53. K. Cameron, 'The Meaning and Significance of Old English "Walh" in English place names', *EPNS Journal*, 12 (1979–80), pp. 1–46. M. Todd, 'The Archaeological

Significance of Place Names in "Walh"', *EPNS Journal*, 12 (1979–80), appendix, pp. 47–50.

54. For example, the Old English version of Matthew's Gospel, Chapter 24, Verse 50, translated the word 'servant' as 'weales'.

55. *EPNS*, vol. 1, part 1, (Cambridge, 1925), p. 18.

56. See V. E. Watts and E. F. M. Prince, 'Old English Walh in English Place Names: an Addendum', *EPNS Journal*, 14 (1981–2), pp. 32–6.

57. A field name in Finchingfield (Essex).

58. A field name in Boreham (Essex).

59. *Cartularium Saxonicum*, 802, W. Birch (ed.), (London, 1885–93). Where the Roman road from Silchester crossed the river Kennet.

60. Ibid., 34. A wharf at Staines where the Roman road from London crossed the river Thames.

61. *Assize Roll* for 1289. An old name for Avebury (Wiltshire).

62. *Codex Diplomaticus aevi Saxonici*, 682, J. M. Kemble (ed.), (London, 1839–48).

63. An Old English form of Ashford.

64. *Cartularium Saxonicum*, 957.

65. Ibid., 674.

66. *Codex Diplomaticus aevi Saxonici*, 682.

67. From a land grant of 955.

68. Smith, part 1, pp. 61–2

69. K. Jackson, *Language and History in Early Britain* (Edinburgh, 1953).

70. Bede, *A History of the English Church and People* (Harmondsworth, 1968), 2.3.

71. M. J. Whittock, 'Place Names: Problems and Possibilities', *Poole Museum Society Newsletter*, 11 (February 1985).

72. C. Nordenfalk, *Celtic and Anglo Saxon Painting* (London, 1977), p. 10.

73. I. Finlay, *Celtic Art* (London, 1973), p. 140.

74. D. Wilson, *Anglo Saxon Art* (London, 1984), p. 114.

75. Ibid., p. 114.

76. R. Bruce Mitford, *The Sutton Hoo Ship Burial, a Hand Book* (London, 1979) 3rd edn, p. 122.

77. B. M. Ager, 'An Anglo Saxon Cruciform Brooch from Lyminge', *Archaeologia Cantiana*, 99 (1983), pp. 59–65. There have even been suggestions that the limited evidence for early English people in Wessex was caused by them being heavily influenced by the native culture. See G. de G. Sieveking and others (eds), *Problems in Economic and Social Archaeology* (London, 1976), p. 323 ff. J.N.L. Myres considered that many of the West Saxons were 'already culturally assimilated to British ways in the last days of Roman Britain'. *The English Settlements* [Oxford, 1986] p. 148; he concluded that much of the pattern of English settlement was established by Saxon shore deployments. The idea of culturally assimilated *Britons* has been explored by C. Hills, *The Blood of the British* [London, 1986] through her principle of 'new pots . . . do not always mean new people.' [p. 9]

78. The brooch and the description of its 'origin' can be found in the New Place Museum, Stratford (Warwickshire).

79. Evison, Hodges and Hurst, *Medieval Pottery*, p. 103.

3 ENGLISH SOCIETY

The Germanic peoples who migrated to Britain in the fourth, fifth and sixth centuries came from a number of different north German, or south Scandanavian tribes. Something of their complexity and history, before the folk movement, and during its earlier stages, has already been discussed (Chapter 1, Continental Origins). However, some of this may be rehearsed again here, before examining how these peoples were translated to Britain.

The major groups that took part in the invasions — according to the literary sources — were the ubiquitous Angles, Saxons and Jutes. Others were Frisians and perhaps Franks. Archaeology supports the latter, as contenders, as it does Swaefe, Alemanni, Swedes, Danes, and possibly Boructuarii or Rugini. All these peoples had peculiar cultural characteristics that identified them as being to some extent different from their neighbours. Cruciform brooches were typical of the Anglo Jutish areas of Frisia, the west bank of the Elbe, Holstein and Mecklenberg. Saucer brooches were typical of the Anglo Saxon regions in Friesland, between the Elbe and Weser, and some regions of the lower Rhine. In a similar way ceramic fashions such as standing arches (stehende Bogen), early Buckelurnen (bossed pots) and chevron decorations may have been associated with Saxon areas. Vertical and diagonal styles were typical of Anglian Fünen and Schleswig. Biconical forms may point to Norwegian, or Danish, origins and corrugated tooling may have been at home in Norway, Jutland and Anglian Schleswig. Simple linear styles in pottery decoration (which may ultimately have had Angle or Saxon origins) were characteristic of the Frisian terpen, whilst small cruciform brooches, square headed brooches and the jewellery known as bracteates were popular among peoples with origins in Jutland (or Sweden). Despite these characteristics there was also much common ground. Much tribal confusion predated the movement to Britain. Because of this '. . .the traditional lands of the Saxons in the valleys of the lower Elbe and Weser were by the later part of the fourth century the scene of a general mix up of peoples resulting principally from the Westward pressure of folk from east Holstein and the southward movement of others from the

Danish peninsular.'[1] It is this great mixing that German scholars have called the *Volkerwanderung* (folk wandering). These scholars have also coined a name for the product of this wandering as it appeared between the Elbe and Ems — the *Mischgruppe*, or mixed group. It was from the mixed group area, and its hinterland (as well as the extension of the former into Frisia), that the majority of settlers set sail on their journey to Britain.

On the continent a curious situation occurred in which many cultures mixed and formed hybrids, whilst items from the original homelands in eastern Holstein or Jutland remained significantly different. In this way some objects can be used to prove very definite points of origin whilst others may point to a far wider area. The key questions are: from which stage of the migration journey did the item come? and whether its owner came through the full melting pot or skirted it? It now remains to be seen how such a situation was removed to Britain.

Bede attributed the colonisation of England north of the Thames (with the exception of Essex) to Angles[2] that is, to tribesmen from Schleswig and Funen. To a large extent he was correct. The cemeteries of east Yorkshire, Lincolnshire and Suffolk bear a distinct resemblance to those of Borgstedt and Anglian south Schleswig. Pottery found at Hanmoor and Sorup on the continent has been found at Caistor by Norwich. Similarly cruciform brooches were popular in the mainly cremating Anglian areas from Norfolk to Yorkshire.

Bede assumed that Saxon settlers accounted for the majority of the southern population.[3] There is, again, a large measure of truth contained in this. Early saucer brooches predominated in the Thames valley, Sussex and the south Midlands. This is indicative of origins in the mixed group area of the Elbe Weser region which, if not purely Saxon, was probably predominantly so. Similarly early standing arch pots are to be found at Abingdon and in Middlesex. At Mitcham and Ham evidence has come to light of highly characteristic styles demonstrably Saxon on the continent, in the fourth century. Even Jutish settlement, for all its problems, does now appear to have been primarily where Bede placed it — in Kent, the Isle of Wight and perhaps to some extent in Essex. There is also a convincing literary tradition which supports such a settlement in southern Hampshire (as Bede insisted).

In short, there is evidence for a Saxon south and a Jutish/Saxon south east — an area of mixed cremation/inhumation rites. In addition there is every reason to assume an Anglian origin for settlers in East and Middle Anglia, the Trent valley, Lindsey and the area of eastern Yorkshire known as Deira. Many came to East Anglia (for example, Caistor by Norwich) and to Deira (for example, Sancton) direct from Schleswig. Such settlers were the dominant influence in Deira from the start. These folk followed mainly cremating rites. So far this is in agreement with Bede. However, the evidence goes far beyond this. It suggests that this picture was not a static one but changed over time. What was a fairly neat pattern by the sixth century was a much more fluid one in the fifth century.

Many traditionally Anglian sites reveal a striking series of Saxon characteristics in the fifth century! Finds at Elkington point to origins in the Saxon culture of Altenwalde in Europe. The great continental Saxon cemeteries of Galgenberg and Westerwanna share similarities of fashions with Lackford (Suffolk), Sponghill, Rushford, Tottenhill (Norfolk), etc. Cemeteries as far apart as Northamptonshire,[4] Lincolnshire,[5] Norfolk,[6] Suffolk,[7] Humberside,[8] and Bedfordshire[9] had close links with the Saxon communities at Wehden, and to a lesser extent that at Quelkhorn. The parallels with Wehden are from so many parts of this country that they argue for a wide scattering of immigrants and the absence of solid blocks of settlers. The pattern of saucer brooch distribution is also revealing. As well as in the areas cited they also appear in Middle Anglia and in the Cambridge region alongside users of Anglian cruciform brooches. Indeed one very early brooch came from Norwich, and fifth-century applied disc brooches have been identified at Luton (star, cruciform, zoomorphic types), Kempston in Bedfordshire (zoomorphic type) as well as in the Thames valley and in the south east.[10]

The distribution of such metalwork and pottery suggests that in the first half of the fifth century many Saxon communities were established in what was to become traditionally Anglian territory. Many were in close proximity to Roman roads and towns and may have been part of a planned deployment. At about this time Anglian settlers were also arriving at Caistor by Norwich, Loveden Hill and other sites. By the latter half of the fifth century this had substantially altered. The later waves of immigrants, north of the Thames, were more in tune with a south Scandanavian culture that was to dominate the life of East Anglia, Lindsey and Deira from this time onwards. After the revolts of the 450s and 460s Saxon influence

Figure 3.1: Major Proto English Sites in North West Europe

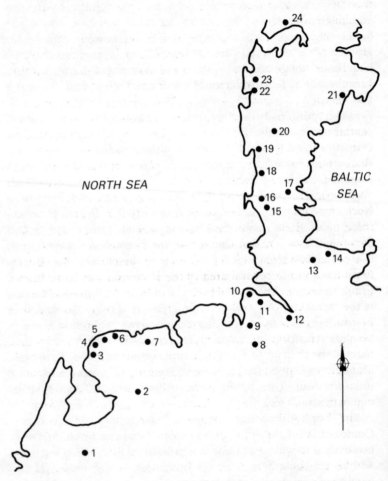

Key to Sites on Map :
1.Wageningen; 2.Wijster; 3.Kimswerd; 4.Beetgum; 5.Hoogebeintum;
6.Raard; 7.Ezinge; 8.Mahndorf; 9.Feddersen Wierde; 10.Galgenberg;
11.Westerwanna; 12.Stade (Perlberg); 13.Bordesholm; 14.Preetz;
15.Traelborg; 16.Drengsted; 17.Galsted; 18.Ribe; 19.Fourfeld;
20.Grinsted; 21.Mogelby; 22.Velling; 23.Molbjerg; 24.Thisted;

waned in favour of this Anglian character, recognised by Bede. The users of Saxon Buckelurnen cremation pots, in the later fifth and early sixth centuries, seem to represent a shift of emphasis into the southern Midlands and onto the established Saxon communities of the Thames valley. This expansion was not related to Roman administration.

The situation is further complicated by reference to other tribal groups. Some settlers in Northamptonshire[11] and Bedfordshire[12] had Danish or Norwegian antecedents; others in Bedfordshire,[13] Lincolnshire,[14] Cambridge,[15] Humberside,[16] Norfolk,[17] Suffolk[18] and Essex[19] had Swedish ones. The handmade imitations of Frankish pots found at Sancton may indicate immigrants from central and south Germany. These may have been Alemanni, or Boructuarii, or Rugini tribesmen and their families. To be fair to Bede he may not have omitted these tribes. In his *History of the English Church and People*, Book 5, Chapter 9, he described the abortive mission of Bishop Egbert to evangelise the tribes 'of whose stock came the Angles or Saxons now settled in Britain'. Among these tribes Bede noted the Frisians, Rugini, Danes, Huns, Old Saxons and Boructuarii. The archaeological evidence may support this contention regarding at least some of these tribes. The Boructuarii lived in the general area of the Ruhr and may have been a Frankish people. The Rugini had moved from the Baltic to Moravia in the fourth century. Although this does not assist in locating them as invaders of Britain, their participation in the Hunnic invasion of Gaul under Attila (defeated at Troyes in 451) may have brought them to the right place at the right time.[20] Such circumstances might also help to explain Bede's rather surprising reference to Hunnish warriors. Such men may even have been involved in the earlier deployment of the English in Britain in the 420s or 430s. From 425 Aëtius employed an army of Huns (reputedly 60,000 strong!) in Gaul. The case against their involvement in this earlier deployment, however, is the distinct possibility that Aëtius threatened Vortigern and his English allies. A later involvement (in the 440s and 450s) would not come up against this problem as by then the Huns had moved out of the position of being loyal to Aëtius.

We are on much firmer ground when we consider Frisian influence. The Byzantine historian Procopius made them and the Angles the primary inhabitants of Britain, in addition to the native British. Whilst this was simplification to the point of inaccuracy it is true that Frisians did take part in the invasions. Anglo Frisian pottery has been identified at a number of sites in Eastern England. This type of pottery — often well made, often with simple linear decorations — was a hybrid whose styles ultimately originated in Angeln or east Holstein. Its incidence at Westerwanna, Wehden, Issendorf and as far away as Preetz shows that it may be risky to consider it as purely Frisian in origin. However, it is found in Holland at Rhenen, Wageningen and Rijnsburg. The latter two sites have close parallels in the eastern English cemeteries at Lackford (Suffolk), Eye (Suffolk) and St John's, Cambridge.[21] At least some of these English potters may have originated in the coastal colonies of Frisia. A more specifically Frisian influence may be discerned in the so-called long bossed type pots. These have been found in north-east Kent, the lower and upper Thames valley, Sussex and the country between the upper Stour and the Ouse. There may have also been other Frisian influences in pottery found along the Thames at Mucking, Mitcham, Ham, Dorchester on Thames, Sutton Courtenay and at West Stow and as far away as Lindsey. By the sixth century Belgian parallels existed in at least two sites in Northamptonshire. The Frisian input was not limited to pottery types. Combs (from the first half of the fifth century) link East Anglian sites with Friesland, Groningen, Nieder Sachsen and Kastell Deutz, near Cologne. At York their identification was assisted by the presence of Frisian cremation urns.[22]

All this evidence shows that Bede's simple geography needs to be treated with caution. It was clearly not as stable as he knew it, but had been prone to fluctuations over time. Even at its most static each area must have had noteworthy minorities. Some of them formed by an alien ruling house — such as the Swedish dynasty buried at Sutton Hoo — others simply small groups of men and women who had chosen homes at some distance from others of their culture. Such cases clearly gave rise to the Saxons remembered at Saxton (Cambridgeshire and Yorkshire), Saxon Dale (Nottinghamshire) and Saxham (Suffolk); the East Saxons at Exton (Hampshire); the Kentishmen at Conderton (Hereford and Worcester) and Canterton (Hampshire); the Angles at Englefield (Berkshire), Englebourne (Devon) and Engleton (Staffordshire); Mercians at Markfield (Leicestershire); Swaefe (Swabians) at Swaby, Swaton (both in Lincolnshire), Swavesey, Swaffham Bulbeck and Prior (all in Cambridgeshire), and Swaffham (Norfolk). The fact that such names arose does demonstrate that such recognisable differences were the exception not the norm. However, the fact that it could happen points to common elements of language and culture that transcended the differences. Both on the continent and in the actual process of the migration the proto English tribes were coalescing to form a generally homogeneous people despite cultural distinctions and at times a dimly remembered folk memory of tribal names that originated in an era when such distinctions had been of greater political importance.

The early groups of immigrants clearly came to this country under the authority of their clan leaders. The word 'clan' seems to be more realistic than 'tribe' since no tradition from the period suggests the co-ordinated movement of tribal groups. As long ago as 1947 the respected historian Sir Frank Stenton concluded that 'unlike Gaul, Spain and Italy, Britain was invaded not by tribes under tribal kings but by bodies of adventurers who according to their own traditions were drawn from three distinct Germanic peoples' (that is, Angles, Saxons, Jutes).[23] Whilst we may wish to modify something of the tribal simplicity, the rest of the statement is clearly sound. This throws us back to asking: what do we know about the authority structures of Germanic peoples in the migration period?

As early as the first century AD the Roman historian Tacitus noted dual traditions among the German tribes. He was aware that kings ('reges') existed, whose legitimacy was based on birth but that this system also had alongside it one in which generals ('duces') were chosen, on the basis of courage.[24] His account is very general and it is not plain whether such a duality existed in one tribe or whether some were monarchical and others not. Neither is it at all clear which applied to the so-called Ingaevones from whose numbers came the proto English. Some light may be shed on this by reference to the eighth-century work of Bede. On the subject of the continental — or 'old Saxons' — he wrote that they '. . .have no king, but several lords who are set over the nation.' These lords governed through lesser nobles or 'reeves'.[25] Apart from these references — one 400 years too early, the other 300 years too late — there is no firm analysis of the basis of English or proto English leadership. We are forced back to the early traditions concerning the landings in Britain. These do not condescend to explain. They simply state what to them was obvious, or desirable, for people to believe.

The early traditions that have survived imply that each major English kingdom was founded by leaders of divine descent. Some are known from the *Chronicle*'s accounts, others from separate genealogical material. This applies to the kingdoms of Kent,

Wessex, Bernicia, Deira, Mercia, East Anglia, Lindsey and Essex. The sole exception is Sussex and here it may be that the obscurity of this kingdom, after the fifth century, led to the loss of its early royal genealogy. It may even mean that the original ruling house was eclipsed. The curious fact is that in no *Chronicle* entry is any incoming ruler actually described as a king. This has led to the accusation that lineages which we have are pure fabrications and that even those names below that of Woden were created to fit, or even cover, political realities.[26] The height of this cynicism is perhaps expressed by Michael Wood who doubted whether the royal pedigrees went back even as far as AD400. He saw the genealogies as the products of the '. . . descendants of the illiterate condottieri who had seized their chances in the fifth and sixth centuries'. His comparison of Hengest of Kent, or Wuffa of East Anglia, with the mercenary leaders of the Congo in the 1960s has an evocative ring and an undoubted appeal to the modern ear.[27] However, it is a clashing anachronism whatever its attractiveness. It is unlikely that the reality was either as simple or as crude.

The early rulers, who claimed divine descent, appealed not only to pre-conversion society in England. They must be seen against the backdrop of continental German culture and the recitation of king lists by the scops, or bard. Indeed within such a milieu the 'belief in descent from a god was an important ideological principle in the ordering of society among the early Germans'.[28] The placing of Woden at the head, or pivot point, of such a genealogy was a mythological statement about the antiquity and legitimacy of the line so described. It does not instantly catapult every name on the list into the realm of fairy tale. It would be wrong, and needless, to declare that the Mercians did *not* descend from King Offa of Angeln just because a chronicler thought that Woden stood five places above his name in the king lists. The very universality of the name simply testifies to the common north German culture of the colonists (the exception being that of Essex in which the dynasty claimed descent from the god Seaxnet — who may be identical with Tiw the war god). The fact that Wessex, Bernicia, Kent and Deira also all claimed descent from either Baeldaeg or Waegdaeg may simply imply Anglian antecedents in all these dynasties,[29] although the description of the founders of Wessex — Cerdic and Cynric — as ealdormen may imply Saxon origins, reminiscent of Bede's eighth-century account of Saxon government. This is not impossible given the cultural mixing that went on before, and during, the invasions. A similar explanation may remove any problems concerning similarities in the cult names, above Woden, in the genealogies of Wessex, Bernicia, Kent and Lindsey. These explanations score lower on cynicism but may be more firmly rooted in the Germanic material. They assume that the founders of most of the kingdoms were of noble birth. This would at least explain how they were able to raise and equip a warband. Noble status, however measured, must have been a prerequisite for this. If noble, then they are likely to have been related to royal houses and to have had a genealogy of their own. It is better to assume them to be footloose cadet branches of ruling dynasties than to think of them all as lowly mercenaries without any formal legitimacy. Such a scenario of landless nobility would explain how Hengest and Horsa appear in Nennius as driven in exile form Germany. There are echoes of later Viking experiences in this.

It should not be taken for granted, however, that all the genealogies are of an identical nature. Some of the lists stand out for special attention. The obvious one is that of Mercia. The descent from a historical ruler of the continental Angles makes it noteworthy. It may also help explain how the Mercian royal family brought other Anglian peoples under its authority in the seventh century. On the other extreme is Lindsey. Both its chronology and nomenclature make it possible that this really is a forgery designed to fit political necessities.

So far the term 'genealogy' has been used as if identical with a 'king list'. This may be a mistake. Clearly they were designed to be accepted as genealogies. They run poetically — 'X son of Y, Y son of Z', etc., but this at times may be an expediency. It is possible that some were, in fact, successive rulers who were not father and son. This was undoubtedly true of fifth- and sixth-century Kent and possibly Wessex too. In those cases the phrase 'king list' is more accurate than that of 'genealogy'. Since we have no way of knowing how widespread this tendency was, the former term will be used as well as geneaology from now on and in the Appendix 1. This characteristic may explain the practice of joint kingship and of rival kings that feature so predominantly in later English history. This is easier to understand if we admit that succession may have passed to any member of the royal house and not necessarily to the eldest son. This would create a situation in which many princelings vied for the throne and in which nobles looked back to a past generation in which a previous member of their line held the throne, if briefly. Alternatively a number of royal families may have existed within one kingdom and the fiction of orderly descent may have masked a reality of division and even rivalry.[30] This would explain some of the otherwise unknown kings who appear and then vanish in the genealogical records of almost all of the kingdoms over the centuries after AD600. It would also explain how in 626 Edwin of Northumbria could invade Wessex and kill five kings! J. Morris actually went as far as saying that in Wessex a high kingship was established on an Irish model. This 'elective monarchy' based on regional dynasties was, in his view, a Saxon answer to the 'strong central monarchy of the Angles on the continent and the Mercians in Britain'.[31] Clearly kingship was no simple matter in either theory or reality. After the death of Cenwalh of Wessex (*c.*672) Bede described how '. . .underkings took over the government of the realm'. The *Chronicle*, however, records an orderly (if genealogically complex) succession. Clearly 'reality'is sometimes not what we see but what we choose to see! Nevertheless it is fair to assume that many of the monarchies with 'divine descent' probably did relate to noble and royal families on the continent. Some did look back to a relatively highly centralised system of government in Angeln whilst others had roots in a more loosely-knit 'Saxon concept'. However, it is too ambitious to follow the interpretation given by Morris. The West Saxon royal house seems to have had Anglian connections and in the sixth century the Mercians of the Trent valley were only one of many royal houses whose traditions have been lost, whilst its survived. Also, the movement to Britain may have caused massive dislocations in the tribal structures. Tacitus and Bede were witnesses of these events from too great a distance and cannot relieve our curiosity.

This leaves the many rulers whose lines and traditions have not survived. We know that many such existed in the Midlands and in the Thames valley. There may have been many equivalents to the later underkings of the Hwicce (in the south west Midlands) or the princes of the Gyrwe (in the fens) or Middle Angles (about Cambridge). None of them claimed divine descent and it may have been this that differentiated them from their overlords.[32] The former being rulers *de facto* and the latter *de jure*. This of course may simply be reading back later interpretations into earlier history. There is a proverb that runs

Treason never prospers. What's the reason?
— If it prosper none dare call it treason.

It may be that some of the early local rulers did have legitimate genealogies which rivalled those of the rulers who came to lord it over them. This would explain why such traditions were suppressed — if not exterminated. Those who gained supremacy would have hardly encouraged the transmission of rival genealogical material. ('Treason never prospers . . .'!) There is, though, no firm evidence for this assumption and so it is best to assume that the local dynasties were composed of recognised clan leaders, or successful warriors, with the proviso that some *may* have had a more exalted status.

Whatever the technical status of the chief, or king, he played a central role in the Germanic heroic society. It is worth rehearsing some of the poetic epithets used of him. He was the 'folces hyrde' or 'shepherd of the people';[33] he was the 'protector of warriors';[34] he was 'the kindest to his people, the keenest for fame'.[35] Not only did he guard the wealth of the people he was also the one who rewarded his warriors and so cemented the bond within the ruling class of warrior aristocrats. The chief was both 'the warden of ring hoards'[36] and the 'ring giver'[37] — the 'guardian of the treasure'[38] and the 'giver of treasure'.[39] When a king was described as a 'gold friend'[40] or 'gold giver'[41] the sentiments employed were not merely those of crude materialism. A chief's gifts to his warriors were part of an intricate reciprocal relationship. The warrior gave his loyalty to his chief and prized it above his own life — it was a deep commitment. In return the chief rewarded his warrior and gave him status. He made him 'a gold resplendent warrior, rejoicing in his rings'.[42] This is the language not merely of acquisitiveness but of status and esteem acquired through loyal service and heroism in battle. This giving was part of the king's role as the protector and supplier of the needs of his warriors. In the earliest of English poems — *Widsith* — Eormenric, King of the Goths, may have been a ruthless and frightening monarch in the early lines of the poem, but he was renowned for his generosity and so was his wife Ealhhild. The historicity of these statements is irrelevant. They do not purport to be a chronicle. They are expressions of what was central to the *idea* of noble kingship. This is particularly important in this poem as the poet consciously preserved an ancient king list of the peoples of north Europe. It was a poem about kings and about the ideal of kingship. The themes are not fully developed but they are clearly discernible.

If the king fulfilled one part of a relationship of reciprocity, the warrior filled the other. He was a member of the king's closest companions. The comitatus of Tacitus, the 'heorthwerod', or 'hearth companions' of Old English poetry. Warriors were the king's 'table companions'[43] because they were his 'battle companions'.[44] Such men made up the nobility of service. They owed their social position to the service that they rendered to their lord. They should be differentiated from the nobility of birth. This latter group represented those whose status was upheld by their membership of landed families who exercised traditional authority. Such men must have made up the majority of local leaders in the early period. This group must have lost out to the king's men in the process of kingdom building. In such a process the exponents of warfare must have gained at the expense of traditional authority.

War and heroic acts were central to a warrior's way of life. It was his *raison d'être*. The warriors were 'war proud people'.[45] When the *Chronicle* accounts tell of the acts of chiefs and their warbands it is this system that was in operation. The scale must have varied with the prestige of a chief. The greater his renown the more attractive would have appeared the membership of his warband. The larger the warband the greater the momentum towards violent expansion, both to reward the king's companions and to increase the leader's prestige. If violence was not the only binding factor in the heorthwerod, it *was* the dominant one.

So far the words 'king' and 'chief' have been used as interchangeable terms. This, in the migration period, is not without historical foundation. Kings could rule lands as limited as the Isle of Wight or as large as East Anglia. Later they could be of divine descent or lack this characteristic. It was only time and the pride of greater rulers that forced local kings down to the status of sub-kings and princes; that accorded them lesser titles such as 'regulus' or 'patricius'. The word king may predate the migration since it was used in the Old German form 'cuning' and the Old Norse 'konungr'. However, it was not until the ninth century that it was used in the Old English form 'Cyng'. Its original meaning, expressed in the earlier form 'cyning', was 'son of the cyn' ('kin'). It probably meant no more than 'member of the ruling family'. It was thus a loose and flexible term that could give way to alternative titles such as 'brytenwealda' ('wide ruler') or 'hlaforde' (from the Old English 'hlaf-

weard' or 'guardian of the bread'). This title can be found in the
Chronicle entries for 922 and 924 (MS A). Its later meaning may
have been that of 'over lord'. In a similar way the word 'cynedom'
('kingdom') — from the word 'cyning' — was in less common usage
than the word 'rice'. The latter was an older word than either
cynedom or cyning and was related to the Gothic 'reiks' and the
Latin 'rex'. The usual old English form of 'X acquired the kingdom'
was 'X feng to rice.'

So far the talk has been of kings, chiefs and warriors. It is these
who dominate the heroic poetry and the earliest *Chronicle* entries.
This is hardly surprising. The literary material was produced to
record the doings of their families and their own legitimacy. Poetry
and *Chronicle* give us a 'king's eye view of the world'. Below them
must have been other *de facto* authority leaders and then the broad
mass of peasant farmers. Such authority figures are not documented
but must have existed. Some must have been village headmen; some
simply the most experienced agriculturalist in the community;
others a patriarch of the local leading family who had acquired
property, slaves, a following of his relatives, and other pioneers
prepared to throw in their lot with him. It was surely something like
one or all of these that underlay the place names that now end in
'-ingham' and 'ing' ('the settlement of X's people', 'the people of
X'). In the fluid generations of folk wandering, sea passage and
settlement such figures must have meant more to the average
immigrant than the more socially conscious warriors and aspiring
kings. However, history is often written by the ruling class and
whatever their contribution history has consigned them to near
oblivion. It is now time to turn to the study of this group and to begin
to examine what can be salvaged. Firstly, place name evidence will
be examined followed by the archaeology of the rural English settlement, the weapons of the colonists and the nature of their religious
beliefs.

Place Name Evidence for the Early English Period

A large number of English place names contain the element 'ing'.
Some contain it as a final element (for example, Hastings (Sussex))
whilst others have it as a middle element (for example, Woking-
gham). For many years it was thought that this element dated from
the earliest years of the English immigration. This view has now

changed. Before this debate is considered it may be helpful to see how this element was used in the Germanic world.[46]

(1) The basic use had the meaning 'son of. . .'. For example, the West Saxon genealogy (which in modern English is 'Cerdic, son of Elesa, Elesa, son of Esla) would have read 'Cerdic, Elesing, Elesa, Esling'.

(2) It could be used as a personal name that had once meant 'son of' (a patronymic) but had lost that function (for example, Deoring).

(3) It could also mean 'the people of. . .' and include an entire household.[47] In Old English this took the form 'ingas'. This could then give rise to a place name such as Hastings or 'the people of Haesta'.[48]

(4) It could also be used in the sense 'X's place' or 'the place of X' such as Clavering (Essex) which means 'place of Clover', or Lawling (Essex) which means 'place of Lealla' — a personal name.[49]

(5) As a medial element with the final element 'ham' it meant 'farm/village of the people of X' (for example, Gillingham (Kent) or 'ham of the Gyllingas, or Gylla's people'). Ham was an ancient word[50] but other final elements, such as 'tun' were not so ancient. It became more common as ham fell into disuse.[51] It had a meaning of 'enclosure/farmstead'. Some experts think that its meaning was 'tun of X' or 'tun of X's people'[52]. Others think that both exist in different place names.[53]

Traditionally it has been thought that these small groups, as represented by the 'ingas' place names, gave rise to the earliest English place names. This view began with the work of J. M. Kemble in the nineteenth century.[54] Names in 'ing' were thought to be the oldest, followed by those in 'ingaham' (or 'ingham').[55] These were followed by other elements compounded with 'ing'.[56] The earliest dominated in the counties with an early history of English immigration (see figure 3.4) and, it was thought, must have represented those who 'proudly bore the name of the leader who had led them across the seas and had triumphantly settled them in a new land. . .'.[57] Some represented warrior bands of kings, others farming communities.[58] Many confident assertions were made on the basis of these assumptions.[59]

Figure 3.2: Areas of England with Frequent Use of the Place Name Element 'Ham' and Those with Infrequent Use of the Element

Areas with frequent use of 'Ham'
Areas with rare use of 'Ham'

Since the 1960s these assertions have been challenged. Some of the names, it was recognised, were not formed from personal names and seemed to lack antiquity.[60] More damaging was the work of J. M. Dodgson[61], Cox[62], Kuurman[63] and Gelling[64] who pointed out that the oldest archaeological sites did not have ingas type names. The new opinion is that these names are not from the migration period but from that of colonisation and the period of political consolidation. The new chronological sequence established by this is: names with 'ham' (often linked to the Roman 'vicus'), 'ingaham', 'ing'. The problem is that ham place names are not numerous enough in ancient areas and the oldest strata may in fact be made up of topographical names (also the latest type of name too!) based on water supplies.[65] This would give an order that may be expressed as the following model:

Table 3.1: Model of Settlement Names and Political Processes

Stage	Political process at work	Settlement name type
1	*Immigration*: direct movement from continent	Topographical type
2(a)	*Settlement*: period of integration with existing society. Embryonic social cohesion into new and larger social groups	Ham
2(b)	*Colonisation*: increased expansion and emergence of clan leaders over hamlet head-men	Ingaham
3	*Political consolidation*: clan leaders extend authority, mature settlements expand and English territory expands	Ingas
4	*Kingdom building*: local aristocrats with necessary resources and prestige develop capability of subduing territories and dividing them among their warbands	Non-specific as based on military aristocrats not a 'grass roots' consolidation

This model represents the early stages of the conquest as a piecemeal affair and expresses the slow development of Germanic political structures in this country. (For distribution of 2(a), (b) and 3, see Figures 3.2, 3.3 and 3.4).

Concerning the ingaham/ingas place names some interesting distribution patterns can be discerned (from a sample of 157 ingaham place names and 168 ingas), as shown in Table 3.2.[66]

Although these patterns are not from the earliest period of English history they are nevertheless revealing and very relevant to

Table 3.2: Distribution Patterns of Ingaham/Ingas Place Names

1(a) Ingaham place names		(b) Ingas place names	
Rank order	(%)	Rank order	(%)
1. Norfolk	26.75	1. Sussex	26.78
2. Lincolnshire	14.64	2. Essex	14.28
3. Yorkshire	12.10	3. Norfolk	11.30
4. Suffolk	9.55	4. Kent	8.92
5. Kent/Northumberland (each)	5.09	5. Suffolk/Yorkshire (each)	6.54
6. Essex	3.82	6. Surrey	4.76
7. Surrey/Isle of Wight (each)	1.91	7. Lincolnshire	4.16
8. Berkshire	0.63	8. Berkshire	2.38
		9. Northumberland	0.59

2(a) Ingaham

Essex+Kent+Lincolnshire+Norfolk+Suffolk = 59.85% of the total

(b) Ingas

Essex+Kent+Lincolnshire+Norfolk+Suffolk = 45.20% of the total

(c) Ingaham plus Ingas names

Essex+Kent+Lincolnshire+Norfolk+Suffolk = 52.30% of the total
(−Kent =45.23% of total)

3   Total of Ingas names plus Ingaham names

Rank order	(%)
1. Norfolk	18.76
2. Sussex	13.84
3. Essex/Lincolnshire/Yorkshire (each)	9.23
4. Suffolk	8.00
5. Kent	7.07
6. Surrey	3.38
7. Northumberland	2.76
8. Hampshire/Berkshire (each)	1.53
9. Isle of Wight	0.92

the English colonisation and political consolidation of their power in this country. The figures in 1(a) show a high concentration of early colonists in eastern England. Although this is supported by the archaeological record it is not reflected in the literary sources. This reinforces the need for caution in using and evaluating these sources. For example, Kent is well represented in the literary sources but cannot be ranked higher than 5, on the basis of place name evidence. The ingas ranking in 1(b) shows that the colonisation process may have occurred later in Sussex than in East Anglia, and would explain the unexpected prominence of this county. This may also have applied to Essex. The continued importance of Norfolk can also be noted. The eastern emphasis of the

Figure 3.3: Place Names in Ingaham

██ MEAN [M] — Mx2	
▨▨ Mx2 — Mx3	
▤▤ Mx3 — Mx4/x5	Areas with National Average,
⠿⠿ Mx6 — Mx7	or Above, Totals

Figure 3.4: Place Names in Ingas

MEAN [M] — Mx2
Mx2 — Mx3
Mx3 — Mx4
Mx4 — Mx5

Areas with National Average,
or Above, Totals

material is further exhibited by 2(a) and 2(b), whilst 2(c) is included to show the great importance of the East Anglian/Wash area. This is also brought out by the figures in 3. (Sussex appears so highly due to its high incidence of ingas names.) Yorkshire also should be noted and this must be corroborative proof regarding the campaigns of Octha and Ebissa in the north of England. It is worth mentioning that Wessex features poorly in each table and it is clear that the early English population on the south coast, west of Sussex, must have been small in the fifth and sixth centuries. One note of caution should be sounded and that is that some low ranking areas may, with fresh study, be shown to have a respectable incidence of the earlier strata of topographical names.

When the figures are transferred to field examples then they turn up other interesting features. In East Anglia the ingaham names cluster along the coast between the mouths of the rivers Thurne and Glaven,[67] and along the banks or tributaries of the rivers Deben[68], Little Ouse, Orwell,[69] Waveney[70] and Yare.[71] These speak volumes about sea-borne colonist making the most of riverine routes into the heart of the country.

The Society and Lifestyles of the Early English

Having examined the evidence left on the map it now remains to consider the physical evidence unearthed by archaeological excavations. Before the clues are studied it is necessary to state a number of cautions. Firstly, the clues that we have are often gained by non-systematic methods. Much of it has come to us as the result of chance discovery which only then has been followed by serious excavations. Estimates vary as to how representative our present state of knowledge is. In 1971 the approximate number of early English funeral urns that had been discovered stood at 4,000.[72] Between 1971 and 1973 the excavations at Lovedon Hill, in Lincolnshire, and Spong Hill, in Norfolk, added some 1,500 to this total.[73] While it is unlikely that such major finds will continue into the twenty-first century the basis for evaluation could alter at any time. Secondly, the areas covered by archaeological research are varied (for example, ceramic funeral items, domestic structures, health and demography, jewellery, metalwork, weaponry, etc.). It is vitally important to pull together the findings from various sources in order to gain an overall picture. The alternative is to 'drown' in a sea of facts and specialist opinion. Thirdly, the items recovered from any one site may not be representative of all that once existed at that site. Time can alter or destroy some clues: flax, horn, leather, sinew, textiles and wool can be totally destroyed under normal climatic conditions; wood may leave only damp patches in the soil; a purple stain is all that remains of silver under some conditions; bronze may turn to green powder; pottery can become so decomposed by wet soil that it has to be taped in order to lift the soggy mass from the earth; archaeological techniques (as we have seen) can destroy slight traces of evidence (this may be particularly true where huts were supported by flimsy stakes or where the use of cross-braced uprights and sleeper beams may have avoided the need for deep bedding); acid sands can destroy an entire body including the bones and the teeth. The fourth caution is that advances of a technological nature may revolutionise older interpretations of the evidence. In the summer of 1984 an Iron Age Celt's body was discovered in a peat bog near Wilmslow (Cheshire). The 1,500-year-old body received the latest scientific treatment. The skull was zero radiographed at the Royal Marsden Hospital in order to achieve an X-ray picture with an exceptional definition. The inside of the skull was viewed with the aid of a fibre optic endoscope. The body hairs were studied under an electron microscope while the internal organs were dissected by Dr James Burke of Nottingham. Prior to this the organs had been scanned by a nuclear magnetic resonator and a computerised tomography scanner at St Thomas's Hospital, London. The incision on the neck became the object of attention of Ian West, a forensic scientist from Guy's Hospital, London. The point has surely been made. Even allowing for the fact that Wilmslow Man constituted something of a historical curiosity, scientific advances made accurate analysis much easier. Such a bevy of equipment was not available for the study of the Danish proto English bog people discovered in the 1950s, (for example, Tollund Man, Grauballe Man, etc.). An example of this phenomenon, more relevant to the period under scrutiny here, comes from the research project at Sutton Hoo. This site was first excavated in 1938–9 when a bodyless barrow was found to contain a hoard of treasure sometimes claimed as the grave goods of the East Anglian King Raedwald.[74] Despite careful searches no definite trace of a body could be found in the bone-dissolving acid sand. More recent excavations — such as the British Museum digs of 1965–71 — and research on the items found in the barrow, failed to establish the identity of the ancient owner of the treasure. However, by 1985 new technology had been made available. The Sutton Hoo Research Project began to use a soil sounding radar machine (produced at the Scott Polar Institute, Cambridge). This machine was designed to have the capability of 'mapping' shapes beneath ground surface without resort to damaging digging. Also the use of vinamul — a polymer — has meant that elusive silhouette burials can now be converted to three dimensions as the polymer holds the black stained sand (all that remains of the body) together. In this way form has returned to bodies otherwise destroyed by the acid sand. Had such techniques been available in 1939 the Sutton Hoo 'mystery' might never have arisen. Thousands of children might then have learned a different interpretation of history since the Schools Council 11–16 Project (*What is History*) could hardly then have justified the title of one of its studies — 'Sutton Hoo, the mystery of the empty grave'! As Martin Carver, director of the excavation project, has put it: 'The evidence is very fugitive and vulnerable, the answer has to be in technology.'[75] The use of modern techniques may be contrasted with the experiences of W. F. Grimes who was present at the excavations of 1938–9. Grimes (later professor of archaeology at the London University and director of the Institute of Archaeology) was then assistant archaeological officer at the Ordnance Survey Department. He excavated such fragile remains as wood and metalwork with '. . . a curved packers needle, which was very sharp — when it started out — and an ordinary glue brush!'

Having taken all of these cautions into account it is possible to gain an insight into the lifestyles and conditions experienced by English men and women between AD410 and 600. One of the first facts that can be established, with a fair degree of certainty, is that these people constituted a minority of the population of Britain. Demography of the Dark Ages is notoriously difficult but despite these difficulties a consensus has emerged. It is likely that the population of the ex-Roman diocese of Britain fell from over three million to just under one million between 410 and 600. It only began to rise again in the seventh and eighth centuries and did not accelerate rapidly until the tenth century.[76] This analysis by J. C. Russell was followed by a similar, if more extreme, analysis by Richard Hodges.[77] In his *Dark Age Economy* he produced a logarithmic graph which illustrated a population of about 250,000 in AD400 followed by an increase to 700,000 in AD500 and a drastic drop to about 250,000 by the last quarter of the sixth century. His arithmetical graph gave a population of about 350,000 in 400 which fell to 250,000 by the 440s, rose to 600,000 by 550 and plummeted down to under 200,000 between 550 and 590. Unfortunately Hodges did not offer corroborative evidence alongside his graphs. Neither was he specific as to whether he intended to represent the population of the entire country (English and British) or whether his work applied only to English areas. His figures would seem to be far too low to imply the former and too high for the latter, which in the sixth century has been assessed as having been between 50 and 100,000.[78] However, this field of study is full of difficulties. Using the formula employed in the calculation of the last set of figures and applying it to the more recent cemetery discoveries the numbers of the English can be gauged as a minimum of 65,000 and a maximum of 130,000 by the mid fifth century.

Similar problems have arisen when attempts have been made to calculate life expectancy. A rather small sample of skeletons has led to a rather speculative set of life spans of 34.7 years for males, 33.1 years for females in rural areas (36 years for men, 29.9 years for women in urban areas).[79] Other research has suggested even lower figures of 33 years for men, and 27 years for women in the fifth century.[80]

We reach much firmer ground when attempting to outline living conditions. The waves of English settlers who swamped the earlier controlled deployments were agriculturalists. Their villages may have been related to Romano British farms but they were not related to any government policy. Most sites, founded after the mid fifth century, had no obvious link with state policy. The siting of one of these new villages probably owed more to a farmer's eye for land than an administrator's eye for the cost-effective deployment of a policing force. River routes seem to have played an important part in helping to site a village. The early topographical names show how crucial an abundant water supply was for people and their animals. Other factors must also have been important. Soil type would have dictated something of the attractiveness of an area. 'Islands' of sand and gravel in areas of workable clay seem to have been popular. They provided dry sites for villages. If the 'island' was too large then it probably deterred settlers from siting villages on it. Alluvial soil was also cultivated. In Lindsey the chalk impregnated soil at the foot of the eastern scarp of the Wolds was popular as it made for a fairly light and fertile soil. Elsewhere in Lindsey the small area of gravel on the west of the Wolds was also farmed. Along the upper Thames the settlers at Benson, Harwell, Wallingford, etc. farmed the soil overlying upper green sand and gault. The earlier topographical sites followed the streams into the Lambourn Downs. In many areas chalk uplands may have been cultivated from the earliest times. As a rough rule of thumb good soil was found in much of East Anglia (away from the Fens), north Kent, the Sussex coast, much of the Midlands and much of the coast between the Wash and the Humber. Medium quality soil was to be had in areas of Hampshire away from the New Forest, east Sussex and west and central Kent. Poor soil covered much of southern Essex and the New Forest.[81]

The availability of mineral deposits in an area must also have affected its attractiveness, as must have the availability of firewood and building materials. Equally important was mast and acorns for pigs and pastures for their long wool sheep, goats and oxen. Open water was a source of fish and other edibles. The newcomers must have had a mixed farming economy geared to near self-sufficiency.

Roads must also have played a part. The remnants of imperial routeways would have provided hard ways through heavily forested areas and over rough land. This is particularly important given the huge areas of the country which were still forested despite Roman and pre-Roman deforestation. Large forests covered much of Essex, west Sussex and the mid Severn in the fifth century. The woods of Sussex probably extended into Kent and those of Essex may have reached as far as the Chilterns to the west. In addition there were large forests to the north of the Solent and to the west of it the forest of Selwood blocked routes into what is now Somerset. The importance of roads through these areas should not be underestimated. Those that crossed the forest of Andredesleag must have provided the way by which warriors and settlers from Sussex reached the Thames in the 480s and 490s. Without them this brief period of 'Greater Sussex' could not have been achieved. As well as Roman roads a plethora of smaller trackways must also have existed. The early English must have made use of these. In reality both rivers and roads must have been used. Key sites may have been where both forms met at river crossings. Many early English villages were near shallows where rivers could have been crossed. The English place name element 'ford' may have once expressed more than a description of a simple topographical feature. At times it may have been used as a quasi habitative element.[82]

The importance of routeways increased as embryonic markets became established. The reality of such trade can be demonstrated by reference to similarities in fashions of pottery shape and decoration. In some areas the villages that traded with each other were fairly close together (for example, the fashions which linked the cemeteries of the Cambridge region). At other sites there is evidence to suggest that some peddlars travelled large distances. By the sixth century the Cambridge region had commercial links to both east and west. The parallels in pottery fashions that have been found at Barton Seagrave (Northamptonshire) and at Kettering (Northamptonshire) reveal infiltrations into the upper reaches of the river Nene and its tributaries, whilst the pots found at Lackford suggest relations with the Angle settlers of west Suffolk. The inhabitants at Lackford also enjoyed some degree of intercourse with the communities of western Norfolk and some (Caistor by Norwich, Markshall) even further to the east. This is evidence left by commercial centres and peddlars. It also shows that the area, later known as 'Middel Engle' ('Middle Anglia') experienced some degree of fusion as early as the mid sixth century. Further north this had happened by the late fifth century. By this time the ceramic centres of Sancton and Elkington were both producing exuberantly bossed pots (Buckelurnen) of a comparable design. Clearly the workshops of Lincolnshire and the Yorkshire Wolds found more to promote unity than division in the great river system of the Humber. A prolific, if more geographically contained, commercial enterprise was that of the Illington-Lackford potters. Some 220 examples of their work have been discovered at ten sites including Castle Acre, Little Wilbraham (Cambridgeshire), Rushford (Norfolk), St Johns, Cambridge, West Stow Heath.[83] This workshop supplied western parts of Suffolk and Norfolk, with outliers in the Cambridge region. The reasons for this particular restriction are unknown. An exception to this was the so-called Lackford/Thurmaston 'ladybird potter', whose characteristic designs have been found as far apart as Suffolk and Leicestershire. However, this may have been due less to a wide marketing technique than to the wanderings of an itinerant craftsman. Such a phenomenon would help explain similarities between pots found in Norfolk, the Trent valley, south Lincolnshire and the Yorkshire Wolds. The mobility of potters would explain this as well as the other possibility of travelling salesmen working from a fixed distribution point.

Early England was a society made up of scattered villages. By the sixth century these villages, as we have seen, were drawing closer together. While self-sufficiency must have been the norm with regard to most agricultural products this was not the case when it came to luxury goods such as jewellery or some funerary ware. These themes of agricultural life and developing trade provide a balance to the martial themes that dominate the English literary sources. For most early Englishmen everyday reality was based on plough and home, not on military adventure. In such communities the arrival of peddlars must have provided a rare diversion from the endless cycle of agricultural pursuits. Such communities must have been very closely knit. They could also be very intense. Blood feuds between communities were not uncommon. The system known as 'wergild' ('bloodprice') was an attempt to reduce the violence of these feuds. By it each class in society was allocated a money value and the compensation due for a wound varied according to the nature of the injury and class of the one injured. The system was devised to replace revenge with economic transactions. It was an old system being mentioned by Tacitus. However, the tight-knit communities often preferred vengeance to compensation. The nature of these communities can be glimpsed at in the rhymes known as Gnomic Verses. They express the outlook of lower-class English society. Many must be very old indeed. They are unpretentious and sometimes mere truisms: 'Frost must freeze, fire eat wood.' At other times their simplicity affords us a look into a forgotten society. At such times we are far from the upper-class concerns with royal pedigrees and campaigns. We are, for a moment, in a more simple, perhaps more fundamental, world — the world of the early English village. 'Unhappy is he who must needs live alone' complained one verse. For such a man solitude meant estrangement from the village community. He was an 'eardstapa' — a wanderer (a grasshopper!). He lived his life dislocated from kin and cultivators of the land. Another writer recorded how

There should be terror of the grey wolf.

For the man apart from the rural community life was spent in the realm of the 'grey wolf'. A poetic tradition stated that he who lived among the wolves would be destroyed by them. The truth of this was as much spiritual and sociological as it was zoological. The woods and wolves meant real danger to a lone man but this was only half the story. Such a situation was also highly symbolic. It stood for social isolation and cultural alienation. Such isolation made a man less of a man and more of a wolf.

The other side of this coin was that close-knit communities were often socially sealed to outsiders. A man may have been as much aware of his danger in entering such a community as in being forced to leave his own: 'Often a man passes by the village, afar off, where he knows he has no certain friend.' If close-knit villages offered home and security to the 'in-person' they were quite capable of hostile parochialism with regard to the 'out-person'. The Russians have a proverb — 'Man is a wolf to man.' We may recall, there should be terror of the grey wolf.

All of this may sound melodramatic. If it is then it is historic melodrama. The themes outlined above were very real elements in Old English poetry and must have dominated the minds of men and women before AD600 as well as afterwards. In Old English the word for an exile ('wraecca') also meant 'wretch, wanderer, unhappy man'. It may be contrasted with the word's development in Old High German, where it became synonymous for 'adventurer, knight errant' and eventually became the Middle High German and German 'recke' or 'warrior, hero'[84] The English etymology is symbolic of the man cut off from his own. In the poem entitled *The Wanderer* the poet told the story of a man who had lost his chief. The loss of status so caused was compounded with separation from home. Like the symbol of the grey wolf this separation was made to be a symbol of social disintegration. The hero complained how

All is full of trouble, all this realm of earth
Fate is changing all the world.
Here our wealth is fleeting, here the friend is fleeting,
Fleeting is the man, fleeting is the kinsman.
All the earth's foundation has become an idle thing.

In a similar vein the Old English poet made the central character of the poem, *Deor*, elaborate the theme of a poet who had lost his place to a rival and was thus forced to experience a desperation similar to that expressed in *The Wanderer*:

how harsh and bitter is care for companion
to him who has few friends to shield him.

Deor's only consolation lay in the phrase 'thaes ofereode, thisses swa maeg' which may be translated as 'that went by this may too'. For a man separated from his home this was clearly the best that could be said.

The early English communities were probably added to each spring as new immigrants made the sea crossing to Britain. This time of year was best suited to travel. Storms would have ruled out a winter passage. The Gnomic poets knew the difficulties of winter sea journeys and concluded that: 'Weary shall he be who rows against the wind'.

More graphic is the account in *The Seafarer* in which the poet contemplated his past life:

> aching hearted on ice cold seas,
> having wasted whole winters, the wanderer's beat,
> cut off from kind. . .
> hung with hoar frost, hail flew in showers.

The idea of winter cutting a man off in an alien port was taken up by the writer of the poem *Beowulf*. During the famous account of Hengest in Frisia the poet recalled how Hengest was left at Finnsburgh[85] and at least one reason for this was climatic.

> He was prevented from passage of the sea
> in his ring beaked boat: the boiling ocean
> fought with the wind, winter locked the seas
> in his icy binding; until another year
> came at last to the dwellings, as it does still,
> continually keeping its season,
> the weather of rainbows. . .[86]

What was true of the warrior Hengest must have been equally true of thousands of anonymous English people *en route* to Britain.

The types of boats used in the crossing are something of a mystery. Very few have survived from this period. The Nydam boat was discovered in Schleswig in 1863 but was clearly designed to be used in the sheltered waters around the Baltic islands. More relevant was the ship unearthed at Sutton Hoo. This vessel (27 m long) was propelled by 40 oarsmen and probably by a sail as well.[87] It was steered by means of a large steering oar over the stern, or possibly by a side rudder. As this ship was built around AD600, other similar, if smaller, ships may have been employed in the fifth century. A smaller vessel (15.25m long) was found at Snape (Suffolk) in 1862–3.

Having examined the clues so far it still remains to see what kinds of dwellings were used by the people who have been described. The most common type of dwelling in early English villages was the sunken feature building (SFB in gazeteers and journals). These huts had a floor set below ground level. At Sutton Courtenay many were some 3–3.9 m long, 2.4–3 m wide and sunk to a depth of 0.45–0.6 m below ground level. At Mucking many of the 208 sunken huts measured 4 m long by 3 m wide. Some huts of this type were used for industrial purposes, others were homes. Some were converted into rubbish pits. The latter use has led to the common assumption that all such huts were squalid and 'little better than holes in the ground'.[88] There is however an increasing amount of evidence which suggests that such a generalisation is unjustified. Some sunken feature buildings exhibit some sophistication. At West Stow it is likely that wooden floors were constructed above ground level. In such a building the sunken feature was probably a cellar under a suspended floor.[89] If this was a general feature it would force us to re-evaluate the lifestyle associated with such buildings.

Excavations have shown that sunken feature buildings were very numerous in early English villages. At Canterbury six were discovered close to a Roman road and were probably the 'abodes of settlers of rank and file, or mercenaries'.[90] At Porchester similar huts were built near a finely carpentered well. They have also been found at Catterick, Dorchester on Thames and at Latimer villa. This type of hut continued to be popular into the fifth and sixth centuries. At West Stow many of them were found near the remains of pits and hearths. These wood- and reed-built houses may have had hearths protected by a mud shield in order to preserve the combustible material. The West Stow site was used for over 200 years. At Mucking (Orsett) well over 100 such huts provided shelter for mercenaries guarding the river route to London. Other large groups of SFBs have been excavated at Abingdon, Butley (Suffolk), Caistor by Yarmouth (Norfolk), Cassington (Oxfordshire), New Wintles (Oxfordshire), Radley (Berkshire), Rickingshall Superior (Suffolk), Sutton Courtenay, Thetford, Wykeham (North Yorkshire), etc.

The layout of early English villages has posed a problem to scholars. They appear to be significantly different to continental examples. The English sites seem to exhibit a low level of planning in their layout. This may have been due to the greater amount of space available on sites in this country. This may have encouraged the 'spilling out' of settlements. However, at Chalton Down and at Catholme (Staffordshire) an orderly plan of farm houses and ancillary buildings has been discovered. It may be that this 'difference' is not as total as was once thought.

A more serious question has arisen over the relationship between SFBs and larger framed buildings. On the continent many settlements grew up with a mixture of the two types. Some of the framed buildings were 'long houses' used to accommodate both animals and people. Some were barns and other ancillary buildings. Alongside these structures were SFBs. At the inland site of Wijster there were 80 major buildings alongside 140 SFBs (the site being occupied from the second to the fifth centuries). It has often been assumed that the long houses were used by the upper classes and the other types were used by lower-class English people. At Warendorf, in Westphalia, small huts clustered around a hall in a way reminiscent of Wijster. In Britain though this pattern did not reproduce itself. Few framed buildings have been discovered relative to the numbers of SFBs unearthed. Does this mean that English society, in Britain, was different to that of the proto English? This question has led to the following speculations:

1. The migrations may have altered the economic base of these communities. It may be this that is reflected in the layout of excavated sites.
2. Smaller groups of immigrants may have lived in villages comprised of farm labourers, in this country, at a distance from upper-class landowners.
3. A lower population density than on the continent may have led to a more dispersed settlement pattern.
4. The early examples may not have been made up of villagers as such but rather of mercenaries or farm labourers grouped into 'single class' units.
5. From AD500–900 depressions tracked further north and this may have led to climatic changes that made the animal end of a long house superfluous to requirements.
6. The excavated villages may be atypical. They may represent failed enterprises. The successful (and typical?) English villages may lie under modern ones.

These options may help explain the different patterns but may be unnecessary! It is possible that many sites did have framed buildings but that these were destroyed by older techniques of archaeology. In this way the clues left by post holes, stake holes, post pits, post trenches, sill beam trenches, slots or stone patterns (with their shallow foundations) may have been missed in an attempt to get at other (often Roman) remains. This is a distinct possibility as some major sites may have had a mixed pattern of buildings. At West Stow the post holes (representing three 'halls') were found on a small knoll. The largest of these was 10 m in length. Even if, as some experts insist, these 'halls' were really barns, others cannot be so easily dismissed. At Sutton Courtenay the SFBs were built around an open space that may once have been the site of an above-ground building. At the Eynsham site of New Wintles framed buildings were built alongside SFBs. At Mucking (Orsett) there may have been at least one framed building and one (7.3 m long) dominated the much smaller community at Mucking (Linford). Remains such as post holes and post-in-trench structures may indicate as many as 26 above-ground buildings at Catholm. Here SFBs constituted a minority!

The new material may make the older theories redundant. The chalk downland site of Chalton has already been noted. This West Saxon (or South Saxon) village with its post-in-trench, above-ground buildings (similar to Roman types) may point the way towards many such sites awaiting discovery on the downs of Wessex. Whilst it is still possible that English villages, in Britain, did experience important developments it is likely that these were not so revolutionary as was once thought.

The first immigrants who established villages in the fifth and sixth centuries lived in an environment that was often hostile. Not only did they face British opposition but the presence of aspiring war lords meant that they may also have been threatened by those of their own culture. Due to these factors the ownership of weapons was a fundamental necessity. This does not mean that the English were 'a nation in arms'. The professional fighting man constituted a minority of the population. Campaigning was carried out by kings, chiefs and their companions. The responsibilities of farm and home prevented the average man from taking part in such activities. Nevertheless the English farmer might have had to defend his home from human or animal marauders. To do so he had a fair range of weapons to choose from although only a few of them would have been within his price range.

The most common weapon was the spear. The cemetery evidence from Mucking suggests that here, as elsewhere, spearmen were the predominant group.[91] Spear shafts were often made of ash wood. The iron spear tip was riveted to the shaft through the socket. The tip could vary in length from a few centimetres to 1.5 m. A simple leaf shaped tip was common and in the sixth century an angular concave sided blade was popular.[92] Sometimes the blade was pattern welded. This entailed twisting bands of iron together to form a plait. This was then hammered to form a hard, flexible blade. At times the spear head was formed from a sharpened wooden shaft. The early cemeteries have also given up various kinds of shields. These were often made from a round limewood board. This was sometimes covered with leather as with one example from Petersfinger in Wiltshire. Some shields were formed from layers that resembled plywood. It has often been assumed that laminated shields were the norm but it is now recognised that this is probably a gross generalisation and lamination was but *one* of the techniques that were used in the making of a shield.[93] An iron boss was often placed at the centre of a shield. A hollow behind it allowed the hand to comfortably hold the shield grip. Poorer owners often dispensed with the boss. Shields varied in size. They could be as small as one found at Petersfinger which measured 30 cm in diameter, or as large as the one found at Ringmere, in Sussex, which was 76 cm in diameter. Some were even larger such as the one found at Sutton Hoo (91.4 cm in diameter) which was notable for stylised animal metal decoration and a 'sword ring' which was probably attached to the lower half of the shield. Mound 2 at this cemetery may also have once contained a shield. The dragon's head plate which has survived points to a Swedish origin or inspiration (parallels exist from Ulltuna, Vallstenarum, Valsgarde and Vendel).

Various forms of knives and swords have also been found in graves. Such weapons as swords and the larger knives were not placed in the graves of the average English farmer. They were the weapons of warriors. Perhaps the most famous fighting knife was the scramasax. This was a single edged weapon and was in use in this country as early as the sixth century. One found in Yorkshire (at Uncleby) was 60 cm long. Another one, from the Thames at Wandsworth, was 71 cm. Some were made as small as 35 cm, others as large as 75 cm long. In addition to the scramasax other smaller knives were also used.

The most aristocratic weapon of all was the sword. Such a weapon was the product of many hours of work and was of immense value. A well-made sword was often a family heirloom. They were passed from father to son. This type of ownership was described by the *Beowulf* poet:

> The earls ran to defend the person
> of their famous prince; they drew their
> ancestral swords to bring what aid they
> could to their captain Beowulf.[94]

The swords used against the monster Grendel clearly possessed a great mystique. The same was true of Beowulf's sword. It was

> The ancient heirloom, the hard ring patterned sword,
> Treasure of the Heathobards.[95]

Beowulf's sword even had a name. It was called Naegling. Similarly the warrior hero Waldhere (known from an eleventh-century Old English version of an early-seventh-century Bavarian poem) had a sword named Mimming. This sword was supposed to have been made by the god/culture hero Wayland the blacksmith. In the later Celtic romances concerning Arthur he was credited with owning a sword called Caliburn (later Excalibur). It is clear from this habit of personifying them that swords were considered to have much symbolic, as well as functional, power. Metalworking was not regarded as a merely mechanical pursuit. Behind it lay centuries of semi-religious veneration of the craft. The sword maker was more than a craftsman. He created a weapon capable of both protecting and taking life, a weapon used to gain fame. The acquisition of fame was a vital part of Germanic heroic society. Without a sword a warrior could not fulfil his role. His sword was an extension of his own personality. It was not merely a tool. It was an integral part of being a warrior. This elevated the prestige of metalworking in ancient societies and in modern primitive ones. A Japanese Samurai sword was manufactured with great solemnity. 'Its forging was a religious act that took place after the workshop had been purified and prayers had been offered to the deity of the sword.'[96] Even in the twentieth century, hunting societies have been studied who refer to their knives as 'the sharpness at the thigh'. Such a circumlocution being designed to avoid speaking the name of the weapon.

To do so, it is thought, would be to capture its mystery and minimise its power. These attitudes sound strange to modern, Western ears. They would have sounded less alien to an English warrior in the fifth or sixth century.

The type of sword used in the migration period was not unique to that era. It is known by the technical name of a 'spatha'. It was a two-edged weapon with a fairly thin blade and a rounded tip. Sometimes the blade was pattern welded and it was this that caused Beowulf's sword to be described as 'ring patterned'. The hilt of such a sword was often very simple as was the guard, or quillon. The earliest swords were made with straight pommel bars and guards. Horn, bone, wood or leather was used in their construction. Because of decomposition these are often missing from excavated examples. Due to their high price swords are a rarity in most excavated cemeteries. At Kingston only two out of 308 graves contained swords; at Biffrons there were swords in only seven out of 150 graves; at Sarre the proportion was one sword to every ten inhumations and this is unrepresentatively high; at Holy Well Row cemetery, in Staffordshire, there was found to be only one sword in 100 graves; in 123 inhumations at Burwell in Cambridgeshire there were none. It is difficult to give a national average but it may not be far wrong to assume that perhaps only 1.5–3 per cent of inhumation graves can be expected to contain such a weapon.

If swords were luxuries, helmets were even more so. Only two from the period before 600 have been found. The most famous of these is the one found at Sutton Hoo. It was probably made in this country although it bears a resemblance to helmets found in Swedish boat burials at Valsgarde and Vendel. The interlace pattern on the crown, visor, cheek guards and neck is the type of Germanic animal art known as Style II. Similar decoration is known from graves 11 and 12 at Vendel. The Sutton Hoo helmet may date from the sixth century[97] and may have been the work of a Swedish craftsman who had settled in England. Alternatively it may have been the work of an East Anglian metalworker who had absorbed Scandanavian influences. The other helmet was found at Benty Grange (Derbyshire) in 1848. It was formed from a frame work of iron bands with a silver nose guard. The metal may have been covered with horn. On top of the helmet a boar had been fixed. This animal was a symbol of masculine authority.

As rare as helmets are finds of arrows. Only at Chessel Down, on the Isle of Wight, has a bow (and hazlewood arrow shafts) been found. At Lowbury Hill (Berkshire) a find in a barrow burial may once have been an archer's brace. As rare was the wearing of chain mail. It has been found at Benty Grange and at Sutton Hoo. It is fitting that helmets and mail were found together — both must have been rare and costly items (the mail in the Suffolk boat burial was riveted and welded, not butted together as was once thought).

The creation of weapons was inextricably mixed with religious mythology. Unfortunately no detailed account of early English pagan beliefs has survived. Such beliefs were defeated and scattered by Christianity. Our most detailed accounts are from later Norse legends. It is not a satisfactory approach merely to read these back into the minds of the early English. Nevertheless some clues have survived. Some of these can be gleaned from a study of Tacitus. Other clues survive in genealogies and place names. Some tattered ones were recorded by later Christian writers.

The three principal deities of English pagan religion were Woden, Tiw and Thunor. Woden was the deity equated with Mercury by Tacitus. He appears in Norse legends as Odin — the 'All Father'. He was the principle god but had not always occupied this position. It is likely that his cult was in the ascendance immediately prior to and during the migration period. His name, which appears in Old High German sources as Wuotan, seems to have been derived from 'furious', 'the excited one'. In the twelfth century, Adam of Bremen noted 'Woden id est furor' ('Woden, that is frenzy'). He had connections with the 'hunt of the dead', was associated with sacrifice and the granting of wisdom. As south German tribes began their incursions into Roman territory his cult grew in popularity. In early English genealogies it was Woden who was made to stand at the head of the king lists. He was clearly associated with military prowess and aristocratic authority. He was also credited with the ability to appear in disguise as Grim, 'the masked one'.

One of the most enigmatic of pagan deities was Tiw or Tyr (also known as Tig). He, like Woden held a position of prominence. The name seems to have an etymological link to that of Zeus. Tacitus was probably thinking of Tiw when he wrote of a god called Mars Thincsus or 'Mars of the assembly'. This indicates that Tiw had a dual role as war god and as deity associated with law making. This particular aspect of his cult was introduced to the Roman fort of Housesteads in the third century AD by the regiment Cuneus Frisiorum Aballavensium (from Frisia) or perhaps the regiment

Numerus Hnaudifridi (from Germany).[98] In later sagas Tiw is described as one handed. Tiw's complex authority and his association with both Zeus and Mars may imply that his cult was older than that of Woden. The likelihood is that Tiw was the old sky god, and chief of the gods, but lost his position to Woden. His authority over warfare being a last vestige of his old authority.[99] It may be the name of Tiw that was engraved (in the form Teiwa) on a helmet unearthed at Negau in southern Austria. The lettering would support Tiw's claim to great antiquity. It is an early Germanic type dating from the third to the first centuries BC. There is every likelihood that Tiw was synonymous with Seaxneat (Saxnot, Saxnote), the eponymous founder of the Saxon peoples. A ninth-century charm refers to the trio of Saxnote, Thunor and Woden. The replacement of Tiw by Saxnote makes sense if the two were indeed identical. The genealogies reveal that the displacement of Tiw/Seaxneat was virtually complete by the mid fifth century. Only the East Saxon dynasty claimed descent from Seaxneat. The cult of Tiw was associated with the rune ' ↑ '. This has been found on funeral pots between the Ems and the Weser. In England the rune was used at North Elmham on two pots. On one of these it was followed by an attempt to spell out the god's name in full.[100] It was used on pots at Caistor by Norwich (in at least four cases), Kettering (three cases) and Loveden Hill (three cases). In each case the rune's most likely function was as a charm to protect the dead.

The third major early English deity was Thunor. He later became known as Thor. He appears in Old High German sources as Donar and was associated with Hercules in Roman works of the first century. He was credited with power over weather. Like Tiw, Woden and the goddess Frig his name was attached to that of a weekday. There was probably no greater significance in this than an attempt to replace days named after Roman deities with the names of those Germanic gods with the most similar attributes. In this way Tiwesdaeg (Tuesday) superseded that in memory of Mars; Wodnesdaeg (Wednesday) that of Mercury; Thunresdaeg (Thursday) that of Jupiter and Frigedaeg (Friday) that of Venus. The cult of Thunor was associated with the swastika. This symbol has been found on funeral pots of the fifth and sixth centuries. He was associated with rites of passage — in these cases, death. At Lackford[101] and at Illington[102] the swastikas were made to confront 'wyrms' or serpents. The idea behind this was probably that

Thunor's power would 'confront' the cosmic serpent of destruction and preserve the dead person. This idea is a very old one. It was rooted in Indo-European mythology and can be found in Indian symbolism as early as the second millennium BC. An annular brooch discovered at Hunstanton (Norfolk) had a swastika worked into its centre. It was probably worn as a charm. In later Norse legends Thunor (Thor) was made to carry a hammer and wear a magic belt which doubled his strength.

In addition to this trio other, lesser, deities were also revered. The wife of Woden was Frig (later Norse Frigg). Her name was derived from 'loved one', or, 'noble kinswomen'. In Old High German her name was Frija. She may originally have been Tiw's wife but later became attached to Woden as the cult of Tiw lost ground to that of Woden. In later Legends Frig was made the mother of one Baldr.

The religious beliefs inherited by the fifth-century immigrants to Britain were not part of a unified whole. Rather they were an amalgam of ancient religious concepts. Other, older, beliefs often existed just beneath the surface. Sometimes they became assimilated to the new cults. At other times these older deities became a second race of lesser gods. A kind of religious sub-culture. By the time of the migrations the dominant religious beliefs were masculine and military. However, earlier beliefs were centred on feminine fertility cults. Tacitus named the Anglii as one of the Ingaevone tribes who worshipped an earth goddess named Nerthus. Nerthus was a spring/fertility deity who, even as Tacitus wrote, was giving way to male intruders. There is evidence for this in the name Ingaevone which was formed from the name of their legendary founder 'Ing'. The worship of 'Ing' was a male counterpart to that of the earlier earth mother religion. His very name was related to the word for 'son of. . .' and emphasised his masculinity. Nerthus later changed sex to become the Scandanavian 'Njorthr', father of Freyr who was also 'Ing' (Ingunar Freyr). The totem animal of Ing was the boar. On the one hand this was a fighting animal and stood for warrior prowess. On the other hand it was an earth rooter. It entered the earth and disturbed the soil. It possessed a curious religious dichotomy. Such a totem animal may have represented a transition from an earlier female fertility cult to a later masculine warrior cult. It is highly significant that at Issendorf, in north west Germany, a funeral pot was decorated with the figure of a pig. It may have been a symbolic representation of a dead body being placed in the disturbed earth. As such it may represent a throwback to the earlier cult. Some fertility deities survived into the migration period as the godesses Erce, Eostre and Hretha.

The older fertility cults may be faintly discerned in English genealogies. The king list of Wessex[103] records a list of names *above* that of Woden. Some of these were thought of as semi-divine ancestors. Others represent the old fertility cults. Manuscripts B and C of the *Anglo Saxon Chronicle* head the list with Sceaf.[104] This name is that of the father of Scyld who founded the Danish dynasty and was sometimes called Scyld Shefing (Scyld, son of Shef or Sceaf).[105] The name Sceaf is probably to be understood as 'sheaf' and represents a vegetation cult. In German legend Scyld was found, as a baby, in an open boat accompanied by a sheaf of corn. Manuscripts A, B, C, E and F also mention another name above Woden and that is Beaw. As with Sceaf this name is probably a remnant from a fertility cult, and means 'grain'. It is significant that these names were placed above (that is, *before*) the name of Woden.

Vegetation cults are not the only substrata in the genealogies. Culture heroes can also be found. Some of these must have been regarded as semi-historic characters who had achieved semi-divine status over time. Geat appears in the material for Bernicia, Lindsey (as Geot) and Wessex. Heremod, the Danish king in *Beowulf*, appears in the West Saxon list five places below Sceaf. Godwulf was put in the lists for Bernicia, Lindsey and Wessex. He may also appear, in the form Folcpald, in the Kentish material preserved in the *Historia Brittonum*. His name may represent the ruler called Folcwalda ('folkruler') who was father of the Finn who appears beneath Godwulf in the lists of Bernicia, Lindsey and Wessex. This Finn was probably meant to be the same as Fin Folcwalding ('Fin son of Folcwald') who the poet knew as king of the Frisians in *Widsith*. He was regarded as king of the east Frisians by the compiler of the *Beowulf* poem. Similar, though obscure, elevations of semi historic figures may underlie the names Frealaf and Frithuwulf who appear in the material from a number of kingdoms.[106] The same may be true of the Frithuwald in the genealogy of Wessex and the otherwise unknown Hrathra, Hwala, Itermon, Sceldwea and Taetwa who accompany him. A number of these names are common to a number of lists and were obviously drawn from a common mythological pool.

Creation myths are not represented in the early English sources. However, Tacitus wrote that the Germans considered that the creator of humanity was named Twisto. His son, Mannus, was the founder of the human race. The later Norse writers thought that Woden killed the giant Ymir and created the world from his body. He also, in this process, made man. The cosmology of the early beliefs can be pieced together from later evidence. Detailed and much developed forms of it can be found in thirteenth-century Icelandic sources. Much of it was recorded in the *Poetic Edda* and the *Prose Edda*. The poetic version is known from a manuscript called the *Codex Regius* (of the 1270s). The prose version was edited, in the 1220s, by the Icelandic scholar Snorri Sturluson. According to these later versions the earth was known as Middangeard[107] and was surrounded by sea. In this sea lived Mithgarthsormr, the cosmic serpent. He was pictured as biting his tail. This vivid image of self-consumption may represent a number of ideas: it may imply death consuming all; it may imply a source of the destructive energy at work in the world: it may represent a cycle of becoming and the regeneration of basic life forces. The earth itself, it was thought, was supported by a great tree. In the ninth century Rudolf of Fulda wrote that the continental Saxons described this as 'the universal pillar, sustaining all things'. At the foot of this tree lay a well from which came Wyrd. Wyrd, or destiny, was the irresistible force that shaped the existence of all things — animal and matter.

The fact that the English, of the fifth and sixth centuries, believed in Mithgarthsormr can be demonstrated by reference to three types of evidence: funeral pottery, poetry, place names. The sign of the snake, dragon or 'wyrm' has been found on a number of cremation pots. It was made to confront swastikas at Illington, Lackford and Sancton; it can be discerned in the zoomorphic curves found on some Buckelurnen; it has been noted as an 'S' curve on pots from Lackford and West Keal (Lincolnshire). These types of decoration have also been found on the continent at Westerwanna and at the terp of Beetgum near Leeuwarden. In three examples from Lackford the wyrms have a head at both ends. This may typify the ability to devour, so characteristic of Mithgarthsormr. These wyrm patterns may have been held to represent devouring destruction by cremation or alternatively a dreadful guardian of the dead. It is probable that the symbol should be regarded as ambiguous. Where it confronts swastikas its character was probably meant to be destructive; on its own it may have been meant as a charm. At Sutton Hoo finely crafted dragon heads were placed on the helmet and twelve such heads were used as decorations on the edges of the shield.

The Gnomic Poems also contain references to wyrms in their capacity as guardians of the dead. One such poem runs: 'Draca sceal on hlaewe, frod, fraetwum wlanc', or 'The dragon (wyrm) shall be in the burial mound, ancient, rich in treasure.' The guardian wyrm was a common theme among Germanic poets. In *Beowulf* the hero was made to kill a dragon guarding 'a golden store of rings'.[108] In another myth the hero Sigurd (Sigemund, Siegfried) was pictured as having to kill the dragon Fafnir to gain his treasure.

These ideas were common among ordinary English people. A number of place names mean 'dragon burial mound' or imply a wyrm guarding a spot. Examples include Drakelow (Bedfordshire, Derbyshire, Hereford/Worcestershire), Dragley (Lincolnshire), Drechowe (a field name in Yorkshire), Drakehow (as Drechowe) and Wormwood Hill (Cambridgeshire).[109] The myth clearly had a grip on the minds of the early English farming communities.

All of these examples serve to illustrate the vivid superstition which dominated the outlook of early English men and women. Some of these superstitions have survived in riddles, curses, folklore and the kind of folk medicine preserved in the tenth-century manuscript called *Lacnunga*, in the British Museum. These ideas express the thoughts of people dominated by an environment that they could not begin to explain. Lacking scientific interpretations of the universe they relied on vivid picture language and metaphors. It is surely wide of the mark (indeed patronising) to describe such phenomena as 'earth magic' (let alone existential psychiatry!) as some modern authors have. This implies that we are able to read back our own social and pseudo-scientific concepts into the minds of those whose outlook was radically different to our own.

Before this study of pagan religion is left it may be helpful to note other references to pagan beliefs or practices preserved in place names. They are categorised as follows:

(1) *Place Names Containing the Name of a Deity*

  (a) *Frig*. Freefolk (Hampshire), Frobury (Hampshire), Froyle (Hampshire), Frydaythorpe (Humberside).
  (b) *Grim*. Grimes Graves (Norfolk), Grimsbury (Berkshire), Grimsbury Castle (Oxfordshire), Grims Ditch (Essex, Hampshire, Hertfordshire, Oxfordshire, three in Wiltshire). Grims Hill (Gloucestershire).

(c) *Thunor.* Thunderfield (Surrey), Thunderley Hall (Essex), Thundersley (Essex), Thungridge (Hertfordshire), Thursley (Surrey), Thurstable (Essex).

(d) *Tiw.* Tuesley (Surrey), Tysoe (Warwickshire).

(e) *Woden.* Wansdyke, Wednesbury (Staffordshire), Wednesfield (Staffordshire), Wensley (Derbyshire), Woodnesborough (Kent).

(2) *Place Names Meaning 'Heathen Temple'*

(a) *Containing 'weoh'/'wih' as in the Gothic 'weihs' or 'holy'.* Patchway (Sussex), Weedon (Berkshire, Northamptonshire), Weeford (Staffordshire), Wembury (Devon), Weoley (Hereford/Worcestershire), Weyhill (Hampshire), Willey (Surrey), Wye (Kent), Wyfordby (Leicestershire), Wyham (Lincolnshire), Wysall (Nottinghamshire), Wyville (Lincolnshire).

(b) *Containing 'hearg' as in the Old High German 'haruc' or 'grove', 'holy place'. The original meaning may have been 'stone altar'.*[110] Harle (Northumberland), Harrow (ex Middlesex), Harrowden (Bedfordshire), Harrowdown (Essex), Peperharrow (Surrey).

(3) *General Superstitions*

(a) *Names containing 'hob'/'puca' or 'goblin'.* Hobditch Causeway (West Midlands), Poppete (Oxfordshire, Sussex), Puckeridge (Hertfordshire), Puckington (Somerset), Pucklechurch (Avon). 'Puca' names were often associated with disturbances in the ground such as Puckpit, near Winchcombe and Puckham Scrubs, shown as an earthwork on the 1:25,000 OS map (both in Gloucestershire).

(b) *Names containing 'thyrs' or 'giant'.* Thirspot (Cumberland), Thursden (Lancashire), Thursford (Norfolk), Tusmore (Oxfordshire). The belief in giants was also expressed in poetry. Large scale remains being classed as their work. A Gnomic Poem runs: 'Ceastra beoth feorran gesyne orthanc enta geweorc' or 'Cities (earthworks?) are seen from afar, cunning works of giants'. In the poem *The Ruin* (about Bath?) the poet pondered on 'snapped rooftrees, towers fallen, the work of the giants, the stonesmiths moulders'. The early English also believed in 'dwerg' ('dwarfs'), elves, 'haelwella' (wishing wells) as well as the more sinister 'waelcyrian' ('corpse choosers'), the hand maidens of Woden, etc.

(c) *Totem names*. Swineshead (Bedfordshire, Gloucestershire, Lancashire, Wiltshire, etc.), Shepshed (Leicestershire), Hartshead (Lancashire), Broxhead (Essex, Hampshire). At these places the heads of pigs, sheep, deer and badgers may have been used for ritual purposes. At the Suffolk site of Butley pits full of ox heads have been discovered. One skull was placed on a spearhead. At Frilford the head of a pig was buried in a pagan cemetery and at Soham (Cambridgeshire) the head of an ox was buried in a similar fashion. More sinister practices may have led to the place name Manshead! (Bedfordshire, Leicestershire, Nottinghamshire). It is possible that some of the immigrants practised human sacrifice. Roman authors noted such tendencies in the first century. In some of the graves at Mitcham extra human heads were present, implying either human sacrifices or head hunting! In a study of 19 graves from Finglesham (Kent) there was found to be a total of twelve extra skulls. Also at Finglesham and at Camerton, Fathingdown (Kent), Mitcham, Sewerby (Humberside) and Worthy Park there is evidence to suggest that women, in isolated incidents, were buried alive. At Sewerby the burial was on top of the richly furnished grave of an older woman.

These last items bring us to the subject of death. The rites of passage associated with this event deserve special attention. There was no uniform practice concerning the disposal of the dead. Different practices flourished in different parts of England at different times. Whether or not the English settlers used sanctified burial sites varied throughout the country. In general the English sites were not placed over older ones. This may have been due to the fact that many later English villages were not related to Roman centres.[111] Nevertheless a substantial minority of cemeteries were placed close to, or on, earlier burial grounds. At Frilford and long Wittenham the burial grounds were sited close to Roman cemeteries. At Kirton Lindsey and at Loveden Hill (both in Lincolnshire) the English placed their cemetery near a prehistoric site. At Abingdon a Bronze Age ring ditch was used. This is reminiscent of continental practices. At Galgenberg bei Cuxhaven and at Westerwanna the great cemeteries were centred on burial mounds of the Neolithic or Bronze Age. When the English cemetery at Spong Hill was excavated in 1979 it was discovered that the site had supported human settlements for millenniums. Mesolithic flints were found in the ploughshare along with Neolithic flints and pottery. Bronze Age pots were found in four pits and a ring ditch revealed by the excavation may have been the remains of a Bronze Age burial mound. Roman pits and ditches were also found and this author noted coarse grey Romano British pottery as well as English cremation pottery when he surveyed the site in the summer of 1985. In 1984 work at Sutton Hoo produced similar results. This English cemetery may have originally covered over four hectares and had been a folk centre for some 3,000 years having five main periods of occupation: Neolithic, Beaker, Bronze Age, Iron Age and early English. Sometimes (as at Cirencester, Denton villa, Girton, Greetwell villa, and Lackford) Roman buildings were used for burials.

The earliest burial ritual was cremation. This was practised in the Elbe Weser region and in Angeln. In this country it was particularly popular in the Anglian areas on the east coast. In some of these areas it continued throughout the pagan period. Great cremation cemeteries were established, on Humberside, at Sancton and further south at Loveden Hill and South Elkington. Others existed at Caistor by Norwich, Illington and Lackford. The greatest number of excavated cremation cemeteries are to be found in Norfolk (see Figure 3.3) which contains 17 per cent of the national total, Lincolnshire (11 per cent) and Suffolk (9 per cent). The use of the rite also extended into the east Midlands. It can be found along the rivers linking into East Anglia (for example, Cambridge, Kempston, Kettering, Newark, Thurmaston). Inhumation was also practised at most of these inland sites. In some cases this may indicate changing beliefs. At others the rites may have been mixed from the start. Some may have experienced intrusions by inhuming folk.

The actual process of cremation seems to have taken place in a trough in the ground. During the burning the temperature reached around 460 degrees centigrade. Such heat melted bronze and glass jewellery. It would have incinerated any grave goods. As the *Beowulf* poet noted: '. . .the dark wood smoke soared over the fire. . .until the body became ash, consumed even to its core'.[112] Such a process called for a marked amount of skill. In the 1950s Joan Kirk suggested that the art of cremation was practised by certain people only. Cremation, in her view, may have occurred at a limited number of crematoria linked to recognised cremation cemeteries.

Figure 3.5: Graph to Show Incidence of English
Cemeteries (According to Rites) in Counties with an
Overall High Rating

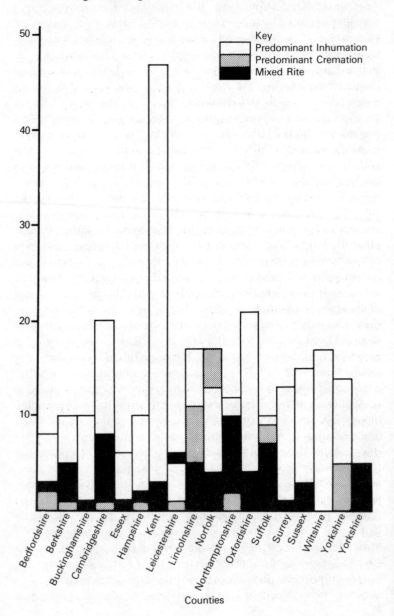

Counties

Water transport may have been used to transport bodies to these places. There is every likelihood that Kirk's assessment is correct.

Sometimes animals were cremated with humans. At Illington dogs, horses, oxen, pigs and sheep were burnt. At Sutton Hoo 1.1 kg of burnt bones were deposited on the Byzantine silver dish. Human ashes were sometimes placed in cooking pots and bronze bowls. Usually special funeral pots were used. It is this funeral ware that has provided modern scholars with the bulk of their ceramic evidence. Sometimes miniature grave goods were placed among the ashes (for example, at Abingdon, Illington, Sancton, Worthy Park). Sometimes these consisted of manicure sets made up of combs, knives, shears and tweezers. These may indicate that the body was shaved before it was burnt. Cremation urns were often laid out in rough rows. Sometimes they were covered with stones (as at Castle acre) or a small cairn (as at Thurmaston). At Spong Hill a lid for one urn (not actually found with a pot) was decorated with a small carved figure, 14.5 cm high. The figure (unique both in this country and on the continent) is seated with his hands supporting his head.

The beliefs behind these cremations are difficult to interpret conclusively. It is possible that the burning was intended to release the spirit of the dead person. This belief may have given rise to the deliberately holed urns of Anglo Frisian type. The early 'window urns' found in Cambridgeshire, Kent and Lincolnshire may have been designed to serve a similar purpose. The glass set into the pot may have been intended as a portal through which the spirit could escape.

Inhumation was also practised and gradually replaced cremation in most areas. Although it is often inferred that this was a later form of rite, some proto English tribes practised it on the continent. It was known along the Rhine and in Jutland. Even if it was a later development from cremation this should not be over-stressed. Under Roman and Christian influence many English communities may have adopted inhumation soon after their arrival in this country. Because of this the 'flight from cremation' should not be used too rigidly in dating cemeteries. The rite was popular in Deira and Bernicia, the south east, Sussex, the south Midlands and Middle Anglia. Of the total number of predominantly inhumation cemeteries excavated (see Figure 3.5) 47 per cent are in Kent, 21 per cent in Oxfordshire, 20 per cent in Cambridgeshire, 17 per cent in Wiltshire, 17 per cent in Lincolnshire, 15 per cent in Sussex, 14 per cent in Yorkshire, 13 per cent in Norfolk, 13 per cent in Surrey and 12 per cent in Northamptonshire. Whilst the Lincolnshire, Norfolk and Suffolk examples indicate the futility of looking for uniformity of rituals (ranking very highly as cremation counties) the overall emphasis of the statistics is towards the south of England (with the exception of Yorkshire). On the Thames cremation was a popular rite but was outnumbered by inhumations. This is true of sites as far apart as Berkshire, Kent and Surrey. Abingdon has the highest ratio of cremations to inhumations but even here the latter rite predominated. As settlers moved away from the Thames the distance from the crematoria might have assisted the adoption of inhumation. British influence must also have helped in this.

Inhumation cemeteries were often sited away from villages. This may have been because it was thought that the unburnt dead inhabited their graves. This may have led to a fear of ghosts. The placing of grave goods with the inhumed dead may substantiate the hypothesis that inhumed corpses were considered to live in their graves in a more marked way than cremated corpses. Women were often buried with their jewellery. In Anglian areas fashionable girdle hangers were included. At Kingston and at Kempston work boxes were also buried. Men were often buried with their weapons. In Anglian areas wrist clasps were sometimes added to the stock of brooches. Often food was put in the grave too. In the Cambridge area and at Holy Well Row eggs were buried; hazel nuts have been found at Faversham; beech nuts were put in a grave at Hitchin (Hertfordshire); oysters were placed with a body at Sarre; an ox head was laid between a man's feet at Girton; the jaws of sheep and cuts of meat, as well as cowrie shells, have been found in some cemeteries. At Sewerby the body of a dog (or wolf?) was draped over a man's body, and was probably meant as a guard or a companion. Of these animal offerings only dogs and horses seem to have been buried whole. Ornaments were buried with the rich dead. A glass beaker, from the sixth century, was found at Mucking. At Finglesham beakers were excavated in graves 203 and 204. Some of this glassware may have been manufactured in the Rhineland. Some of it may have been manufactured in Kent. Buckets were found in graves at Long Wittenham and in grave 600 at Mucking. The former was probably made in Frankish territory and was found with a Frankish cauldron. At Taplow (Buckinghamshire) the early-seventh-century mound contained a drinking horn complete with silver gilt mounts and a bronze bowl from Coptic Egypt. The Sutton

Hoo mound also contained a coptic bowl. This mound also contained an iron standard, a sceptre, a lyre, silver bowls and spoons, drinking horns and vessels, a Byzantine silver dish and other items! The Sutton Hoo mound also concealed a ship measuring some 27 m long.[113] Another mound at this site once held a ship which was 8 m long. West of the great ship burial in mound 1 another ship burial was sited on a promontory. Unfortunately this was excavated prior to this century and the site is now covered by a plantation. At Snape (Suffolk), on the river Alde, another boat (15.25 m long) was discovered in 1862. Pseudo boat burials occurred at Caistor by Yarmouth. Here at least twelve graves were constructed by laying pieces of a boat over a body. These boat burials are from the early seventh century although the Sutton Hoo boat must have seen service in the late sixth.

In some cemeteries corn was burnt and sprinkled over the bodies (for example, Marston (Northamptonshire), Sandy (Bedfordshire)). At Camerton it was found in 42 graves. It had been sprinkled on the upper half of the body only. The corn had not been used in the burial of babies.

The positioning of bodies was not uniform. At Abingdon one skeleton was found lying face down with its left arm across its forehead. Sometimes a body was laid on top of another one, or side by side. Children were often buried beside adults. This may mean that they were put into any available grave. At Chadlington (Oxfordshire) a corpse was decapitated (to stop it from walking after death?). The orientation of bodies was often irregular, until the east-west pattern of Christian burials. Some cemeteries had a predominant orientation (for example, east-west at Abingdon) but often there were many variations from the norm. At Worthy Park it was a 'chaotic arrangement'.[114] Children's orientation sometimes differed from that of adults. Why this should be so is not clear, nor is it clear why heavy flints were thrown onto the heads of dead children at Winnall (Hampshire).

The mixing of funeral rites is best seen in the mixed cremation/ inhumation cemeteries. Mixed cemeteries were popular in Middle Anglia. Northamptonshire has 13 per cent of them, Cambridgeshire has 10 per cent (see Figure 3.5). At Girton pottery from the same workshop was used for both rites. This despite the fact that the rites represented radically different views of the nature of the after life! Were mixed marriages allowed between the two communities? If so, was the rite followed matrilineal or patrilineal? So far these fundamental questions remain unanswered. What is likely is that pagan religion was fractured and turning to agnosticism. Bede described how a Northumbrian noble responded to the preaching of the Christian Paulinus:

> Man appears on earth for a little while: but of what went before this life or of what follows we know nothing. Therefore if this new teaching has brought any more certain knowledge, it seems only right that we should follow it.[115]

Such sentiments would probably have been at home in the mixed-rite communities of the sixth century. To such a scene of cultural chaos and doubt the Christian Gospel offered a sound and persuasive alternative.

One more rite remains to be considered in detail and that is the practice of mound burial.[116] The earliest use of this rite is difficult to assess.[117] There is evidence, however, to suggest that it began in the early sixth century. At Finglesham at least seven barrows were raised over inhumation graves. Grave 204 was probably so covered around 525 AD. The small barrow over grave 203 was probably built between 550 and 570. The forms of barrow burial used in this country were:

(1) *Primary inhumation*: a barrow built over an unburnt body
(2) *Primary cremation*: a barrow built over a burnt body
(3) *Secondary inhumation*: an unburnt body placed in a pre-existing Neolithic or Bronze Age barrow.
(4) *Secondary cremation*: a burnt body placed in such an ancient burial mound.

The use of barrows clearly had geographical limits. The Derbyshire hills contain 21.5 per cent of all primary inhumations and 16.5 per cent of all secondary inhumations. Wiltshire is well represented with 13.5 per cent of all primary inhumations and 28 per cent of all secondary inhumations. Kent has 20 per cent of all primary inhumations and Sussex has 15 per cent of all primary inhumations and 4.5 per cent of secondary inhumations. It is noteworthy that a number score highly on both types of barrow inhumation. It was once thought that secondary burials predated primary ones.[118] The Finglesham evidence undermines this theory. It was also once thought that barrow burial began in Sussex. It was thought that from here it spread into Kent and from there was spread as a result of Kentish power and prosperity at the end of the pagan period.[119] This concept of a single cultural source is now less appealing. It is just as possible that the English of Derbyshire evolved their own rite. This is especially likely if isolated cases of barrow burial were indigenous to continental Germanic culture.[120]

Barrow burial was related to inhumation. Very few such burials were primary cremations (only two in Derbyshire, one in Kent, one in Oxfordshire, two in Suffolk, one in Surrey, one in Sussex). Only one secondary cremation is known (at Risby Poor Heath, in Suffolk). This may be because the dead were thought to live in the large barrow. Such a belief would relate more effectively to inhumation.

Societal attitudes towards barrow burial varied. In Wiltshire and the Peak District the secondary burials were often isolated. In Yorkshire whole communities used a prehistoric tumulus. Similar differences can be discerned regarding primary inhumations. On the Isle of Wight and in Kent and Sussex they have been found in clusters. Elsewhere such burials were often isolated (for example, Asthall barrow (Oxfordshire), Taplow). This may have been because away from the primary foci of barrow burial the rite was only used for the most privileged aristocrats. The high incidence of such burials in Derbyshire and Wiltshire may indicate that in these areas a nomadic, campaigning, warrior society lasted well into the seventh century.[121]

Barrow burial therefore can be dated from the early sixth century onwards. It was a development of inhumation practices. Primary and secondary aspects of the burials cannot be used as a fixed dating mechanism. The fashion was known nationally but was particularly popular in some areas. It was probably a symbol of rank in all areas but especially so in those areas away from the primary foci of the fashion. The barrow was a lasting memorial. A Gnomic Poem runs: 'Beorh sceal on eorthan grene standan' ('The barrow must (will ever) stand, green upon the land'). The funeral rites which accompanied a barrow interment may be hinted at in the *Beowulf* poem. After the death of Beowulf his people — the Geats — built

A barrow on the headland,
it was high and broad, visible from afar. . .
they buried rings and brooches in the barrow. . .
Then twelve brave warriors, sons of heroes,

rode round the barrow, sorrowing,
they mourned their king, chanted
an elegy, spoke about that great man.
They exalted his heroic life, lauded his daring deeds. . .

Such a description may be an echo of rites that were conducted at a primary or secondary barrow inhumation. In *Beowulf* the poet made these events follow a cremation. This practice of heaping grave goods on a primary cremation is unknown to archaeology. It may be that the poet confused two traditions.

Notes

1. J. N. L. Myres, *Anglo Saxon Pottery and the Settlement of England* (Oxford, 1969) p. 22.
2. Bede, *A History of the English Church and People* (Harmondsworth, 1968), 1.15.
3. Ibid.
4. Newark.
5. Loveden Hill.
6. Illington, Markshall, Spong Hill.
7. Lackford.
8. Sancton.
9. Sandy.
10. V. I. Evison, 'Early Anglo Saxon Applied Disc Brooches, Part 2, in England', *Antiquaries Journal*, 58 (1978), pp. 260–78.
11. Helpstone.
12. Kempston.
13. Kempston.
14. Sleaford.
15. Girton.
16. Sancton.
17. Caistor by Norwich, Mundesley, Spong Hill, Wormegay.
18. Lackford.
19. Hornchurch.
20. J. Campbell, 'The Lost Centuries' in J. Campbell (ed.), *The Anglo Saxons* (London, 1982), p. 31.
21. J. N. L. Myres, *A Corpus of Anglo Saxon Pottery of the Pagan Period* (Cambridge, 1977), p. 39.
22. A. MacGregor, 'Barred Combs of Frisian type in England', *Medieval Archaeology*, 19 (1975), pp. 195–8
23. F. Stenton, *Anglo Saxon England* (Oxford, 1971), 3rd edn, p. 37.
24. Tacitus, *The Germania*, 7.
25. Bede, *A History of the English Church*, 5.10.
26. H. R. Loyn, *The Governance of Anglo Saxon England, 500–1087* (London, 1984), p. 13.
27 M. Wood, *In Search of the Dark Ages* (London, 1981), p. 62.
28. H. Moisl, 'Anglo Saxon Genealogies and German Oral Tradition', *Journal of Medieval History* 7 (1981), pp. 215–48.

29. Moisl, *Anglo Saxon Genealogies*, p. 235

30. A point made frequently by P. H. Sawyer, *Roman Britain to Norman England* (London, 1978) and emphasised by P. Hunter Blair, *Roman Britain and Early England, 55 B.C.–871 A.D.* (London, 1963), p. 206.

31. J. Morris, *The Age of Arthur* (London, 1973), footnote to p. 324.

32. Stenton, *Anglo Saxon England*, p. 47.

33. *The Fight at Finnsburgh* (see Chapter 1, this volume, note 26).

34. *Beowulf* (Harmondsworth, 1973), line 899.

35. Ibid., line 3182.

36. Ibid., line 922b.

37. Ibid., line 1012.

38. Ibid., line 1046.

39. Ibid., line 1170.

40. *The Wanderer* (see note 33 above).

41. *The Wanderer*.

42. *Beowulf*, line 1882.

43. Ibid., line 1714a.

44. Ibid., line 63.

45. *The Husband's Message* (see note 33 above).

46. A full analysis can be found in A. H. Smith, *English Place Name Elements* (Cambridge, 1956), *EPNS*, vol. 25, part 1, pp. 282–303.

47. *EPNS*, vol. 1, part 2, p. 42.

48. E. Ekwall, *Concise Oxford Dictionary of English Place Names* (Oxford, 1960), p. 224 and p. 382.

49. Ibid., p. 290.

50. *EPNS*, vol. 1, part 2, pp. 31–2.

51. Smith, *English Place Name Elements*, p. 192.

52. For an insight into the discussion see: Ekwall, *Concise Oxford Dictionary*, p. 264; *EPNS*, vol. 1, part 1, p. 42; P. Reaney, *The Origin of English Place Names* (London, 1960), pp. 114–16.

53. C. Copley, *English Place Names and Their Origins* (Newton Abbot, 1968), pp. 141–3.

54. J. Kemble, *The Saxons in England* (London, 1849).

55. Copley, *English Place Names*, p. 140.

56. A. H. Smith in *Place Names and the Anglo Saxon Settlement* (Oxford, 1956) thought that 'folk names of this kind, in the genitive plural -inga- occur only in those place names combined with elements like ham. . .tun, leah, wic, etc. . . . which belong to a slightly later period when the groups of folk established their permanent homesteads' (p. 229).

57. Reaney, *Origin of English Place Names*, p. 107.

58. Smith *Place Names*, pp. 76–7.

59. R. G. Collingwood and J. N. L. Myres, *Roman Britain and the English Settlements* (Oxford, 1937), p. 368.

60. Smith, *Place Names*, wrote 'The first group of ingas names formed from personal names is ancient whereas the second group formed from older place names could have been created at any time in the Old English period.' (p. 76).

61. J. M. Dodgson, 'The Significance of the Distribution of English Place Names in -ingas, -inga- in South East England', *Medieval Archaeology*, 10 (1966), pp. 1–29.

62. B. Cox, 'The Significance of the Distribution of English Place Name Elements in Ham in the Midlands and East Anglia', *EPNS Journal*, 5 (1973), pp. 15–73.

63. J. Kuurman, 'An Examination of the ingas, inga, Place Names in the East Midlands', *EPNS Journal*, 7 (1975), pp. 11–14.

64. M. Gelling, 'English Place Names Derived from the Compound Wicham', *Medieval Archaeology*, 11 (1967) pp. 87–104 and Gelling (1978), op. cit., ch. 5.

65. M. Gelling, *Signposts to the Past* (London, 1978), p. 118 examines the evidence regarding north-east Berkshire and the Fobbing/Mucking area of Essex.

66. Based on compilations such as K. Cameron, *English Place Names* (London, 1977), 3rd edn.

67. For example, Banningham, Bessingham, Erpingham, Gimingham, Lessingham, Trimingham.

68. For example, Badingham, Cretingham, Framlingham, Heveningham, Letheringham.

69. For example, Barningham, Finningham, Icklingham.

70. For example, Ditchingham, Gillingham, Mettingham, Worlingham.

71. For example, Ellingham, Hardingham, Hassingham, Honingham, Raveningham, Surlingham.

72. L. Alcock, *Arthur's Britain* (Harmondsworth, 1971), pp. 310–11.

73. J. G. Hurst, 'The Pottery' in D. Wilson (ed.), *The Archaeology of Anglo Saxon England* (Cambridge, 1976), p. 294.

74. The claim cannot be verified. Other candidates include Anna and Ethelhere.

75. The *Sunday Times*, 30 December 1984. In August 1985 (23 August), on the BBC television news programme 'Look East', Peter Leach, senior supervisor of the site, announced that in the second excavation season the new technology was being used to support the idea that Christian burials (east-west orientated) were superimposed on earlier and deeper graves of the pagan period (north-south orientated) and that this probably took place in the seventh century.

76. J. C. Russell, 'Population in Europe 500–1500' in the *Fontana Economic History of Europe* (London, 1969), Chapter 1.

77. R. Hodges, *Dark Age Economy* (London, 1984), p. 164.

78. Alcock, *Arthur's Britain*, pp. 310–11.

79. D. Brothwell, 'Palaeodemography and Earlier British Populations', *World Archaeology*, 4 (1972), pp. 75–87.

80. This may be compared to 23.7 years in India in 1890–1900 and the lowest recorded figure of 27 years (male and female) in the Vallee de Niger, Mali, in 1957–8.

81. D. Hill, *An Atlas of Anglo Saxon England* (Oxford, 1984), soil map on p. 7.

82. M. Gelling, *Place Names in the Landscape* (London, 1984), p. 2.

83. J. N. L. Myres *Anglo Saxon Pottery and the Settlement of England* (Oxford, 1969), map 10.

84. *Oxford English Dictionary* (Oxford, 1933), vol. 12, pp. 364–5.

85. The Danish warriors having returned to their homes.

86. *Beowulf*, lines 1130–6.

87. R. Bruce-Mitford, *The Sutton Hoo Ship Burial. A Hand Book* (London, 1979), 3rd edn, pp. 76–7.

88. M. Beresford and J. Hurst (eds), *Deserted Medieval Villages* (London, 1971), p. 174.

89. M. Jones, 'Saxon Sunken Huts: Problems of Interpretation;, *Archaeological Journal*, 136 (1979), pp. 53–9.

90. P. Rahtz, 'Gazeteer of Anglo Saxon Domestic Settlement Sites' (appendix A) in Wilson (ed.), *Anglo Saxon England*, p. 413.

91. See the article 'Mucking, the Anglo Saxon Cemeteries', *Current Archaeology*, 5 (1975–6), no. 50, pp. 73–80.

92. M.J. Swanton, *The Spearheads of the Anglo Saxon Settlements* (London, 1973).

93. H. Harke, 'Anglo Saxon Laminated Shields at Petersfinger — a myth', *Medieval Archaeology*, 25 (1981), pp. 141–4.

94. *Beowulf*, lines 794b–7.

95. Ibid., lines 2036–7.

96. H. Reid and M. Croucher, *The Way of the Warrior* (London, 1983), p. 141.

97. G. Speake, *Anglo Saxon Animal Art and its Germanic Background* (Oxford, 1980), p. 31.

98. D. Breeze and B. Dobson, *Hadrian's Wall* (Harmondsworth, 1978), p. 265. Tacitus made a number of references to Germanic deities. Indeed in one study the author considered that Tacitus' account of the religion of the Semnones was a description of the worship of Woden. J. Westwood, *Albion* (London, 1985), pp. 69–70.

99. B. Branston, *The Lost Gods of England* (London, 1984 edn), p. 186.

100. North Elmham (Spong Hill) pot 1564. See Myers, *A Corpus of Anglo Saxon Pottery*, vol. 2, plate 3b, p. 372.

101. Myres *Anglo Saxon Pottery*, Figures 4, 8 and 49.

102. Ibid., Figure 69.

103. *Anglo Saxon Chronicle* entry for 855 mss A, B, C, E and F. The majority of modern English references to the *Chronicle*, in this study, are from Garmonsway's excellent translation, *The Anglo Saxon Chronicle* (London, 1954), 2nd edn.

104. See Appendix 1. H.

105. In Aethelweard's ms of the *Chronicle* Scef is three places above Taetwas and the name Scyld (below Scef) replaces the usual name of Sceldw(e)a.

106. Bernicia, East Anglia (Frealaf only), Kent, Lindsey, Wessex.

107. Also known as 'Midgard', 'Midgarth'. It was this form (meaning 'middle enclave') which gave rise to 'Middle Earth' in J. R. Tolkien's *Lord of the Rings*.

108. *Beowulf*, line 3054.

109. Gelling *Signposts*, pp. 141–2.

110. Ekwall *Concise Oxford Dictionary*, p. 230.

111. D. Wilson, *The Anglo Saxons* (Harmondsworth, 1971), p. 34.

112. *Beowulf*, from the translation by K. Crossley Holland (Cambridge, 1968).

113. Bruce-Mitford, *The Sutton Hoo Ship Burial*, p. 76.

114. Myres *Anglo Saxon Pottery* note 2, p. 122. See also S. Chadwick Hawkes, 'Orientation at Finglesham: Sunrise Dating of Death and Burial in an Anglo Saxon Cemetery in East Kent, *Archaeologia Cantiana*, 92 (1977), pp. 33–51.

115. Bede, *A History of the English Church*, 2.13.

116. Referred to in passing regarding Sutton Hoo.

117. Although A. Meaney in *A Gazeteer of Anglo Saxon Burial Sites* (London, 1964) considered that a seventh-century date was the most likely one for the start of primary barrow burials (p. 19), she did allow, however, for the possibility that secondary burials may have occurred as early as the mid sixth century in the Peak District, the Yorkshire Wolds and in Wiltshire.

118. Meaney, *A Gazeteer*, pp. 18–19.

119. Ibid., p. 19.

120. See the barrow burial in the *Beowulf* poem.

121. Collingwood and Myres, *Roman Britain* p. 417.

4 THE FOUNDING OF THE KINGDOMS

Despite a bitter resistance, the English established permanent colonies in many areas of Britain. The campaigns of Arthur and Ambrosius were only a temporary set-back to the inexorable process of English settlement. Within two generations of Arthur the English were once again on the offensive. Their advance would never again be as seriously resisted as it was around the years 480–500. Nevertheless all these statements are great generalisations and it would be mistaken to expect a uniform pattern of English settlement. The real picture varied from area to area depending on regional circumstances. In some places the English, of the late fifth century, entered areas of established settlement. These primary settlement areas had a history of Germanic immigration, generations old. In other places the colonists, who followed Hengest and Horsa, were themselves the vanguard of the advance. In addition, conditions were bound to differ as established colonies became over-populated and established an expanding frontier policy to relieve pressure of numbers. In these areas conditions might imitate those of the earliest pioneering settlers, long after such conditions had vanished in the areas of primary settlement. In order to examine the growth of English power it is necessary to study it area by area. The areas relevant to this study are East Anglia and the Wash, the Humber–Trent area, Kent and Sussex, Wessex (Thames valley, Hampshire, Wiltshire) and Britain north of the Humber.

East Anglia and the Wash

Despite the continued emphasis in the *Anglo Saxon Chronicle* on Kent, Sussex and Wessex it does not make sense to begin with those areas. One of the oldest centres of English immigration was East Anglia and the Wash. This is hardly a surprise. English colonists, sailing from the Frisian coast and northern Germany, could cross to this area without sailing south into the English Channel. This area of the east coast was very exposed to English raiders, or immigrants. In addition, the river systems of the Wash and East Anglia — Cam,

161

Ivel, Lark, Little Ouse, Nene, Orwell, Ouse, Slea, Stour, Waveney, Welland, Wensum, Witham, Yare, etc. provided a comprehensive transport network into the heart of Britain. Settlements from the settlement/colonising phase (if not the earlier immigration phase) often clustered close to the river network.[1] This river system linked East Anglia to the east Midlands and to the Lincoln area. Cemeteries dating from before AD 500 (many showing use of cremation rites) have been discovered along the river Nene leading to Kettering, Great Addington (Northamptonshire), and Northampton; along the river Ouse towards Bedford; along the river Cam to Cambridge, Girton, and Haslingfield — and then onto the pathway known as the Icknield Way to Dunstable, and Luton; along the little Ouse to Thetford; along the River Lark to Mildenhall, etc.

This area had known sizeable English immigration from Roman times. Caistor by Norwich, Caistor by Yarmouth, Cambridge, Colchester, Hoxne, Illington, Markshall, Thetford and West Stow undoubtedly had English troops stationed in them before the end of Roman administration. That this deployment was not always harmonious can be illustrated from Caistor by Norwich. Here modern excavations discovered 36 people massacred in one of the town's houses. The killing had probably occurred in the early fifth century. However, it is incorrect to assume that this indicates a major uprising. The killing seems to have been limited to only one house. No other buildings had been burnt down. In fact, this little walled town, of some 14 hectares, probably declined more as a result of economic dislocation than the sword.

As the fifth century progressed immigration increased into East Anglia. Small pottery bowls found at West Stow, Barrington (Cambridgeshire) and Haslingfield, (Cambridgeshire) were probably used by troops stationed in the area after 410. Similar types were used on the continent in eastern Holstein and further west in the Cuxhaven area and at Feddersen Wierde (where occupation ended about 450). The revolt of Hengest and Horsa can only have accelerated the movement into the area. The English population of East Anglia continued to receive fresh arrivals until the end of the fifth century. There is even a possibility that this continued into the sixth. Many of these newcomers came from the Anglian homeland on the continent. There are parallels between pottery found at Caistor by Norwich and types found at Hammoor and Sorup in Schleswig. The later name of the area — 'Eostengla' —

commemorated this racial orientation. It was to be remembered as East Anglia (partly to differentiate it from the lands of the Middle Angles of Cambridgeshire and Northamptonshire). However, this simplifies a more complex situation. There is every reason to believe that the immigrants were racially mixed. The Anglian parallels have already been observed. To this, though, could be added similar parallels with Saxon-type pottery from Wehden–bei–Lehe (north east of Bremerhaven) on the mouth of the river Weser. The clear implication of this evidence is that both Angles and Saxons landed together on the Norfolk coast. A similar picture can be gained from place names. Saxton (Cambridgeshire) and Great and Little Saxham (Suffolk) are from the Old English 'Seax-tun' and 'Seax-ham' respectively. Both refer to Saxon settlers in East Anglia. Other peoples also took part in the colonisation. A number of places around the Wash contain the element 'Swaefas' or 'Swaef'. This is the Old English form of the Germanic tribal name 'Swabian, Suevi or Suebi' (see figure 4.1). The instances are Swaffham (Norfolk), Swaffham Bulbeck (Cambridgeshire) and Swavesey (Cambridgeshire). Another form — 'Swafa' — possibly underlies Swaton (Lincolnshire) and Swaby (Lincolnshire). These latter two have undergone later Scandanavian influence.

Nevertheless it would be incorrect to challenge seriously the degree of Anglian influence between East Anglia and the Humber. It was clearly the most influential cultural factor from the late fifth century onwards. However, it would be wrong to consider it the only factor. Whilst the inhabitants of Saxham, Swaffham, etc. may have stood out due to their uniqueness in their area they were still there. They show that it is a mistake to look for 100 per cent tribal purity in England. Considering the degree of cultural intercourse on the continent this is hardly surprising. An area illustrating this excellently is Middle Anglia (Old English 'Middel Engle'). This people lay south east of the later kingdom of Mercia. Situated on the rivers Cam, Nene and Welland, it was an outlier of the whole Wash complex. It covered much of the modern counties of Northamptonshire, Bedfordshire, Cambridgeshire, north Buckinghamshire and east Oxfordshire. By the mid seventh century it had been annexed by the Mercian King Penda who set his son — Peada — over the territory. It was, however, a culturally distinct area and many finds here show links with the Saxon Elbe Weser region (including window urns and equal arm brooches). However, other finds from the Cambridge area (cruciform brooches) indicate Anglian origins.

It is possible that this mixed little community was a loose alliance of various peoples with no supreme royal family over it. This complexity may underlie a faulty reference to this people in the *Anglo Saxon Chronicle* for 653. Manuscript A describes them as the 'Middle Saxons' whilst manuscripts B, C and E use the correct term 'Middle Angles'. The error may have been inspired by knowledge of mixed ethnic origins rather than by a confusion with the long defunct kingdom of Middlesex. Its influence may have spread as far south west as the Chilterns as well as into the Ivel valley, south Bedfordshire and the area about Hitchin (Hertfordshire). Some of its constituent peoples may have included the Gifle, Hicce and Gyrwe (recorded in later Mercian documents).

The East Anglian area speaks more of complexity and cultural diversity than it does of unity and uniformity. Its ancient division into the 'north folk' and the 'south folk' may indicate it was once two kingdoms. (Bede referred to joint kingship in East Anglia (*History of the English Church and People*, 3. 18, and this may indicate divisions of longstanding.) It is likely that the tribes who inhabited the fens had their own noble families. It is possible that some had their own kings. The people who gave their name to Cretingham (Suffolk) had a name identical with the Gothic tribe called the Greutungi.[2] Such people must have had leaders of substance. However, nothing of their early history has been recorded.

The kings who eventually fused East Anglia into one unit were neither purely Angle nor purely Saxon. Every indication is that the dynasty had strong Swedish connections. According to Nennius, the first king to rule over the East Angles was named Wehha. He was the son of Wilhelm, descended from Hryp, Hrothmund, Trygil, Tyttman, Caser (Caeser!), Woden Frealaf. However, the dynasty took its name from Wehha's son Wuffa. They were called the 'Wuffings' — the 'descendants of Wuffa'[3] The centre of their royal power was about Rendlesham on the River Deben. Their royal burial site was at Sutton Hoo. It was from this site in 1939 that the greatest Dark Age discovery yet made in Britain occurred. The great boat burial and the treasures discovered with it were probably a tribute to the power and wealth of the Wuffings. It is likely that the treasure accompanied the burial of Wuffa's grandson Raedwald — the only East Anglian king to become the overlord of the southern English. However, the Wuffings were comparative latecomers to Britain. Wehha most probably established his power base no earlier than the 520s. When he did so he chose Suffolk, south of the primary settlements in Norfolk. It is possible that the newcomers displaced an earlier dynasty ruling from Norfolk. This dynasty may have included members of the later Mercian royal house. The consolidation of East Anglia probably took place in a period when the local English were recovering from reversals inflicted by the British. The great dykes on the western borders perhaps indicate frontiers established in troubled times and the loss of the Cambridge area to the British.

The Sutton Hoo burial casts light upon the sixth-century origins of the Wuffings. The remains of the shield are similar to ones found in graves at Vendel in Sweden. The sword ring on its lower half is similar to one found at Valsgarde. 'The shield may have been brought from Sweden just before the burial took place. But the probability is that it was an heirloom. . .which fell into disrepair in England.'[4] The sword, pattern welded with multiple chevron patterns, is similar to Swedish work, as is the iron chain work and the great buckle. The purse lid recalls styles found at Bjornhovda and Torslunda. The Swedish connection is also seen in the jewellery (two flat mounts) using cloisonne garnets.

Despite the Swedish influence it would be wrong to regard the influences in the mound burial as purely Scandanavian. The Wuffings clearly ruled a people of mixed culture and much in the mound was unique to Britain. It arose from a fusion of styles. The helmet, though similar to Swedish ones from Uppsala, also has notable differences and is in many important aspects unique to this country. Moreover the Wuffing genealogy betrays confusion at its Swedish end. It is not similar to the royal house of the Svear (the kings who ruled in Uppland — the area with the most striking parallels to Sutton Hoo). It has resemblances to the genealogy of the Geats who ruled south of Lakes Vannen and Vatten in southern Sweden. There is also a possible, oblique link, to the Danish royal house — the Scyldings. It is perhaps fitting that even the royal house of East Anglia reveals racial complexity. An equally persuasive case for links with Scandanavia can be made on the basis of ceramic evidence. One form of pot found in Gotland, Sweden, from AD 350 onwards has parallels in England. Examples include Caistor by Norwich, Elkington, Girton, Hornchurch (Essex), Lackford, Mundesley (Norfolk), North Elmham and Wormegay. There are other parallels to this form in west Jutland. Pottery from sixth century contexts in Gotland is similar to items discovered at Kempston, Sleaford and further north at Sancton. More

Scandanavian influence has been discerned at Helpstone (North-amptonshire) and at Linton Heath (Cambridgeshire). Here, the style of some biconical pots is reminiscent of Norwegian types. These examples make it extremely likely that Scandanavian settlers were present in some areas of East Anglia (and elsewhere) much earlier than the establishment of the Wuffing dynasty.[5]

Essex

To the south of East Anglia lay the kingdom of the East Saxons. Separated from the north by forests it did not really belong to the East Anglian complex. Dense woodland may have extended from Essex to the Chilterns.[6] Even its name shows it to be different. Bede described it as being formed from Saxon peoples. This is in contrast to his description of the northern neighbours of Essex as Angles. It seems likely that Essex enjoyed a rather chequered history. It was never a major centre of population and it did not enjoy the prestige of other English kingdoms.

Essex did not enjoy great prosperity in Roman times. It had the colonia of Camulodunum within its boundaries (probably as an administrative capital for the Trinovantes tribe) but no great villa network. Small-scale potteries, small hamlets, longshore villages on the Thames and the shore fort of Othona (Bradwell on Sea) did not make it exactly a rich area. It must have stood very much in the shadow of Londinium. However, there were areas of strategic importance in Essex. In the east it faced the low countries. More importantly, in the south, its coastline could be used to guard the entry to the Thames estuary. Romano Saxon pottery at Colchester and Great Stambridge indicates the presence of Germanic soldiers there before the end of direct Roman rule. Such soldiers must have constituted garrisons in Roman centres. Later the presence of German mercenaries (AD 410–50) left traces at both these centres and others. The evidence to suggest the presence of these troops is in the form of early carinated bowl pottery (the other sites are Feering, Heybridge, Linford, Little Oakley and Mucking). The most striking of these sites is that of Mucking. It lies about five miles south of Basildon, near the coast. Sited on a bend in the Thames it commands the stretch of the river where the 'Sea Reach' becomes the 'Lower Hope'. It could easily be used to close the Thames to shipping, or at least provide a stationing post in a sensitive area. In the early English period it was comprised of two sites — Mucking (Linford) and Mucking (Orset). Of these two, the latter was by far the most important site. It consisted of over 100 sunken feature buildings and ditches. In addition a framed building possibly stood on the edge of the excavated site. With such a position on the Thames its use by mercenaries seems obvious. That the site had close contacts with Roman society is indicated by mixed Saxon and Romano Saxon pottery in at least two of the huts. The site shows signs of continuity into the sixth century. Over the period of its use its function may have altered. In its later period it may have been used seasonally, provided a transit camp for use by immigrants, or been a permanent village.

On the other sites a similar, if not so intense, English occupation occurred. At Heybridge the five sunken feature buildings may suggest an occupation as old as Mucking. At Little Oakley the evidence — two pits and a hearth — is harder to assess. Two other sites where at least one sunken feature building has been excavated are Bulmer and Chadwell St Mary. Rather more suggestive evidence has come from Great Dunmow and Rivenhall. In the former a framed building was built over a Roman gravel pit. Saxon pottery lay on the floor of a Roman shrine. In the latter a Saxon pot was found in one wing of a Roman villa. It is also possible that at this site a Roman barn was re-used. The fact that the Saxon pottery was discovered under a fallen roof is important. It indicates English occupation before the villa fell into disrepair and total ruin. At Hornchurch the settlers had cultural similarities with Gotland in Sweden. Perhaps this site, situated between the rivers Beam and Ingrebourne, was settled with permission from the authorities in London, only 15 miles away to the west.

The later fifth-century occupation has left continued evidence at Great Stambridge and Little Oakley. There is also ceramic evidence for settlements at Great Chesterford and at Stevenage and Hertford. These last two Hertfordshire sites may have come under 'Greater Essex'. The great Chesterford cemetery may be more realistically regarded as an offshoot of the Middle Anglian community at Cambridge.

The place name evidence that suggests topographical names may be from the migration period may explain some of Essex's place names. A number of the Essex ingas names are in the singular. It is highly likely that such types arose from stream names and not from tribal communities. Examples may include Bocking, Clavering,

Cobbins Brook, Cressing, Fobbing, Frating, Lawling Hall, Matching, Mucking and Tendring. The Mucking area contains many topographical names — Basildon, Bowers, Canvey, Chadwell (with a confirmed early occupation site), Horndon Orsett, Stifford etc.

Whatever the early origins of Essex it seems to have suffered some form of eclipse; in the early sixth century it is highly probable that it was one of the areas that suffered from the British revival at Badon. It is likely that the ruling dynasty of Essex established itself in the early sixth century. Its King Aescwine probably ruled in the decades after 510. Apart from his place in the king lists[7] he is otherwise unknown. He may have established his rule over the demoralised area. Alternatively this may have been done by his father Offa, or grandfather Bedca, before AD 500.

The dynasty of Essex was a peculiar one. Firstly, it claimed descent not from Woden but from Seaxneat (or Tiw). Secondly, the dynasty may not have been purely Saxon. The rejection of Woden was unique. Whether it represented a dynasty of inferior social status or one simply different to the others is not clear. Either way the kings of Essex claimed descent from the warrior god of the Saxon peoples. It is of interest to note that Seaxneat (or Tig or Tiw) was probably part of an older mythological stratum to that of Woden. It is also noteworthy that the cult of Tiw is preserved in the place names Tewin (Hertfordshire) and Tuesley (Surrey). Both areas may have attracted settlers who had cultural affinities with Essex. The cult of Tiw is also associated with the runic symbol ' ↑ '. This sign has been found on pottery in England and on the continent. In England at Caistor by Norwich and at Loveden Hill, Lincolnshire. On the continent at Altenwalde, Galgenberg, and Westerwanna.

There is evidence that the kings of Essex were aware of more than their religious uniqueness. They may also have had peculiar tribal characteristics. In the seventh century Kent suffered a period of being administered by usurpers, or foreign kings. One of these was named Swaefheard of Swefheard. He was a son of the East Saxon King Sebbe. This king had two other sons, one of whom was named Swaefred or Swefred.[8] The importance of these two names — Swaefheard and Swaefred — lies in the first element 'Swaef' or 'Swef'. It is the Old English form of the tribal name 'Swabian, Suebi, Suevi'. The form Swef is an East Saxon form of Swaef, as 'ae' could become 'e' in East Saxon. The implication is that the tribal name was significant enough to be a part of two princes' names. (It is fair to note that the element also occurs in the genealogy of Deira, in the form Swefdaeg. However, there this name appears only three below Woden[9] whereas the East Saxon names were from historic times and must have represented a conscious choice to preserve the tribal name. To suggest that the East Saxon dynasty was established by Deira[10] would be, of course, without foundation.) It has already been shown that there were elements of the Swaefe in East Anglia. A type of pot found at Caistor by Norwich had similarities with styles found in Swabian areas of eastern Holstein and Mecklenburg. The pot at Caistor was probably made after AD 400. This indicates that a movement of this tribe into eastern England is quite plausible.

It can also be shown that the cult of Tiw and the migration distribution of Swaefe was related. The cemeteries of Galgenberg and of Westerwanna (where pots decorated with ' ↑ ' were found) are in the vicinity of Cuxhaven, where the Elbe reaches the sea. In the fourth century a migration of Swaefe occurred. They left the area of east Holstein and Mecklenburg and migrated to the lower Elbe and the region of Stade, near Cuxhaven. This placed them among the tribes using the ' ↑ ' rune. This exact relationship between tribe and belief is found in Essex. Such a phenomenon could have occurred if we assume close relationships between Saxons and Swaefe in the Cuxhaven region. The poem *Widsith* (lines 35–44) may imply this when its writer referred to Swaefe, south of the river Eider, in the company of the Myrgings. It is likely that the Myrgings were a Saxon people. If this is so, the relationship dated from the end of the fourth century. It may also be relevant that the Swaff- names in the Cambridge area came very possibly from Swaefo Saxon communities [see figure 4.1]. In all these cases a picture is slowly building up of a close relationship between the two tribes — both on the continent and in England. This flowered in Essex. Here a Swaefo Saxon noble family established itself in an area of Saxon settlement. Its mixed ethnic/religious character surfaced in the genealogy of the family. However, this was only part of a mixed culture in the area (as shown by Swaff and Tiw place names and the ' ↑ ' rune).

By the end of the sixth century this dynasty had extended its dominance over 'Greater Essex'. This included Middlesex, London and much of Hertfordshire. This region had closer cultural affinities with Kent and Sussex than it did with East Anglia and Cambridge-shire. The kingdom of Middlesex has not left any record of its dynasty or early history. At some stage in its development it may have included the Saxon folk of the Geddings, Gillings and the Mimmas.[11] It also extended itself south of the Thames. This southern province is the only explanation of the name Surrey. Derived from the Old English 'Suthrige' it means 'southern district'.[12] Considering its geographical position such a description only makes sense in terms of Middlesex being the 'northern district'. By a charter of 704 Middlesex was described as a 'provincia' ('province'); this probably means it was a subdivision of Essex. This 'northern district' included the old Roman port of London. The state of London by the fifth century has given rise to much controversy. With the exception of a few finds (for example, a sunken feature building at the Savoy) London has produced no major evidence of early English occupation. This may have been because of the power of Verulamium that overawed the English, north of the Thames. It is possible that the English at Croydon, Mitcham, Shepperton and Taplow were employed by a British power. They, along with the colonists in the Darenth valley of Kent, may have originally been made up of troops dependent on London. Such troops may have resisted incursions by other English people. This would help explain the lack of evidence for English occupation in London. Alternatively, the real reason may simply have been that London's power was eclipsed in the late fifth century. Such a loss of economic importance may have deterred colonists from entering it. This lack of trade may help explain the relative poverty of the English Thames-side settlements at Horton Kirby, Northfleet and Riseley.

Historians who argue for the continuity of London as a major centre face a major problem. If its occupation continued to be significant why did its trade not help to enrich the Thames-side Saxon communities? To this of course it may be answered that the trade along the Thames was not an integral part of London's survival. However, such an assertion puts an axe to the root of the argument. Roman urban centres were based on trade. Their sophistication was a superstructure raised on an economic foundation. They relied on a money economy and the marketing of surpluses. Both these were severely dislocated from the 450s onwards. Indeed Roman coin production and supply was geared to the army's expenditure.[13] The departure of the Roman military would have meant that by the 430s coins were no longer the common means of exchange. Without them (that is, without money trade) it is incon-

Figure 4.1: East Englian Place Names Containing
Swæfas, Swæf, Swafa

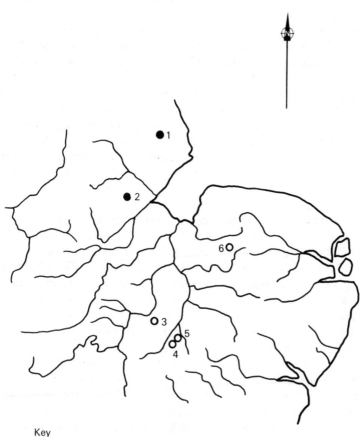

Key
O Place Names containing Swæfas or Swæf
● Place Names possibly containing Swafa

1 Swaby, LI; 2 Swaton, LI; 3 Swavesey, CA; 4 Swaffham Bulbeck, CA;
5 Swaffham Prior, CA; 6 Swaffham, NF;

ceivable that London could have continued as a viable urban unit.

That London experienced something of a hiatus is self-evident. However, this does not mean that it was totally deserted. It is likely that British squatters continued to use its declining facilities until English settlers began an occupation from the mid sixth century onwards. The city may have preserved *something* of its original economic function until the late fifth century.[14] By 604 London (and with it Middlesex) had passed into East Saxon hands. London had become the capital of Greater Essex. This may indicate the beginnings of a revival of trade along the Thames. At this time the king of Essex was Aescwine's grandson Sabert. His father Sledd(a) had married Ricula (or Ricola) the sister of Ethelbert of Kent. By 604 Sabert 'ruled the province under the suzerainty of Ethelbert, who . . . governed all the English peoples as far north as the Humber'.[15] This clearly demonstrates something of the dynamics of kingdom building. One kingdom (Essex) absorbed a lesser (Middlesex) only to be subdued by a greater kingdom (Kent). Such a process must have repeated itself time and again in the fifth and sixth centuries.

The later history of London lies outside the scope of this study. However, a glimpse of it may help to give an impression of the importance of its reviving trade. In 604 Ethelbert of Kent allowed London to become an episcopal see. Its first bishop was Mellitus, appointed by Augustine, archbishop of Canterbury. When Sabert of Essex died (converted through the preaching of Mellitus) the kingdom of Essex reverted to paganism. Mellitus was expelled from London. It was some years before the church was re-established in London as 'the people of London preferred their own idolatrous priests, and refused to accept Mellitus as bishop'.[16] By the third quarter of the seventh century the kings of Kent had a royal hall in the city, their authority in it having temporarily declined with the death of Ethelbert in AD 616. By the 640s the city had once again become a commercial centre. The legend 'Londvniv' found to be stamped on an issue of gold coins (tremisses, or, thrymsas) bears this out. Further evidence of the revival of the money economy is found in the form of silver coins called sceattas. These proto-pennies — some stamped with 'Lvndonia' — may date from as early as the 650s,[17] although other numismatists prefer dates as late as the 680s, 690s, and even 730s for the London issues. By this time London's trade was probably well established with the continental centres of Quentovic, Dorestad and Domburg. It is this that underlay the reference to London, in the law codes of Hlothhere and Eadric of Kent (673–85). The city was described as 'Lunden-wic'. We may translate this as the 'market town of London'. Such a translation of 'wic' is open to criticism but any other meaning in this case is difficult to imagine. The element was clearly added to the name without any earlier reference to such a use, regarding London. However, London's growing power contrasted sharply with the political insignificance of Essex. It did not have the population, or the pretensions, of many of the other kingdoms. It was from first till last in the shadow of the other kingdoms. Its greatest asset — London — would have attracted the desires of other, more powerful, states. Essex was, as we have seen, subject to the kings of Kent by 604. It later passed under the authority of the East Angles and of the kings of Wessex. It was not to regain its independence as 'from the middle of the seventh century Essex was little more than a dependency of Mercia. . .'[18]

The Humber–Trent Area

The rivers Humber, Trent, and their tributaries, provide a vast routeway into the east of England. The river Humber was not a racial or a tribal boundary in early English times. Ceramic evidence, from the seventh century suggests similar fashions in Yorkshire and in Lincolnshire. This is similar to the Thames valley where Surrey and Middlesex were linked by the river not divided by it. It would perhaps be correct to refer to the English, who settled on both banks of the Humber, as 'Humbrensians'. Nevertheless the Humber did *become* a political boundary. Those living to the north of it came to describe themselves as the 'Nordanhymbrorum Gens'.[19] But this was not always the case and although Bede used the form 'Nordanhymbri', in the eighth century, early alternative forms existed, such as the 'Transhumbrana Gens' or the 'Ultra Humbrenses' — even the simple 'People of the Humber'. Despite this the political divisions along the line of the Humber became more important than cultural similarities.[20] In this study, and for the sake of convenience, this simplistic division is adhered to. The area south of the Humber will be studied separately from that north of it.

South of the Humber there existed a number of kingdoms. The collective term 'Sutangli' ('South Angles/English') and 'Sudanhymbra' ('Southumbrians') was occasionally used to describe them. The *Anglo Saxon Chronicle* (MS E) uses it when it describes (year 449) how from Woden sprang the royal houses 'of the peoples dwelling south of the Humber'. However, such a term could not make sense of the political and cultural diversity south of the Humber. It was too general a term to pass into common use. When reference was made to the people south of the Humber it was usually in the form of a catch-all phrase designed to describe overlordship. A case was when Bede described the overlordships of Aelle, Ceawlin and Ethelbert who held 'sway over all the provinces south of the river Humber . . .'[21] Normally the peoples were described by their separate titles.

The most martial people living immediately south of the Humber were called the Mercians. In Old English its form was 'Mierce' or the 'people of the frontier'. Whether this was a frontier with the British or with Englishmen over the Humber is impossible to tell. The original Mercia — the 'Myrcna Landes'[22] — was around the valley of the upper Trent. This river provided a route, from the sea, into Nottinghamshire and Leicestershire. Into this area colonists might also have migrated from the Fens, using the rivers Soar and Welland. This Mercian people later came to dominate the whole of the Midlands. They exercised political authority over many other tribes — some of which had their own dynasties. However, no Mercian king is mentioned in the sources until the seventh century. Bede referred to one, Cearl King of the Mercians,[23] whose daughter, Coenburg, married Edwin of Northumbria. There is no other reference to this king and he did not appear in any later chronicler's Mercian king list.[24] The first Mercian king mentioned in the *Chronicle* is in the year 628. In this year the West Saxons fought Penda at Cirencester. This Penda went on to establish a military reputation that facilitated the absorption of lesser peoples into Mercia. For instance he subjugated the Middle Angles and set his son Peada over them.

This period of Mercian ascendancy occurred later than the year AD 600. Before this time the Mercians were no more than one of the many English peoples establishing themselves in the Trent valley and its environs. Even their dynasty lacked stability. The case of the otherwise unknown Cearl illustrates that no one noble family had asserted itself in the Midlands prior to the 620s or later. The later house of Mercia was named the 'Iclings'. They took their name from an ancestor ranked five above Penda. His name was Icel ('(Ic) iL' in the manuscript *Cotton Vespasian B6. fol. 108 foll.*) Allowing 30 years for a generation he must have flourished in the 470s, his son

Cnebba in the decade after 500, his son Cynewald (Cynewold, MS C, *Anglo Saxon Chronicle*) in the 530s, his son Crioda (Creoda, MS C, *Anglo Saxon Chronicle*) in the 560s and his son Pybba (Pypba in *Cotton Vespasian*) in the 590s. None of these kings has left any literary evidence other than that in the king lists. In their own lifetimes they can have been little more than members of one warrior family among many in the east Midlands.

An area of early colonisation was along the Warwickshire Avon. This area is famous for the sites at Baginton, Bidford, Blacklow, Gibbet Hill, Stratford and Stretton. At these sites continuous occupation from 500 onwards is reflected in an undisturbed ceramic sequence. At Baginton a cemetery was discovered of a mixed cremation/inhumation type. A sunken feature building was also excavated at the town. At Bidford the mixed cemetery began being used around 500 and contained about 187 inhumations and 150 cremations. Near this cemetery excavated post holes possibly indicate that animal pens were erected here. The presence of wattle and daub, querns and other post holes may indicate a small farmstead. Excavations at Blacklow Hill have revealed pits and post holes cut into the bedrock. The layout of these remains — circular *and* square in shape — along with two pagan graves (one with a seaxe) has led to the identification of the site as some kind of religious structure. The remains are on the eastern end of a spur of land facing the sunrise. At Gibbet Hill a number of burials occurred along the line of the Roman road — Watling Street. A number were actually dug into the road surface itself. These graves are probably from a very early period although an exact chronology is difficult to establish. The picture is similar at Stratford. Here the mixed cemetery probably came into use soon after AD 500. At Stretton on the Fosse a cemetery was juxtaposed with pits, sunken features and a ditch dug in the shape of a trapezium. The tribal nature of these colonists is unclear. It is highly likely that they constituted Angle settlers from Middle Anglia. Very possibly some of their roots lay in Northamptonshire and possibly Leicestershire. The villages of Phepson and the Whitsun Brook (Warwickshire) commemorate offshoots of fenland tribes. The Wixna tribe, who gave rise to Whitsun Brook, have left evidence of their migrations in Cambridgeshire and in Middlesex. The name Phepson is derived from the tribe name Faerpinga. The place name means tun ('farmstead') of the Fepsaetan (probably meaning 'the settlers of the Feppingas tribe').[25] This must be related to the district 'In-

Feppingum' mentioned by Bede.[26] According to his account this was an area of Middle Anglia in which Bishop Diuma was buried in the 650s. It is probably this tribe which appears, in the form 'Faerpinga', in the *Tribal Hideage* (possibly compiled by the Mercian King Wulfhere who died in 674). If in fact these communities had their original homes in Middle Anglia then they probably reached the Warwickshire Avon via the river Welland.

Before we look at the diverse peoples of what later became Mercia we must pause to consider the case of Lincolnshire. This area has preserved a record of something of its dynasty if not its history. By the seventh century it had lost its independence and was a bone of contention between Northumbria and Mercia. It eventually passed permanently into Mercian hands in the 680s, in the reign of the Mercian King Ethelred (AD 674–704). Prior to this it had been an independent kingdom. The name of this kingdom — Lindsey — was itself an anachronism. The Roman form of Lincoln was 'Lindon' or 'Lindum Colonia'. It was related to the Welsh word 'llyn' or 'lake', a reference to a widening of the river Witham. The name later became 'Lindcolne' and finally 'Lincoln'. The name of the kingdom was formed by adding the old English word 'eg' ('island') to the word 'lindon'. This gave the forms 'Lindissi' 'Lindissae', 'Lindesse', 'Lindissa'. The modern form is Lindsey. This area faced English colonists coming down the Trent *and* the Roman road from the Humber. From the south, colonists from the Wash could reach the area via the rivers Whitham and Slea. At Sleaford some 600 English graves have been excavated. This mainly cremation[27] cemetery was probably in use by the end of the fifth century and continued into the sixth century. Sleaford may have been a transit camp for colonists moving north. The English buried there had clearly lived against a backdrop of warfare. Several of the skulls bore signs of severe wounds received some years before death. The Lincolnshire area had also attracted other immigrants from the fifth century. At South Elkington the cremation cemetery may originally have contained as many as 800 urns. From here there are ceramic parallels with Holland and Frisia, although some pieces are reminiscent of types found in Anglian Schleswig. The important cemetery at Loveden Hill has already been mentioned, in other contexts, but suffice it to say that both it and Elkington may have been used as early as the first half of the fifth century. To this list we might also add Kirton Lindsey and Ancaster. This last site is only five miles west of Sleaford and has a commanding position on the

Roman road — Ermine Street. The presence here of Romano Saxon pottery (group F, 'chevron and dot' type) probably indicates the presence of English troops — perhaps two generations before the first colonists at Sleaford.

The colonists in Lincolnshire were at first of mixed culture. By the mid fifth century users of Anglian and Anglo Frisian pottery were arriving on the east coast. The smooth well-made Anglo Frisian types (from Holland/Belgium) have been found at Hough on the Hill (Loveden Hill complex) and Sleaford (we have already noted Saxon types at Elkington). However, from the late fifth century onwards the Saxon element was submerged by a greater influx of Anglian settlers. This infusion of peoples brought Lindsey culturally closer to southern Scandanavia than to the Saxon lands of the Elbe Weser/terpen areas.

The modern county of Lincoln is divided into three areas: south of Lincoln are the Parts of Kesteven, south east of it are the Parts of Holland, north and east are the Parts of Lindsey. The major signs of settlement, after 450, come from south of Lincoln — in the Parts of Kesteven. These include Loveden Hill (approx. 17 miles south west of Lincoln), Sleaford (about 17 miles south of Lincoln) and the remains of a fairly extensive English village at Woolsthorpe (about ten miles south west of Loveden Hill). There may also have been a settlement at Caythorpe (within two miles of Loveden Hill). The distribution of sites north of Lincoln lacks the intensity of those in Kesteven. A notable exception is Elkington. However, it is separated from Lincoln by the Wolds and may have belonged to the coastal plain to the east (it is only twelve miles from the sea). Other archaeological research has produced single examples of huts at Bagmoor, Salmonby and Willougton; pottery and slag has been recovered from Mantom and Messingham; loom weights and other domestic finds have been discovered at Normanby. The larger settlement at Barton on Humber was clearly a product of its proximity to the riverine trade route.

This distribution may indicate that the north of Lindsey did not see large-scale land seizures following the revolts of the mid fifth century. It may also be indicative of the Wash being the primary source of immigrants. This may have meant a survival of British power in the area until the sixth century. Clearly, a close relationship with the British is implied by the adoption of the name Lindsey. Kesteven also has origins in a British word. In this case the word was the British 'ceto', or 'wood' that gave rise to the district name. The linear earthwork known as 'King Lud's Bank' may represent a British attempt to control English immigration from the rivers Welland and Gwash, overland to the middle Trent. The earthwork blocked the ancient routeway known as Sewestern Lane.

A more revealing example of British influence can be found within the king list of Lindsey itself. The sixth-century King of Lindsey — Caedbaed — bore a British name. Its first element, 'cad', was the British word for 'battle'. The first king after Woden was named Uinta — a name suspiciously similar to Venta (the Roman name for Caistor by Norwich). Does this indicate a place name personified? Or is it some reference to dynastic origins in East Anglia? Even the chronology of the king list is rather peculiar. Allowing 30 years for a generation the following framework appears: Caedbaed ruling *c*. 600; Cueldgils ruling *c*. 580; Cretta ruling *c*. 550; 'Uinta' ruling *c*. 520. This places the mythical origin of the dynasty, in Woden, no earlier than the 490s.[28] This may mean that the dynasty was founded comparatively late, and then that it contained British elements. Such a construction would explain the lack of mythological elements at the top of the king list and an inability to make a train of relationships that dated from earlier than the end of the fifth century. The names before Woden have probably been lifted from a common Germanic store.

The works of Bede may even contain a hint that some form of urban existence survived at Lincoln itself. During the time the Christian missionary Paulinus (under Northumbrian patronage) preached in Lindsey (in the 620s) it is recorded that he met a high ranking official at Lincoln.[29] The official's name was Blaecca. Bede gave him the Latin title of 'praefectus', or 'prefect'. The Latin is a rendition of the Old English 'gerefa' or 'reeve'. The story implies that civic life had to some degree, survived in Lincoln. Paulinus went on to build 'a stone church of fine workmanship' there. Again hardly likely if the capital of Lindsey had been a crumbling ruin. Perhaps, a little like London, it was beginning to revive. Perhaps it had never fully succumbed. Excavations at the Flaxengate site revealed buildings used in the post Roman period and walls robbed of material. There is evidence, though, of a population decline from the mid fourth century onwards and of a retreat to the improved defences of the walled city.[30] Perhaps a remnant of this population continued to live within the city walls up to the time that Paulinus met the reeve. A hanging bowl, discovered in the early 1970s on the site of St Paul in the Bail, may support this contention. It was constructed in the seventh century from tinned copper alloy and stood 25 cm in diameter with an extra rim soldered to it. On it were three bird like escutcheons of tinned bronze and enamel construction. Between them a craftsman had worked three small trumpet spiral motif or 'triskeles', similar to decorations on the hanging bowl found at Sutton Hoo. This may indicate a Celtic craftsman, or at least a Celtic market, resident in the city, in the early seventh century. The name Blaecca is of interest. It alliterates with the names of three Kings of Lindsey. They were Bubba (*c.* 640), Beda (*c.* 670) and Biscop. (*c.* 690). Perhaps Blaecca was a junior member of the ruling dynasty. It would help to explain his high office. It would also explain how his conversion assisted Paulinus in his mission to the kingdom.

Other constituent elements of the later kingdom of Mercia are more difficult to trace. Many of them are merely names without any historic flesh to fill out the bare bones. For example, of the Mimmas who gave their name to Mimms (Hertfordshire) nothing, apart from the place name, is known! The names of many of them are recorded in a document called the *Tribal Hideage*, which may date from the time of Offa of Mercia in the 760s, although an earlier date in the seventh century is possible. Whatever its date of composition it contains names of some tribes that are probably of great antiquity. The *Tribal Hideage* was a taxation document. Its scribe listed peoples subject to, or clients of, the Mercian kings. The controversies over its exact date and over the mathematics of its calculations, concerning the lands of the subject peoples, are not relevant to this study. Its importance lies in the probability that some of the tribal names date back to the sixth century, if not before. They constituted the proto Anglian kingdoms of the Midlands. Many of them may once have had their own separate dynasties. All must have had their leading noble families, drawn from the Angle warrior aristocracy. In the 650s many of these noble families still survived. When the pagan King Penda of Mercia led his army to the river Winwaed in 656 (to face Oswy (Oswiu) of Bernicia), he went in the company of 30 sub-kings! Many must have been drawn from the Anglian peoples of the Midlands. However, the very title 'sub-king' is indicative of changes in their status. They had, by the 650s, lost their independent status, and they were succumbing to the inexorable dynamics of kingdom building, noted elsewhere.

The study of the tribes in the *Hideage* cannot constitute well-rounded history. Too much of the evidence has been lost or suppressed. It is sufficient to record those names of tribes that were probably established by AD 600 and to note any evidence concerning them that may have survived. The list begins with the 'Myrcna lands' — the territory of the Mercians. The next tribes — 'Wocen Saetna', 'Westerna', 'Pecsaetna', 'Elmed Saetna' — were probably established after AD 600. The next is 'Lindsey' and 'Hatfield Chase'. The next tribe is that of the 'Gyrwa' or 'Gyrwe'. This tribe, with a north and south subdivision, took its name from the old English 'gyr' — 'mud, filth, marsh'. They had their home in the Fens, around the Wash (in this province was 'Medeshamstede' or Peterborough). Their lands extended into Northamptonshire, the old county of Huntingdonshire, Lincolnshire and the county of Cambridgeshire. According to a late source (*The Book of Ely*), 'The Gyrwas are all the southern Angles living in the great fen, in which lies the Isle of Ely' (Cambridgeshire). In the 650s the south Gyrwas were ruled by a prince named Tondbert; he probably represented a dynasty rooted in the sixth century. Bede also described Jarrow (Tyne and Wear) as 'in Gyrwum'[31] — this may imply that this area was colonised from the Fens. Alternatively it may have taken its name from another marsh. The next tribes are the 'East and West Wixna'. Their name has left traces in Wisbech (Cambridgeshire), Uxbridge (Middlesex), Uxindon Avenue, Harrow (Middlesex) and Waxlow (Middlesex.) These have been absorbed into Greater London. Members of the tribe may also have migrated to the Whitsun Brook (Warwickshire). The next tribe is that of the 'Spalda' possibly originating in the Old English word 'spalde' — 'ditch'. This tribe has left evidence in the place names Spalding (Lincolnshire), Spaldwick (Cambridgeshire), Spalford (Nottinghamshire), and Spaldington and Spalding Moor (Humberside). The latter two may not necessarily be derived from the tribe in the Lincolnshire and Cambridgeshire fens. The name Spalda (alternatively 'Spalde' or 'Spaldas') has counterparts on the continent. Spauwen in Holland was 'Spalden' in 1096; L'espaix in France was 'Spalt' in the eleventh century. Both are etymologically identical to Spalda. The tribal name Spalda may have been brought from the continent in the late fifth/early sixth centuries. The home of the next tribe, the 'Wigesta', is unknown. The tribe that follows the Wigesta is that of the 'Herefinna'. Corruptions of the name include 'Hersinna' and 'Herstinna'. Its name may survive in Hurstingstone Hundred (Cambridgeshire). The following name — 'Sweord Ora'

— was probably taken from the Old English 'sweora' — 'neck' and 'ord' — 'point'. A twelfth century writer referred to a peninsular, in Whittlesea Mere, south of Peterborough, as 'Swere point'. This is in all likelihood a remnant of the tribal name. The river Ivel gave rise to the next tribe name 'Gifla' but the name survives in Northill and Southill (Bedfordshire). The next tribe — the 'Hicca' — gave rise to the name of the Hertfordshire town of Hitchin. The next three tribes — 'Wihtgara', 'Noxgaga', 'Ohtgaga' — are otherwise unknown. After the Ohtgaga, this section of the *Tribal Hideage* closes with a total. Up until this point the *Hideage* has taken a generally southerly direction. There is a possibility that the Noxgaga and Ohtgaga were not Angles but Thames valley Saxon peoples. This contention is examined later in this study.

The second section of the *Hideage* opens with the 'Hwinca'. This tribe was identical with the kingdom of the Hwicce in Gloucestershire, Worcestershire and Warwickshire. The name is preserved in Whichford, (Warwickshire), Wichenford (Hereford/Worcestershire) and Wychwood (Oxfordshire). The Oxfordshire example shows a spreading of the tribal settlement. Other examples of this can be traced in Whiston (Northamptonshire), Wichnor (Staffordshire) and Witchley Green (Leicestershire). The place name Edgcote (Northamptonshire) is derived from a solitary migrant and is in the form 'the Hwiccian'. A poorly-attested tradition gives an alternative name for Worcester as 'Hwicwara Ceaster' (literally the 'Hwicce dwellers' city' (fortress)). The better preserved evidence for Worcester's etymology suggests the meaning 'fort of the Wigoran tribe'. *This* Anglian tribe is otherwise unknown. The Hwicce were a numerous and powerful tribe. It is likely that racially they were mixed in their origins. Seventh-century kings of the Hwicce included Eanfrith, Eanhere, Osric, Oswald and Oshere. Later recorded kings were Ethelheard, Ethelweard, Ethelric, Eanberht, Uhtred and Aldred.

After the Hwinca the direction of the *Hideage* plunges south again before rising back into the Warwickshire region. It is possible that the Hwinca are misplaced in the list and should come after the tribes attendant on the next item — the 'Ciltern Saetna' — the Chiltern settlers. Given this southerly beginning of part 2 it is likely that those tribes before and after it, except the Hwinca, were in the valley of the Thames, or at least the south Midlands. This idea may receive support from a tenuous identification of the 'Hendrica' as a Berkshire tribe inhabiting the land to the west of Reading (in the crescent formed by the Berkshire Downs).[32] The 'Unecunga' therefore may represent the inhabitants, south of the Thames, beyond the Goring Gap (in the valley of the river Ock and the Vale of White Horse). After the Unecunga the list returns north to the 'Aro Saetna' in Warwickshire. This is hardly surprising if we accept that the Hwinca are misplaced and out of the geographical trend intended in the document. The last identifiable tribe is another displaced Middle Anglian people — the 'Faerpinga'. The last four cannot be identified; they are the 'Bilmiga', 'Widderiga', 'East Willa' and 'West Willa'.

Before we leave Mercia there is one more of its constituent elements that may repay study. We have already dismissed the Westerna as a tribe that was established after AD 600. However, there may be some tenuous evidence that may lead us to question this assumption. The kingdom of the Western (in later texts 'West Angles' and 'Westan Hecani') is better known as the 'Magonsaetna'. Its first recorded king was called Merewalh. He lived in the 650s. The tenth-century tradition preserved in the records of Hyde Abbey, that he was a son of Penda, is probably false. However, he is likely to have been related by marriage to this powerful dynasty. It is probable that this underlay the claim, in a charter of Athelbald of Mercia (716–57), that Merewalh's daughter was a relative of his. Even if there was a separate dynasty in the west Midlands its establishment was probably no earlier than the 640s at least. However, there is evidence of Anglian settlers in this area before this date. The place names Beslow, Longslow, Munslow, Onslow, Peplow, Purslow, Whittingslow (all in Shropshire), Wolferlow (Hereford/Worcestershire) may record the burial mounds of Anglian chieftains (named, Betti, Wlanc, Mundel, Andhere, Pyppa, Pussa, Hwit(t)uc, and Wulfhere respectively). Such chieftains may have constituted the proto kingdoms of the west Midlands in the first half of the sixth century and undoubtedly represent 'a generation of pagan Angles, of aristocratic status, who were among the first English settlers in the marches'.[33] Since the 'M' alliteration found in the names of the ruling family of the Magonsaetna is not reflected in these names, it is likely that the dynasty of Merewalh was imposed upon a group of earlier confederates. These confederates may even have moved into the area in the late sixth century (by way of the rivers Avon, Severn and Teme, or by using the Watling Street from Gloucester to Wroxeter). There is some evidence to support this view. The name Magonsaetna may be derived from the the British town called Maund (Hereford/Worcestershire) or the Roman name for Kenchester (Hereford/Worcestershire) — 'Magnis'. Both are derived from the Romano British for 'rock'. However, if this is true it necessitates an assumption that English settlers were in the area before 550. This is because, after this date, changes in the Welsh language would have prevented the word 'magnis' from giving rise to 'magon'. This leads to the obvious question — is there any evidence of English colonists in the west Midlands in the sixth century? The answers are ambiguous but might provide some clues. English metalwork, of the type used by mercenaries, has come from Caerwent and the Cirencester/Gloucester area. If this area had links (as is likely) with the kingdom of Powys then such troops may have been familiar with the area in question. At Wroxeter some clues may be found in the remains of the Roman city of Viroconium. Here the Roman basilica area was cleared (*c.* 460–500) and replaced by a timber hall (38 m x 15 m) and other wooden buildings.[34] These buildings probably belonged to a British chieftain. Some aspects, however, may indicate English influence. Two buildings with post holes and a sleeper beam slot (possibly to hold a building's beam or a foundation for one) may be very early English.[35] This may indicate the use of Germanic mercenaries by the British authorities in eastern Powys. This base was abandoned by the British in the early sixth century because the area was 'under some kind of threat, and was no longer considered to be easily defensible'.[36] The threat may have come from mercenaries within the region or from early settlers penetrating from the Warwickshire Avon. In addition the remains of post holes and a framed building at Hen Domen Castle (Powys) may also be early English.[37]

The evidence discussed above is limited and open to criticism. However, it could help to explain the origins of the kingdom of the Magonsaetna and push its origins back into the sixth century. If this is so, we can identify three main phases: firstly, a mercenary phase; secondly, a proto kingdom phase of warrior aristocrats; thirdly, the subjugating of the previous two phases by a dominant dynasty in the phase of kingdom building. This may appear too much, built on too little, to many. To others it may reveal familiar characteristics of processes studied, by reference to more substantial evidence, elsewhere. Before we leave this area there is a curious characteristic, concerning the names of the Magonsaetna nobles that should be noted. This is that a number of them reappear either within Shropshire, so as to suggest the route of the migrants into the marches. The name Hwituc also appears in Whixall ('Hwituc's halh', or, 'nook', 'recess', 'remote valley')[38] which is some 30 miles to the north of Whittingslow ('Hwituc's burial mound'). The name is singularly appropriate for a land holding some distance from a man's settlement and home. The name Betti is the most intriguing. In Shropshire the place Beslow ('Betti's burial mound') is in the parish of Wroxeter on the upper Severn. However, the name also appears in Besford ('Betti's ford') only ten miles north of Wroxeter and on the Sleap Brook, a tributary of the river Tern, which itself joins the Severn in the vicinity of Wroxeter. Curiously enough, nine miles north west of Besford is Bettisfield (which may mean 'Betti's open land') and this too is on a tributary of the Tern. It is four miles west of Whixall. The riverine nature of the distribution of names in 'Betti' is remarkable, as is the proximity of Bettisfield to Whixall. Furthermore another Besford exists in Worcestershire on the Avon and close to its junction with the Severn. Does this distribution suggest a migrant's route? Originally a Hwiccian, or from the Warwickshire Avon, the Betti of Besford (Hereford/Worcester-shire) would have followed the Avon and Severn to Wroxeter (his base?). Further campaigning, or expansion of his party, along river routes, gave rise to Beslow (Shropshire) and Bettisfield on the borders of Clywyd. Such expansion may have been in the company of Hwituc who, like Betti, was buried to the south of his most wide-ranging exploits. Only six miles to the east of Besford (Shropshire), and on the Tern itself, is Pyppa's burial mound. The otherwise unknown Pyppa and Betti may have had close links when alive. Only five miles northeast of Besford (Hereford/Worcestershire) is Peopleton — the 'tun (farmstead) of the people of Pyppel'. The name Pyppel was probably related to the short form Pyppa which was formed by the addition of an '-A' suffix to the stem 'Pypp'. If this is so, then we have the amazing coincidence of Betti and Pyppa appearing together on the lower Avon and again on the upper Severn/Tern. Surely the balance of evidence suggests that both Betti and Pyppa migrated from the Avon in the same generation and possibly in the company of the other nobles buried in Shrop-shire and that this took place before the consolidation of the west Midland kingdom. The fact that so many of the tribal names in northern Shropshire were based on topography[39] suggests that they consisted of loose bands of colonists who took their name from local geography, long after they first arrived, in order to give coherence to a confused situation. The exception is the Magonsaetna. As we have seen this name may indicate an older tradition of colonisation and may have had its origins in an early sixth-century precedent that led to later settlers arriving from the established communities in the vicinity of the Warwickshire Avon. In this way a continuous thread of English minority occupation may predate Merewalh by over 100 years. The picture might be clearer if we possessed a more detailed knowledge of the frontier policy, employed by the rulers of the Welsh kingdom of Powys. Unfortunately we do not. We do know that in the 640s its prince — Cynddylan — was an ally of the Mercian Penda. It is likely that Cynddylan's father — Cyndrwyn 'the stubborn' — employed a similar system of *realpolitik*. Such a situation may have led to the employment of limited bands of English warriors. It may even have allowed a controlled settlement policy — particularly if small groups of English had previously been employed by the authorities of Powys, and before them the Roman Civitas of the Cornovii. At no point should it be assumed that such settlement was anything but tiny.

Wessex

The early history of the West Saxons is fraught with controversy. There is controversy concerning almost every aspect of it: the chronology is suspect; the route followed by the colonists is suspect; the name and race of the founder of the dynasty is suspect; the very unity and coherence of the king list of Wessex is suspect. All this despite the fact that the early entries of the *Anglo Saxon Chronicle* leave more room for Wessex than for any other kingdom. The problem of Wessex is a crisis in the sources. The main source is the *Chronicle*. Much of it is probably drawn from primary sources, based on oral transmission and church records. However, there is every likelihood that aspects of the *Chronicle* have been censored and altered to please West Saxon nationalism — or more correctly the West Saxon royal house. Its chronology, for the period 410–550, is likely to be speculative. Moreover the literary sources appear to clash with the archaeological ones. Whilst the *Chronicle* indicates a West Saxon thrust north from the Solent, the archaeological evidence points to intense English colonisation in the Thames valley. The *Chronicle* does not make one direct reference to these Thames valley settlers. It doggedly follows the adventures of the royal warband (the Gewisse) that landed near Totton (Hampshire), as if they alone were the source of the West Saxon population! All this may make the study appear rather hopeless. However, some form of coherency can be salvaged from this confusion, with patient study of the various primary and secondary sources available. What should be borne in mind is that such a study cannot hope to provide a problem-free explanation of events. On almost all points some ends must remain untied, some edges appear a little frayed. Given the complex nature of the problem, any neat and tidy history of Wessex should cause suspicion!

To ease part of the problem it may help to outline some of the terminology that will be used in this section. The following terms will be used throughout:

1. *Thames valley Saxons* — denoting settlers both along the river and in its environs.
2. *Gewisse* — denoting the royal house of Wessex and its associated warband of warriors.
3. *West Saxon* and *Wessex* — denoting the community formed by the fusion of 1 and 2.

The earliest inhabitants of Wessex settled in the area of the upper Thames. They were the primary focus of settlement. Here the cemeteries and communities clustered along the rivers, especially along the Thames. Of the larger cemeteries (with 20–150 burials) some 17 practised inhumation and two cremation. Cremation was in all likelihood the earlier rite. However, it was probably abandoned early on and so the inhumation cemeteries and the 13 definite mixed rite examples may still claim to be early. Cremation may have turned to inhumation under the influence of Romano British inhabitants who practised the latter rite. A number of cemeteries enjoyed a long period of use over several generations.[40] The presence of Romano Saxon pottery at Oxford and Abingdon probably indicates the stationing of German troops there in the decades before 410. There is also evidence for German settlers, in the period, at Dorchester on Thames.[41] At Abingdon archaeological excavation has uncovered at least three sunken feature buildings and post holes. At Dorchester one small building, of fifth-century type, had a half-timbered upper structure and other buildings in the town indicate a continued occupation into the sixth century and beyond. At least one sunken feature building appears to have been sited in relation to a Roman street. As we have already seen the settlement at Dorchester was very possibly part of a defence system under the authority of Silchester. In the period 410–450 this system was extended. Ceramic evidence suggests the planting of colonists at Brighthampton (Oxfordshire), Cassington (Oxfordshire), Frilford, Long Wittenham, Wallingford, Reading, Lower Shiplake and Aston next Remenham, as well as continued occupation at Dorchester and Abingdon. Dorchester was an ideal site to act as the centre of this colonisation. It was a 'pagus' — a small Roman town — in the heart of the Thames cornlands.[42] It occupied a key position where the river Thame joins the Thames and from it the upper Thames and the valley of the Ock could be overawed, by detachments of Germanic troops. The town had been fortified at the end of the second century AD. It probably played a part in the government system as the administrative centre of a country district within the framework of the tribal region. The town may also have been a nodal point in the imperial postal service and in the collection system which provided grain for the military. After 410 the accommodation of its military garrison degenerated from good quality masonry buildings to wattle and daub huts built over sunken floors.[43]

It is clear that this area of primary settlement received continued waves of new immigrants. At Cassington over 25 sunken feature buildings have been discovered; at Cassington (Purwell farm) another 20; at Eynsham at least three and one framed building; at Spelsbury (Oxfordshire) one; at Standlake (Oxfordshire) a large community; at Stanton Harcourt (Oxfordshire) at least two SFBs; at Sutton Courtenay (Oxfordshire) 31 and a framed building and post holes. Other examples of sunken feature buildings include Upton Nervet (Oxfordshire), Wooton Hordley (Oxfordshire), and Yelford (Oxfordshire). At New Wintles the settlement covered some three hectares. It consisted of some 17 sunken feature buildings in association with at least three framed buildings. At this site loom weights, trackways and animal enclosures were found.

Over most of this area, Saxon immigrants spread out from the established Thames-side communities. By the late fifth century it is likely that much of the valley of the Ock was experiencing inroads by English farmers. North western Berkshire and neighbouring Oxfordshire reveal a concentration of topographical place names, now thought to be typical of the immigration phase. Many are formed from stream names (Balking, Ginge, Lockinge, etc.); others arose from crossing places (Frilford Garford, Shellingford, etc.); others contain the Old English word 'ieg' or 'dry land', 'island, in a marsh' (Charney, Goosey, Pusey, etc.); the Old English word for spring, 'wielle', is prominent (Brightwell, Coxwell, Harwell, etc.) as is the term 'hamm', often used in terms of a 'water meadow' (Marcham, Shrivenham, Wittenham, etc.).[44] The picture is one of farming communities developing from the military sites as fresh immigrants altered the previous settlement patterns. At one or two sites continuity of occupation can be traced from Roman times. The case of Dorchester has already been noted but another is that of Shakenoak villa. Here English settlers wove, and worked iron, from the fifth through to the seventh century. It is a classic example of site continuity. English cemeteries were sited close to Roman centres at East Shefford, Frilford and Long Wittenham.

By the early sixth century outliers of the Thames valley Saxons existed as far away as Fairford (Gloucestershire). There may even have been contacts with the English community at Bidford on the Warwickshire Avon. The route to Bidford may have been along the river Evenlode to Moreton in Marsh (Gloucestershire) and then by way of Icknield (Ryknield) Street to Bidford. The river is navigable, to small boats, as far as Moreton.

There is still debate as to the route by which the Saxons reached the upper Thames. Two possibilities have received much attention — by way of the Thames or by way of the Icknield Way over the Chilterns. Both have some virtue, both also pose problems. The Thames valley route is perhaps the most obvious. The cremation cemeteries at Lower Shiplake and Reading may provide a link between the communities of Abingdon, Frilford and Long Wittenham and those of the lower Thames at Croydon, Northfleet and Shepperton. However there appears to be something of a ceramic gap in the middle Thames below Reading. This may be explained by the inhospitable nature of the Berkshire heaths. Perhaps colonists avoided settling here and waited until they reached the more attractive alluvial gravel terraces above Goring. It is clear that in time this river route gave rise to substantial English land holdings. The place names (in Oxfordshire and Berkshire) of Sonning, Reading, Goring, Pangbourne and Bensington are all examples of the 'ingas' type. They denote communities formed round a central leader. The fact that by the early Middle Ages, Sonning, Reading and Bensington were very substantial manors may indicate well-established and highly significant English communities. However, this information does not assist in the present study. The 'ingas' type name is not typical of the immigration phase or of the secondary phase of settlement. It seems to date from the period of political consolidation that preceded the phase of kingdom building. In other words these names and their subsequent history do not shed light on the original settlement patterns. Other evidence must be relied on. So far we have reviewed the ceramic evidence but this is not unambiguous. Some specific pottery types of north Kent and Surrey are not found on the upper Thames. Similarly some of the fashions of Oxford and Middle Anglia do not appear in Northfleet or Croydon, on the lower Thames. Whilst this does not rule out the river route it does indicate that the option is not without problems.

In the first half of this century another possibility was offered by the renowned archaeologist E. T. Leeds. He noticed that it was possible to trace cultural similarities between the communities of the upper Thames and others in south west Cambridgeshire/Bedfordshire and the area between the upper Ouse and Oxfordshire. He particularly noted the similarity in jewellery found in early graves. All the areas revealed a taste for equal arm brooches and early saucer brooches. These types of brooch were typical of the Saxon homeland between the rivers Elbe and Weser. A similar pattern was later seen in the distribution of a type of pottery vessel known as 'Buckelurnen with feet'. This type of pot has an interesting distribution in England. It would seem to indicate a spread of settlers from East Anglia through Middle Anglia and on to the upper Thames sites such as Harwell and East Shefford.[45] These Buckelurnen had their origins in the same European context as the equal arm and saucer brooches. Leeds believed that the evidence pointed to Saxon settlers making their way to the Thames from the cultural mix of Middle Anglia. The question is — was Middle Anglia the source of the Saxons of the upper Thames? If it was then the obvious route to follow into the south Midlands was that of the Icknield Way. It is at this point that this option meets a problem. Whilst early Saxon communities at places like Luton seem to be on the route to the Thames there are significant gaps in the settlement pattern. There is a wide gap between the sites at Luton, Kempston, Stevenage (and others in Middle Anglia) and those along the upper Thames. Along the line of the Chilterns there are no early cemeteries. This gap between the Thames and the upper Lea (about Dunstable) is a serious stumbling-block. Until the eighth century this was a very wild area. The ecclesiastic Eddius described it as the 'deserts of Chiltern'. It was probably a British enclave until the late 570s and a refuge for robbers until the Middle Ages. Apart from the cemeteries at Kingsley and Bledlow there is no sign of early cremations or settlement for a full third of the route between Mentmore (Buckinghamshire) and Wallingford. If early English travellers did use this route they made little attempt to settle along it, or bury their dead along it. This problem is particularly frustrating considering the attractive parallels in pottery. A number of solutions have been offered to this dilemma. It has been argued that the Britons of Buckinghamshire and east Oxfordshire may have allowed Saxons to pass through their territory but not suffered any villages springing up.[46] Alternatively the travellers may not have felt sufficiently at ease to carry out the rite of cremation and the graves that do exist are those of stragglers.[47] Another possibility is that the Icknield Way was not the major route from the north east. Travellers may have come from the Fens along either the rivers Ouse or the Nene. From here they could have reached the upper Thames by way of the river Cherwell. Alternatively the similar fashions in pottery and metalwork may have been due to the activities of pedlars and peripatetic metalsmiths.[48] There is, however, an inconsistency in one part of this large argument. There is evidence that the Saxons on the upper Thames and in Middle Anglia did not enjoy joint pottery facilities. Whilst their remains show similarities in style (for example, brooches and stamped pendant triangle style decorations on pots) they did not, in the main, enjoy trade from the same workshops.[49] This was also true of the communities on the Warwickshire Avon (for example, Baginton). What this may indicate is that the colonists on the upper Thames and Warwickshire Avon had at least part of their origins in Middle Anglia and the Fens. However, at some early period intercourse with these areas was disrupted. This would explain how three peoples of similar culture had dissimilar trade patterns. What caused this dislocation is unclear. It may simply have been that from the late fifth century the original Middle Anglian homeland received an influx of Angle immigrants. Such an alteration of the population may have had repercussions on the fusion of the diverse Middle Anglian peoples. It may also have brought them more into the trade orbit of the Nene valley and west Suffolk.

The likelihood is that the Thames valley English received reinforcements from all these directions in varying degrees. This may explain why the Thames valley did not succeed in offering a serious monarchical alternative to that of the Gewisse, which was imposed upon them in the late sixth century.[50] It is highly possible that by this time such a disparate people may not have experienced sufficient political fusion. Alternatively it may be argued that they did have a common Saxon culture and that any trace of their native nobility was erased by later west Saxon chauvinism. If there is any evidence of this native nobility it may be found in the kind of place name evidence already studied with regard to the west Midlands. A number of places within a working distance of the Thames record the burial mounds of warrior aristocrats (others are referred to in charters and land grants). Such aristocratic burials could easily date from after the fusion of the Thames valley Saxons and the Gewisse. In which case a date between the 570s and 650s can probably be envisaged — the final date being dictated by the conversion of Wessex. This must have eclipsed barrow burial among the aristocracy. Although this late date for the construction of the mounds is likely it is also possible that some may have been constructed before the 570s. In this case they may represent the last vestiges of a Thames valley aristocracy.

At Compton Beauchamp (Oxfordshire), a land grant in 955 mentioned the burial mound ('hlaew') of Hwit(t)uc and of Hild. The site is only one mile from the ridgeway which offered a routeway from the Thames at Goring. The distance from Shellingford (an early topographical name) is only four and a half miles. A land grant of 953 for Uffington referred to the burial mounds of Dudda and of Hod. Any of these persons could have led early settlers into the valley of the Ock. Other examples are found in Bledlow (Buckinghamshire) — 'Wine's Burial mound'. Wine meaning 'friend' or 'protector'; Challow Berkshire 'Ceawa's burial mound'. An exception that may prove the rule is that of Taplow. Here a burial mound was opened in 1883. The finds unearthed probably date from the seventh century. However, the richness of the burial almost certainly indicates that the occupant of the mound was a man of wealth and importance who had his own power base. The funeral items may indicate Kentish links.[51] If Taeppa was not a king he was clearly an aristocrat of real power. Whether he was a native Thames valley Saxon, or a client ruler installed by the East Angles,[52] his grave increases the possibility that the other mounds may be those of earlier, if less auspicious, rulers and aristocrats.

Whatever the state of Thames valley authority it was from the south that their eventual rulers were to come. Under the year 495 the *Anglo Saxon Chronicle* records the fateful words: 'Her coman twegen ealdormen on brytene, cerdic 7 cynric his sunu mid V. scipum. . .'[53] or, as translated by G. N. Garmonsway: 'In this year two princes, Cerdic and Cynric, his son, came to Britain with 5 ships. . .'[54] Garmonsway used the title 'princes' as the word behind this entry may be the Latin 'principes'. This is supported by the Latin manuscript 'F', which employs the phrase 'duces duo' — 'two dukes'. However, the manuscripts A and E of the *Chronicle* use the Old English word 'ealdormen' or 'aldormen'.

Their arrival in England was one of a series recorded by the *Chronicle* for the late fifth century. In 477 the arrival of the South Saxon Aelle was recorded; in 495 Cerdic and Cynric; in 501 Port, Bieda and Maegla; in 514 Stuf and Wihtgar. The chronicler was clearly trying to imply that a succession of Saxon adventurers landed on the south coast around the year AD 500. These arrivals tended to have a westward drift, beginning at Selsey Bill in Sussex and ending in the Solent. The idea, floated by some historians, that Cerdic came to Britain from the Celto-Saxon communities on the Loire seems devoid of evidence.

Taken at its face value the *Chronicle* account, up until the 560s, tells the story of the Saxon leaders — Cerdic, Cynric and Ceawlin (father, son and grandson). It also introduces other characters in the early part of the story, of lesser importance and yet others in the later part, of much more importance. There are, however, very real pitfalls in accepting the story at its face value. We will therefore study the account in the following sequence: the identity role and race of Cerdic and Cynric; problems in the early part of the genealogy of the Gewisse in Britain; the early campaign; the campaigns of Ceawlin and the problem of Ceawlin.

Before we begin this, a word about chronology. The dates used in the *Chronicle* are highly suspect. Oral tradition cannot necessarily be relied on for the accurate transmission of dates. Historians have argued for decades over how to approach the *Chronicle's* chronology. Perhaps one of the more radical approaches was offered by Vera Evison.[55] She argued that the arrivals of Hengest, Horsa, Aelle, Cerdic and Cynric were simultaneous and about AD 450. She implied that this was the result of a concerted attack by Frankish tribesmen timed to coincide with the revolt in Kent.[56] Evison adopted an extreme position and one not taken up in this study, as, whilst a possibility, it is not sufficiently supported by the available evidence. Nevertheless the dates of the *Chronicle* are probably very flexible. For the duration of this study it will be accepted that the rough sequence in the *Chronicle* is correct and will not be rejected. The dates used in the various manuscripts of the *Chronicle* will be used with the proviso that they probably represent a legitimate sense of sequence and *not* an exact chronology.

The very names Cerdic and Cynric are controversial. 'Cerdic' was not a Saxon name although he is implicitly Saxon in the *Chronicle's* account. The name was in fact British! In British sources it exists in the form 'Ceretic' or 'Certic'. A man of this name was the Welsh king of Elmet until he was expelled by Edwin of Northumbria in the seventh century. The fact that the founder of Wessex had a British name has led to some wild suggestions. Morris[57] believed that Cerdic was a British leader of the Belgae and was ruler of Venta Belgarum (Winchester). He invited English mercenaries into the south to fight for him and became their leader. His English genealogy was a later west Saxon invention to give legitimacy to the royal line. Cynric (Morris thought) was Irish. The name exists in the form 'Cunorix' from Wroxeter.[58] Morris suggested that he was an ally of the British ruler and his English troops. This version has been taken on board in other, less analytical, works.[59] The best example of this[60] argues that Cerdic bore a British title 'dux Gewissae' and was grandson of Vortigern and great grandson of the British Emperor Maximus. Faced with this fantastic triangle we may not be surprised that 'most writers seem to have missed this point'![61] It will come as some relief to realise that this latter conclusion has arisen from the fact that 'two major books only are the basis of this review: (1) *The Age of Arthur* by the late Dr John Morris and (2) *The history of the Kings of Britain* by Geoffrey of Monmouth'.[62] Needless to say we can swiftly see the limits of such 'a review', if such it may be called, since it finds too much of its material in a Medieval book of unproven sources and in one, at times highly individualistic, interpretation of the evidence.

The theory of Morris needs more attention. It is a valid, if radical, alternative. It is not, however, a necessary one. If we accept a fair degree of cultural exchange between the English and British it is not too much to expect that the offspring of a mixed marriage might bear a name chosen from his mother's side. This simple alternative would make Cerdic the son of an English father and a British mother without recourse to Dr Morris's theory *or* the unlikely 'dux Gewissae'. We are then left with a small warband landing on the south coast under the leadership of a warrior aristocrat who claimed divine descent from Woden. His son may also have borne a name which was a product of a mixed marriage.

The use of 'Gewisse' to describe the followers of Cerdic is noteworthy. At no time was it used in the *Chronicle* but it does appear elsewhere. Bede made several references to it. Concerning the conversion of the West Saxon King Cyngils he wrote of 'the West Saxons, anciently known as the Gewissae'.[63] Cadwalla was described as 'a daring young man of the royal house of the Gewissae'.[64] Agilbert was described as 'Bishop of the Gewissae'.[65] In the Welsh *Annales Cambriae* it was used in the form 'Giuoys'. In the Welsh *Red Book of Hergest*, Alfred of Wessex was 'Alvryt Urenhin Iwys' or 'Alfred King of Iwys'. The word 'Iwys' was a form of 'Giwis' in which the 'G' had been written 'I' as it was followed by a palatal vowel. In an English work called the *Textus Roffensis* it was explained that the Welsh called England 'Gewis'. There is no definite answer as to the meaning of Gewisse or Gewissae. It may have meant 'the confederates'. A much more simple explanation is that it was rooted in the name of Cerdic's great grandfather — Gewis — and was a family name for the ruling house. Morris suggested that it was '. . .the earliest name of the middle Thames Saxons'.[66] But this does not seem reasonable, given the authoritative statements of Bede.

Even if we accept the Englishness of Cerdic the debate concerning him is not closed. At no point in the *Chronicle* is he called a Saxon although the assumption is implicit. Other evidence though points to a racially mixed penetration into southern Hampshire and the Isle of Wight. Bede wrote that Kent, the Isle of Wight and 'those in the province of the West Saxons opposite the Isle of Wight', were descended not from Saxons but from Jutes.[67] Even accepting that the Jutes were a mongrel people the total omission of them from the *Chronicle* account is intriguing. Bede actually referred to southern Hampshire as the 'province of the Jutes'.[68] In the early Middle Ages, Florence of Worcester wrote how William Rufus died '. . .in the New Forest which in English is called Ytene'. This is Bede's 'Iutae' ('Jutes') in a late West Saxon form, in which the West Saxon 'IU' has become 'IE' giving 'Iete'. By the early Middle Ages this would have given way to 'Ytum', or the 'Ytene' of Florence's *Chronicon ex Chronicis*. This was consistent with a tradition recorded by Asser, the biographer of King Alfred. According to this Oslac the Father of Osburg (Alfred's mother) was of Jutish descent. He was descended from Stuf and Wihtgar.

According to the *Chronicle* these two men (one possibly mythical) landed on the Solent nine years after Cerdic and Cynric. In the entry for 534 they are described as the 'nefan' of Cerdic and Cynric. The word nefan is often translated 'nephew' but this may be an over-simplification. The word can mean both grandson and nephew. Possibly they were sons of an unknown sister of Cynric. This would imply that they were grandsons of Cerdic and nephews of Cynric. The exact relationship apart, it means that Cerdic was either a Jute or related to Jutes. In addition he landed in an area either already Jutish or soon to be so.

Jutes were not the only tribe of southern Wessex ignored by the compiler of the *Chronicle*. A number of excavations have revealed equipment of an apparently Frankish nature. At Chessel Down, on the Isle of Wight, Frankish influences can be seen in an early cemetery. More appear in Hampshire and Wiltshire: Frankish rings have been found at Harnham Hill; at Petersfinger one grave produced a sword, axe and a buckle of Frankish type; at Winter-bourne Gunner the decoration on a strap end is similar to ones found from the early fifth century, in Belgium and northern France; other evidence of a Frankish presence has been unearthed at Basset Down and at West Overton (where a cauldron was reminiscent of a type manufactured in the valley of the Meuse, on the continent). This Frankish influence may have linked the area to other settlers in Kent and Sussex. However, there is no echo of either Jutes or Franks in the *Chronicle*. What is likely is that the account has been carefully censored. As it stands the *Chronicle* tells the story of one unified West Saxon house. All other diversity has been suppressed — whether it be mixed marriages, Jutish and Frankish influences or other more ancient Saxon communities further to the north.

It is time to turn to the genealogy of Cerdic.[69] Above Woden the mythical figures of the genealogy have parallels in other English lists. From Woden to Geat the names mirror those in the Bernician genealogy (except for Frithuwald and he was omitted from the West Saxon list by the compilers of the manuscripts B, C and D). This also extends to the two names Baeldaeg and Brand (Brond) below Woden. There is an almost identical parallel with the five names above Woden in the genealogy of Lindsey. Frealaf also appears in the Kent genealogy as does Frithuwulf (in the form Fredulf). The name Frealaf also appears in the East Anglian list. Above Geat the names are similarly taken from a mythological store common to a number of Germanic peoples. At the head of the West Saxon list, in manuscripts B and C (under the entry for 855), are Sceaf and Bedwig. In the more confused manuscript of Aethelweard they are Scef, Scyld, Beo. In this case Scyld had been inserted below the final name Sceaf or Scef. This is not surprising as in Danish legends Scyld, who founded the Danish dynasty, was the son of Sceaf. Since much of this, as with other genealogies, was borrowed from a common heritage too much should not be made of the Danish connection embodied in Sceaf and Scyld.

Below Woden, at least two of the names refer to once historic personages. Freawine and Wig were fourth-century nobles in Schleswig and related to Offa I, king of Angeln. This is intriguing as it indicates an otherwise unrecorded relationship with the royal house of Mercia.

Before we leave the genealogy it is necessary to settle one other issue. This is that it is highly likely that in our references to Cerdic and Cynric an entire generation has been omitted. To understand this it is necessary to turn once more to the genealogies in the *Chronicle*. In the regnal list attached to manuscript A, Cynric is made the son of Cerdic. This relationship was followed by the compilers of the entries for 495, 534, 597, 674, 685, 688 and has been followed so far in this study. In the entry for 855 the genealogy of Aethulwulf of Wessex is listed back to Adam. In manuscript A the order 'Cynric, the son of Cerdic', is given but in manuscripts B, C, and D the order is 'Cynric, the son of Creoda, the son of Cerdic'. An unknown name and a new generation has appeared in these three ancient and reliable manuscripts. In addition, the ninth-century Saxon genealogy in the British museum known as *Manuscript add. 23211* gives 'Cynnric, son of Criodo, son of Ceardic'. What has happened is that the name of Creoda (or Crioda) has been either accidentally omitted or deliberately cut out from some sources. That this is the answer can be deduced from an examination of the sources in the *Chronicle* manuscripts. In the regnal list attached to manuscript A, it is stated that Cerdic and Cynric conquered the kingdom six years after they had landed. Since the regnal list places this latter event in 494 we are left with the date AD 500 for the former event. It is then recorded that Cerdic reigned for 16 years (that is, until AD 516). It is then said that Cynric reigned for 26 years (that is, until 542). However, this is contradicted in the main text where the taking of the kingdom is placed in 519, Cerdic ruled 15 years till 534 and was replaced by Cynric who ruled for 26 years until 560. This is a clear contradiction. Even if we consider the chronology to be suspect we might at least expect it to be internally consistent, within its own chronological framework. However, here there is evidence of an irreconcilable contradiction between the regnal list, at the head of the *Chronicle*, and the main body of the text. The person of Creoda (found at 855) may help to explain this. The situation can be resolved if we assume that Cerdic did reign for 16 years after 500 (that is, until 516 as in the regnal list); however, if we then assume that Creoda then ruled until 534 (a total of 18 years) we can then begin the 26-year reign of Cynric so that it ended in 560 as in the main body of the *Chronicle*. This reconstruction can be defended in the following ways:

(1) It avoids an unrealistic life span for Cerdic.
(2) It preserves the length of reigns of the two characters mentioned in the main text.
(3) It preserves the date of the accession of Ceawlin as 560. This is likely to have some validity as it was nearer to the time when the traditions were put into writing (in the seventh century?).
(4) It fills the missing 18 years with the historic person mentioned in reliable manuscripts for 855.
(5) In the regnal list of manuscript A, Cynric is credited with ruling for 17 years. This is usually regarded as a scribal error and 'missing material' supplied from manuscript B in order to give Cynric a 26-year reign and Ceawlin one of 17 years.[70] However, this may not be the correct interpretation of the material since Ceawlin did not reign 17 years but 24 years (560–84), or possibly 32 years (560–92).[71] What the regnal list may indicate is a confusion between Cynric's rule and the 17, or 18, years of Creoda's rule. It is this confusion that manuscript B attempted to rationalise, only to cause more confusion!

The *Anglo Saxon Chronicle* lists three arrivals of the English in Wessex — Cerdic and Cynric in 495, Port and his two sons in 501 and 'the West Saxons' Stuf and Wihtgar in 514 (who as we have seen, were actually Jutes). What is probably implied by these entries is that the conquest of Wessex followed the arrival of a number of warbands on the coast. At least two of these bands were probably related. The *Chronicle* records that Cerdic and his men landed at Cerdicesora (MS A) or Certicesora (MS E). This probably lay high up on Southampton water near the modern Totton. From here they were to strike north across the New Forest heath. The route lay between Totton and Charford and possibly along the Roman road that intercepts the trackway known as the 'Cloven Way'. From here the route pointed to Old Sarum and on towards the Berkshire ridgeway and the communities of the upper Thames. The battles, recorded in the *Chronicle*, indicate this thrust north to the Thames. This sharply contradicts those who claim that Cerdic fought at Badon, (especially when the battle site is identified as Badbury Rings (Dorset)).[72] He clearly had nothing to gain from a major expedition into Dorset. The imperial estate of Cranborne Chase must have severely restricted the prosperity of the local Romano British farmers. Such a state control of private enterprise would have prevented the area from offering the rich pickings desired by a war chief and his comitatus. Theories that rest upon a mythical raid by Cerdic up the Stour do not fit in with the evidence. There is no proof of any major Saxon thrust into east Dorset before the seventh century.[73] The few finds at Hengistbury Head and a solitary cremation at Iford Bridge (Bournemouth, Dorset) do not contradict this line of argument. They were clearly the result of a slight English drift along the coast. They do not constitute any evidence for serious settlement, or raiding. The geography of the *Chronicle* forces us to conclude that Cerdic's primary aim was to reach the Thames valley.

In 501 the original force was reinforced by the arrival of two more ships. This contingent was led by Port, Bieda and Maegla. The likelihood is that Port took his 'name' from Portsmouth and was an attempt by the chronicler to explain a place name by reference to a mythical person.[74] The names Bieda and Maegla, though, are possibly genuine. Bieda was clearly an Old English name formed by using an 'A' suffix. Maegla may have been a British name, related to Maglos.[75] However, as we have seen, this does not mean that he himself was British. The entry says that after landing they '. . . immediately seized land and slew a young Briton, a very noble man' (MS E). This sounds suspiciously like a duplicate of a later entry (for 508) and may indicate that the whole account of the landing at Portsmouth is an amalgam of legends which formed about a very slim tradition.

By 508 Cerdic and Cynric had begun to face British opposition in strength. In this year they killed a British king called Natanleod at Natanleag (MS A) or Nazaleod, at Nazaleog (MS E). The name has echoes of the last entry, in that it is not likely to be accurate. The name Natanleag survives in the place name Netley, Hampshire. It most likely means 'wet wood' the first element containing an unrecorded Old English 'naet' or 'wet' — not a personal name.[76]

The next *Chronicle* entry is the one that recounts the arrival of Stuf and Wihtgar. This entry is problematic too. For a start it sounds suspiciously like the entry for 495. They are even made to land at exactly the same spot, on Southampton water, as Cerdic and Cynric. The historicity of the entry is not helped by the name of one of the combatants. Wihtgar sounds like an English version of 'Vectis' — the Roman name for the Isle of Wight. If this is so then it follows in the footsteps of Port and Natanleod. This has led some historians to believe that the whole episode is nothing more than a duplicate of the 495 entry. Also it raises the problem that the record of the battle of Ceridices Leag, 527, (or 13 years after the landing of Stuf and Wihtgar) is simply a duplicate of the Natanleag battle, 508 (fought 13 years after the landing of Cerdic and Cynric).[77] However, whilst this may be correct it is likely that a germ of truth lies at the heart of this confusion. We still cannot ignore the likely historicity of the personal name Stuf or the tradition of his Jutish origins. The fact that this is the only entry that directly refers to its chief characters as 'the West Saxons . . .' is noteworthy. It may indicate that the genuine arrival of a group of Jutes was clumsily censored by deliberately modelling their arrival on that of Cerdic and Cynric. The name 'Jute' has been expurgated. This construction of events reconciles the witness of Asser with the confusion in the *Chronicle*.

The entry for 519 has already been dealt with. Its claim that 'In this year Cerdic and Cynric obtained the kingdom of the West Saxons' (MS E) was probably a misplaced record that should have stood at AD 500. This is supported by the preface to manuscript A and by a note in *Aethelweard's Chronicle* under 500 which reads:

Sexto etiam anno aduentus eorum occidentalem circumierunt brittaniae partem, quae nunc vuest sexe nuncupatur.
or
In the sixth year from their arrival they encircled that western part of Britain now known as Wessex.[78]

The implication would seem to be that they seized control of Wessex, or at least southern Hampshire, in about AD 500.

There is a possibility nevertheless that an event of some importance did take place about 520. The *Chronicle* maintains that this year also saw a battle at Certicesford (MS E) or Cerdices ford (MS A). The most likely candidate for the site of this battle is Charford on Avon (Hampshire). The name appeared as Cerdeford in 1086 and means 'Cerdic's Ford'.[79] Aethelweard wrote that the battle took place on the river Avon and this clearly describes Charford. The battle established the northern boundary of the Gewisse. Here the New Forest heath gave way to the open chalk downs of Wiltshire. This northern frontier was not to be extended until 552. It was probably to face this enemy that the earthwork known as Bokerly Dyke was reinforced at this time, by the British of Dorset.

The containment of the English in this southern enclave coincided with the peace of mons Badonicus. It probably indicates a resurgence of British power in the south Midlands that restricted any further Germanic land seizures. It is possible that following this battle Cerdic and Creoda consolidated their power in Hampshire. This may explain how easily the chronicler confused this battle with the original establishment of the kingdom. It may also explain the gloss on the duplicate entry for 527, in Aethelweard, that reads: 'Then after their government was in function, in the eighth year to be exact, they took up arms again against the Britons.'[80]

The evidence suggests a campaign to exterminate the last British survivors on the Isle of Wight. This took place in 530. They slew only a few men there. In 534 the Gewisse gave the island to Stuf and Wihtgar. There is no reason to doubt that this records the establishment of the client kingdom of Wight. It survived until AD 686 when its pagan monarch, Arwald, was killed by Cadwalla, King of Wessex.[81] His pretext for this policy of destruction was the idolatry of the island's inhabitants. However, the attack may indicate a genocidal campaign against a non-Saxon people (Jutes?) — Bede's words would appear to indicate this: Cadwalla '. . .strove to exterminate all the natives and replace them by settlers from his own province'. Such a policy of slaughter would make sense if the island was not a part of the dominant culture of Wessex.

The other entry for 534 records the death of Cerdic. As we have seen this was probably misplaced by the compiler and should have been entered *c.*516. In which case the consolidation of the kingdom, 516–34, was the work of Creoda and his son Cynric. This period was one of limited activity. If we assume that the 514 entry of Stuf and Wihtgar was a confused duplicate of earlier landings — and so was the 527 battle at Cerdicesleag — we are left with a period from 508 until 530 when no major campaigns took place, except the battle of Cerdicesford (519). In the 530s the battles on the Isle of Wight hardly represented a major offensive and the period of inactivity extended into the 540s. In 538 the *Chronicle* records an eclipse of the sun. In 540 another was noted and 'the stars appeared very nearly half an hour after 9 in the morning'. In 544 the death of Wihtgar was announced. As he was probably a mythological figure this was hardly a historical entry. In 547 an entry was made regarding the establishment of the kingdom of Northumberland. It is surely noteworthy that the chronicler could find no oral traditions more exciting than these for a period of some 20 years! The Gewisse were obviously contained within the perimeters of their initial exploits. Considering the initial success of Cerdic it is hardly surprising that the name of Creoda was forgotten. The same fate might have hung over Cynric[82] but for the fact that at the close of his reign he burst out of the containment. This revolt signalled the end of whatever peace had been brought about following Badon.

In 552 Cynric struck north and defeated the British who opposed him. The battle was at Searoburh or Old Sarum (Wiltshire). This identification is given in manuscripts A and E. Manuscript F gives it as Saelesberi (Salisbury, Wiltshire.) The difference is a fine one in terms of geography. Cemeteries such as those at Worthy Park, Harnham Hill and Petersfinger indicate the gradual process of colonisation pushing northwards. Morris interpreted the battle of Old Sarum as being between the British of Winchester and those of Salisbury. Cynric in his view being a mercenary in the pay of the British Cerdic and his political descendants. Alternatively he considered the possibility that prior to 552 the English, in the vicinity of Winchester, had overthrown British authority.[83]

There had been English mercenaries at Winchester since the fourth century. At the Lank Hills site the late Roman cemetery had, by its final phase, come to be used by Germanic folk. The ambiguous evidence of military belt buckles has been unearthed here. More positive clues have come in the form of pots of a south German type, dating from the mid fourth century onwards.[84] As we have seen the authority, in such towns, might have passed into the hands of the German military during the course of the fifth century.[85] If this happened it is another serious blow to the idea of a British power at Venta Belgarum surviving into the first half of the sixth century. Even if it did not happen there is still a serious problem in simply accepting the final conquerors of Winchester as the direct heirs of the original mercenary troops. It is true that by the mid sixth century the town was surrounded by a number of important English cemeteries and even had settlers occupying part of the walled city.[86] However, the case of the Worthy Park cemetery indicates that many of these were not the lineal descendants of earlier folk. Here an inhuming people (possibly related to Sussex and Kent) were superseded in the mid sixth century by a cremating folk. These later intruders fit the *Chronicle* sequence of the Gewisse moving northwards and absorbing other settlers whose presence was either ignored or confused in the construction of the *Chronicle* account. 'The sequence seems to rule out the possibility that the Worthy Park people originated in a controlled settlement concerned with the defence of Roman Winchester'.[87] The evidence suggests that both Winchester and Old Sarum fell to the Gewisse in the mid sixth century. At Winchester the town was already probably ruled by Germans who now accepted the rule of Cynric.

From Old Sarum the options open to the conquering English were limited. To the west the great forest of Selwood would have been uninviting. To the south west the six-mile stretch of Bokerly Dyke cut the road from Old Sarum. To the east lay the dry chalk downs of Hampshire. However, to the north an ancient trackway led towards the Thames valley. This was the line of attack taken by Cynric. In 556 he fought against the British at Beranburh (Barbury Castle, Wiltshire). From this vantage point on the Wiltshire ridgeway he could strike in a number of directions. Some 30 miles to the north east lay the English communities by the Thames. He could reach them by way of the ridgeway path which ran along the northern edge of the Lambourn downs. To the north lay the Saxon community of Fairford (25 miles away, by the most practicable route) and the British estates of the Cotswolds. He could reach these by way of the old Roman road from Silchester — Cirencester. This road was crossed by the Wiltshire ridgeway just north of Barbury Castle. To the east he could follow the Roman road to Staines, via Silchester, or drop south and follow the track of the Harroway into Surrey; his options were open and he had come a long way since the years of relative inactivity during the reign of Creoda.

The explosion of the Gewisse out of Hampshire was to become as important as the initial revolt in the 450s in Kent in establishing English dominance in Britain. It was to wreck what was left of British control in southern England. For a generation the Gewisse were to dictate their own terms to British and English alike. In this they may have been assisted by a most unlikely ally. It is probable that the triumphs of the 550s, 560s and 570s were not merely the results of Germanic military proficiency and tactics. They may also have been favoured by natural ecology. From the 540s the British Isles suffered a series of serious epidemics. Maelgwyn, the British king of Gwynedd, died in a great plague ('mortalitas magna' in the Welsh *Easter Annals*) also known, from Welsh sources as the yellow plague.[88] In 534 the Irish *Annals of Boyle* record 'a great mortality' known as the 'buidhe chonnail'. For 545 the *Annals of Ulster* preserve a tradition of a disease called the 'blefed'. Between 545 and 577 the *Annals of Clonmacnoise* record a disease known as the 'sawthrust', the *Annals of Ulster* one called 'samthrosc' and one called 'scintilla leprae', the *Annals of Clonmacnoise* contain another reference to a disease of 'leaprosie and knobbes'.[89] Earlier, the Welsh annals record the terse note: 'There was plague in Britain and Ireland.'

The exact identification of the disease is fraught with difficulties. A number of options have been put forward by medical experts and historians. The epidemics could have been of smallpox. The later Irish name for this illness — 'bolgach' — appears in the *Annals of Ulster* and those of Clonmacnoise. Alternatively it could have been malignant influenza or measles. The most common identification has made it bubonic plague (*pasteurella pestis* or *p. pestis*). This disease probably appeared in the Middle East in the third century BC where it was described by Rufus of Ephesus. It appeared again in 542–3 in the Mediterranean as the so-called 'plague of Justinian'. Descriptions of victims by Procopius make this identification fairly certain. It is, however, wise to remember that 'the subsequent infections that ricochetted through the Mediterranean coastlands in the following two centuries were not necessarily also bubonic'[90] This proviso has often been ignored by historians, many of whom seem ignorant of the life cycle of *p. pestis* and the ecology necessary for its existence in both endemic and epidemic forms. *P. pestis* exists endemically among burrowing rodent populations. When a series of natural triggers are operated it is transferred to man by rat fleas. Of 17 species of rat flea, only two can constantly carry the *p. pestis* bacillus in their stomach — *xenopsylla cheopis* and *nosopsyllus (cerato phyllus) fasciatus*. The human flea (*pulex irritans*) can only transfer the disease from person to person in the minority of cases when the disease causes general blood poisoning. In the normal order of things the disease is transferred to man from rats. A human epidemic is always preceded by an outburst of the disease among rats (an epizootic). As the rats die so the rat fleas transfer to human hosts. Without the medium of the rat the transfer cannot take place.

The main rat host is the black rat (*rattus rattus*). It lives in close proximity to man and following an epizootic a transfer of fleas can swiftly take place. However, it has long been thought that the black rat did not reach Britain until the eleventh century. This fact seems to have been ignored by a number of historians but recent research may overturn this. Firstly, the monogram page of the illuminated manuscript, the *Book of Kells* (late eighth/early ninth century) may contain rats as part of the native decorations.[91] More important is further material (furnished for this study by the Ministry of Agriculture, Fisheries and Food, Tolworth laboratory, Surrey) which suggests that the black rat has been resident in Britain since late Roman times. Having arrived in the Levant by as early as *c*. 300 BC. *Rattus rattus* has been identified from sixth-century levels in York. This is vitally important as a native population of the black rat would have been a basic requirement before an epidemic of *p. pestis* could break out. This restores *p. pestis* as a viable option but on the basis of evidence that has been neglected in other works. In addition the Irish reference to 'knobbes' may indicate the presence of the characteristic bubonic swellings in the groin and armpits.

Were the plague *p. pestis* it is of interest to examine the potential mortality rate of those infected by it. Shrewsbury[92] estimated the mortality in the initial weeks as 90 per cent of those contracting the disease, and 30 per cent as the epidemic subsides. This would give an average mortality rate, for those with the disease, of 60–70 per cent. A total death rate of 5 per cent of the total population has been suggested in regard to the outbreak of 1348.[93] Other experts have argued for 25–35 per cent as being more realistic.[94] Recent work has indicated that the *form* of *p. pestis* may cause variations — bubonic form = 50–60 per cent die off; pneumonic form = 95–100 per cent die off.[95] It may be noted that when the Japanese used it (in bombs) on a town near Shanghai in the 1940s 98 out of 99 cases were fatal. It is difficult to be precise concerning the actual mortality rate as the medical and zoological experts cannot agree. In one recent debate for the TV programme Timewatch (1984), one school of thought represented by Dr Twig but forward the estimate that *p. pestis* may only infect 0.002 per cent of a total given population. This was countered by Dr W. Bynum of the Wellcome Institute who argued that such infections do not always follow fixed norms. This of course would be particularly true of the impact of such an infection on a population without built-in immunity. This would increase both the 'die offs' and the forms in which the disease manifested itself.

According to the figures quoted above, an outbreak of *p. pestis* could have a serious debilitating affect on a community. Even if the disease were not *p. pestis* — but measles, influenza or smallpox — the effect could be as disastrous. The outbreak of such diseases in a virgin population could cause fatalities to rival bubonic plague.

The English sources make no references to epidemics until 664. This is curious and deserves attention. An answer is that the epidemics of the sixth century did not seriously affect the English colonists but hit the British with whom the Latin world traded. This is highly likely as the Mediterranean was the source of the epidemics. As V. I. Evison has noticed 'The present state of research shows that the routes which brought Mediterranean wares to the western and northern parts of the British Isles in the post Roman period were channelled exclusively in this direction and touched at none of the ports occupied by the Anglo Saxons, with the possible exception of London. . .'[96] Such a trade could easily have transported disease as an invisible import. The most important evidence of this trade comes in the form of amphora (two-handled earthenware vessels) found at a number of sites in western Britain. The dating of these vessels is still rather flexible. They may be from the fifth to seventh centuries (with some fourth-century types) or they may occupy a narrower period of the time from the late fifth–early sixth centuries. The amphora were used for carrying a number of articles in addition to wine. Other articles included oil, chalk, lime, olives, fish sauce, fruit, nuts, beans, lentils and even nails. In Avon and in Somerset, sub Roman Type A, Type B and Type D amphora have been found at a number of sites — Cadbury–Congresbury (Types A, B and D), South Cadbury (Types A, B and D), Glastonbury (Type B). Other sites have also produced amphora remains [97] but these examples of either Type A or B might not be post-Roman. The Type D ware was a grey kitchen ware which probably originated from the Mediterranean, via south-west Gaul, in the fifth-sixth centuries.[98] Another form, the gritty 'Cadbury–Congresbury Ware' may have had a similar origin to Type D.

Other evidence of amphora importation comes in a wide arc from Cornwall to Herefordshire.[99] In Cornwall sites include — Castle-dore, Constantine Bay, Gwithian, Hellesvean, Looe Island,

Mawgan Porth, Padstow, Tingagel, and Trebarveth; in Devon —
Bantham, Exeter, High Peak, Lundy Island and Mothecombe;
Welsh sites include — Bank Cave (Dyfed), Coygan Cave (Dyfed),
Dinas Emrys (Gwynedd), Dinas Powys (South Glamorgan) and
Dinorben (Clwyd). Other examples occur in Argyll, Fife, northern
Yorkshire and the Outer Hebrides. In short a substantial trade link
connected the countries of southern Europe to the non-Saxon areas
of Britain. Such an exclusive relationship almost definitely shielded
the English from the ravages of sixth century epidemics. Even if
such diseases were transmitted to English settlers it is likely that the
Gewisse remained untouched. In their little enclave of Hampshire
they must have remained out of the mainstream of whatever trade
existed between the British and more established English
communities. In addition it should be remembered that what trade
there was between the rival camps was probably conducted by
itinerant peddlars. Such men were unlikely to provide a sufficient
channel for widespread epidemics to break out. The real centres of
disease must have been what remained of the British urban centres
and political centres on the south western hillforts. Here disease
must have accelerated an ongoing disintegration. It must also have
severely damaged the British farming communities of the
Cotswolds and south west. It was against this background of social
breakdown that the revolt of the Gewisse took place. It was so
serious in its repercussions that we might call it the second
Germanic revolt. This puts it on a par with the first revolt of Hengest
and Horsa.

A name which first appears in the account of the battle of
Beranburg dominated the closing decades of the sixth century. The
name is that of Ceawlin, he fought alongside Cynric at Beranburgh,
a certain Cutha at Wibbandun in 568, Cuthwine at Dyrham in 577,
Cutha at Fethanleag in 584, and was expelled in 592. Like Cerdic,
Cynric and Creoda he has been the source of some debate. This is
because the *Chronicle* accounts do not refer to him in a uniform
manner. He appears in the main body of the *Chronicle* as active in
the entries for 556, 560, 568, 577, 584, 592 and 593 (the year of his
death). He was also listed in the pedigrees for 568 (MS A, the
pedigree of Caedwalla) 688 (MS A, the pedigree of Ine), 728 (MS
A, the pedigree of Oswald) and 855 (MS A, the pedigree of Ethel-
wulf). The chronicler omitted him from the pedigrees for 597 (MS
A, the pedigree of Ceolwulf), 611 (added to MS A as the pedigree of
Cynegils,) and 674 (MS A, the pedigree of Aescwine). This is

despite the fact that some names are common to both lists. In at least one list (under the year 688) Ceawlin is described as the grandfather of a man called Cynegils yet in another (under the year 611) he is not described as such!

The matter is not clarified in the genealogical preface to the *Chronicle*. In the compilation of the regnal list to manuscript A he was totally omitted. This was despite the fact that he appears in the main body of manuscript A. In addition he is referred to late on in the preface to manuscript A but called 'Celm'. He is listed as Ceawlin in the preface to manuscript B but is given a reign of 17 years. In the main text of 'B' he is given a reign of 32 years (from 560–92)! When added to the fact that a number of the recorded descendants of Ceawlin have mutually irreconcilable family trees, the confusion seems complete. Not only are we unsure of the identity of Ceawlin, the doubts have spread to cover those — Cuthwulf and Cuthwine — who appear, after 560, in his company. We may sympathise with those historians who have finally concluded that Ceawlin was an interloper among the legitimate heirs of Cerdic. To them he

> . . . led a warband recruited from settlers in the Thames valley, the West Saxons properly so called! At first the ally of the Gewisse, he may soon have become their rival; the annal which records his accession to the kingship of Wessex in 560 possibly conceals a more or less successful effort by Ceawlin to unite the West Saxons of the Thames valley and the Gewisse under his rule.[100]

This is an attractive argument. However, it is an extreme answer to the problem. Others have continued to maintain that, despite the problems, Ceawlin is best regarded as an heir of Cerdic.[101] The case for Ceawlin being a member of the Gewisse rests on three main foundations: firstly, it is hard to imagine that both the Thames valley Saxons and Gewisse followed such a conscious 'C' alliteration in the names of their aristocracy; secondly, the subsequent history of Wessex is more easily explained if some fusion of Thames valley Saxons with a dominating Gewisse took place in the late sixth century. Thirdly, the *Chronicle* evidence can be sufficiently explained. The omission of Ceawlin from the preface to manuscript A can be explained by a confusion over names. In the Northumbrian form 'Caelin'[102] the name could give rise to 'Celin'. This is

probably what lay behind the mistaken form 'Celm' in the general
preface to manuscript A. Similarly if Ceawlin were spelt 'Ceolwin' it
could become abbreviated to 'Ceol'. In this case the name could be
confused with that of Ceolwulf (reigned 597–611) and the two
names conflated. As for the error over the length of his reign, this
has already been explained as a confusion with the reign of Creoda.
The confusion that followed Ceawlin's fall is best seen as a vicious
infighting among the royal house and retinue of the Gewisse (with
the possible addition of some contenders from outside the dynasty).
The confused genealogies are best regarded as confused attempts to
prove genealogical origins from Cerdic. Even if some of these later
kings were interlopers (and this is likely) this does not necessarily
indicate that this was the case with regard to Ceawlin.

Bede recorded that Ceawlin became the second English king to
hold the title of 'bretwalda' (overlord), over all the provinces south
of the Humber. His authority was built upon his military prowess. In
568 he struck against Ethelbert of Kent at the battle of Wibbandun.
Attempts have been made to identify this as Wimbledon in the
Greater London area, but not conclusively. Presumably Ceawlin
used this battle as part of a campaign designed to annex Surrey. At
this battle two Kentish Aldormen were killed — Oslaf (Oslac, MSS
F and E) and Cnebba. Ceawlin fought in the company of a chief
named Cutha. This name was formed from the element 'Cuth' and
an 'A' suffix. Unfortunately, Ceawlin fought alongside a Cuthwulf
and a Cuthwine in later years. When the suffixed form Cutha
appears in the documents, that we have to hand, it is not always
possible to identify which is being referred to!

The next entry (for 571) may help clarify the matter a little. It tells
of an English victory at the battle of Bedcanford. This battle was
won by Cuthwulf (MS A), Cutha (MS E). It is likely that this was the
Cutha of 568. The *Chronicle* does not give him a lineage. To ease
confusion the writer of manuscript E added the explanatory note 'se
Cutha waes Ceawlines brother' ('this Cutha was Ceawlin's
brother'). Similarly the later scribe who copied out manuscript F's
entry for 568 wrote 'Ceawlin and Cutha, Ceawlin's brother'. This
was supported by a later entry (for 597). Under this year King
Ceolwulf traced his origins from Cutha, son of Cynric, son of
Cerdic. This Cutha must have been the Cuthwulf of 571 and
presumably 568. Morris, in a highly individualistic interpretation,
made Cuthwulf the leader of the Haslingfield Saxons. He pictured
him marching down the vale of Aylesbury to meet Ceawlin in the

Thames valley.[103] He cited the distribution of Maltese Cross saucer brooches to demonstrate the movement of Cuthwulf's armies along the Icknield Way and westward into Middle Anglia.[104] His assertion that Cutteslowe (Oxfordshire) is from Cuthwulf is not supported by Ekwall, who gave the meaning 'Cuthen's burial mound'. The name Cuthen was formed from the diminutive suffix — 'in' whereas the short forms of Cuthwulf and Cuthwine were formed from the stem Cuth with an 'A' suffix added.[105] The distribution of brooches is a tenuous piece of evidence. They could as easily mark out the beats of Cambridgeshire peddlars!

Whatever Cuthwulf's origins he died in 571. The battle of Bedcanford cannot be identified with absolute certainty. If it was Bedford then we must assume that the name Beda (in Bedford) and Biedca (in Bedcanford) were interchangeable in personal names *and* in place names formed from them. There is some evidence for this. The candidature of Bedford is further strengthened by the fact that *Aethelweard's Chronicle* gives the name 'Bedanford' (and omits the 'C'). The result of the battle was the capture, or recapture, of Lygean Burg (Limbury), Aegeles Burg (Aylesbury), Egones Ham (Eynsham) and Baenesingtun (Benson). It would seem that the English seized Bedford and then followed the line of the Chiltern scarp.

This battle record indicates that a major part of the Chilterns was in British hands until the 570s. This has led to some accusations that the battle was misdated by a century and should be placed at the end of the fifth century. Others have argued that the battle was fought, not against the British, but against Angles. However, the picture is beginning to emerge of a British power which maintained itself at Verulamium for almost 200 years after the end of Roman Britain. Such a region would have had its north-west boundary formed by the Chilterns. Here the hills fall gently into the London basin. Under its wooded slopes are a jumbled series of long, steep-sided valleys. These may have provided places of refuge for Romano British farmers and deterred English raids until 577. Other evidence may be found in the English settlements of Bedfordshire (at Dunstable, Kempston and Luton). With the minor exception of Dunstable, these settlements reveal a very limited growth rate. Similarly there was little Saxon expansion on the Oxford side of the Thames compared to that on the Berkshire bank. The scenario is one of 'static occupation and tightly contained expansion'.[106]

In Verulamium itself civic life seems to have continued to some extent throughout the fifth century. Civic projects such as the construction of a corn drying plant, the building of a stone barn (or hall) and the laying of a new water main has led to the cautious conclusion that 'there is every chance that urban life continued in Verulamium in some form into the second half of the century'.[107] The entry for 577 may lead us to extend its life span substantially! This community may have been that of the people of Argoed Calchvynydd whose name was preserved among the British of Wales.[108] Under the rule of its king — Cadrawd — it may have been the force that stopped English settlers reaching the Thames via the Icknield Way. Perhaps it was for fear of this people that the East Angles built the great dykes across the Icknield Way. If so, Verulamium's policy met with greater success than that of Silchester to the south. It implies that far from regaining land lost to the English[109] in the fifth century Verulamium remained in control of its hinterland from 410 until 577. This was a considerable achievement. It goes far beyond the assumption that the area captured by Cuthwulf had 'been briefly recovered by some militant Britons'.[110]

Six years later Ceawlin struck again. The *Chronicle* records: 'her Cuthwine and Ceawlin fuhton with brettas. . .and genamon threo ceastra Gleawanceaster and Cirenceaster and Bathanceaster'. Ceawlin struck north to Deorham (Dyrham, Avon), six miles north of Bath. The battle site has traditionally been identified as Dyrham camp. However, this name does not predate the nineteenth century. In the eighteenth century the camp was called Barhill and in the seventeenth century Burrill. In consequence the exact site is unknown. The site is now called Hinton camp. An earth wall and ditch was constructed to make a fortified spur of land that possessed commanding views that stretched to the valley of the Severn. He killed three British kings — Coinmail, Condidan, Farinmail — and captured Gloucester, Cirencester and Bath. The victory opened up the farmlands of the Cotswolds and Severn to the English. At Barton farm, Cirencester, an English warrior's grave was cut through a mosaic pavement. It can be roughly dated by a small stamped accessory vessel placed with the body. The pot is decorated with cruciform stamps and small bosses.[111] The burial can be dated to the approximate reign of Ceawlin. The account may indicate that Bath, Gloucester and Cirencester were centres of regions with their own kings. However, the extent of urban life surviving in them is open to question. The Roman city of Corinium (Cirencester) was a cantonal capital of some 97.1 hectares. In the fourth century it had become the capital of the province of Britannia Prima. It was intimately related to the farming communities beyond its walls. It, like Glevum, must have suffered massive deterioration by the 570s. The most vivid example of this comes from Aqua Sulis (Bath). The Roman drainage system removed from here 1,136,500 litres of spring water daily. When this broke down some two metres of silt built up over the Saxon period.[112] The English poem *The Ruin* (contained in two badly-burnt leaves of the so-called *Exeter Book*) probably describes the state of Aqua Sulis. It may also provide evidence of epidemics in the sixth century which crippled the urban populations:

> Snapped rooftrees, towers fallen
> the work of the Giants, the Stonesmiths
> Mouldereth. . .
> Came days of pestilence, on all sides men fell dead,
> death fetched off the flower of the people;
> Where they stood to fight, waste places
> and on the acropolis ruins. . .

The area cannot have been in a very attractive state by the 570s. Despite this there may have been some activity near the site of the baths. Votive offerings appear to have been made there after 410 and a sub-Roman date is likely for the repairing of the temple precinct floor.[113] In Barry Cunliffe's opinion the Roman house in Abbeygate Street 'continued to be occupied for a considerable period after the nominal end of Roman Britain in 410', although the baths ceased to function in their original form in the early fifth century. However, it is not yet possible to tell how long such activities continued. In the works collected by Nennius, is a source known as *The Wonders of Britain*. In it the writer described a hot lake in the country of the Hwicce tribe (the Bath area). It was, he wrote, 'surrounded by a wall, made of brick and stone'. Bede wrote how Britain had 'both salt springs and hot springs, and the waters flowing from them provide hot baths' (Bede 1.1). This may imply that something of the function of the baths survived the end of Roman rule and into the sixth century at least. Still, the situation must have been highly dilapidated. That the severed head of a girl could be found in the oven of the Abbeygate house obviously suggests the dereliction of this particular property but at what date is not known, nor to what extent this was true of other urban properties in Bath. Such a fate of near desertion, or dilapidation, had probably overtaken all the other major Roman sites along the Avon valley. At Keynsham the villa was inhabited by squatters who laid a hearth over a tessellated pavement. In 1985 excavations between Keynsham and Saltford unearthed evidence of a Roman settlement. It, too, had not survived into the English period.

By the 570s the three cities may have come to symbolise regions rather than examples of sophisticated urban continuity. This is supported by the fact that by the tenth century Bristol (Avon), Cirencester and Gloucester were administrative units with Bristol having replaced Bath. Recent evidence has suggested that a reduced population may have survived at Glevum and at Corinium until the 570s at least. In Gloucester a number of buildings were reoccupied although most of the town was in decay and prone to flooding. The most promising evidence, however, has been unearthed at Cirencester. The evidence suggests that the urban centre continued but was relocated. The site that was probably the centre of urban life in the 570s was the old Roman amphitheatre outside of the main city. This area — known locally as 'the Bull Ring' — probably became a defended area. Sherds of grass-tempered pottery provide some ceramic evidence for occupation. The Bull Ring had its north-eastern entrance reduced to restrict access to the arena. In addition to this doors into two of the amphitheatre's rooms were blocked. Two doors were erected to seal off the amphitheatre and wooden buildings were put up inside the great earth ring. It is also possible that a ditch was dug around it. Such an enclosure would have been easier to defend than the three mile circuit of Corinium's walls. J. S. Wacher of the University of Leicester, who led the dig on the site, posed a vital question — 'was it the amphitheatre, shielding the remnants of the Romano British townspeople which fell to the Saxon advance after the battle of Dyrham?'[114] The answer is almost definitely that it must have been.

The earthwork known as west Wansdyke was very possibly erected as a result of the English victory at Dyrham. It is a single bank with a ditch on its northern side. It runs for eleven miles from the Iron Age fort on Dundry (Avon) to the hills south of Bath. There are a number of ideas as to when it was built and which enemy it faced. It may have been built in the late fifth century against marauding Thames valley Saxons. Alternatively it may have been the work of English settlers as a protection against marauding Angles, either in the late sixth century or after the loss of the Severn valley to Penda of Mercia after 628. Another option is that the work was done by a British authority as a protection against Ceawlin's Wessex. The construction of the west Wansdyke involved the movement of an absolute minimum of some 64,600 cubic metres of earth. This must have involved a minimum of some 7,000 man-days and possibly double this. It is easier to imagine that this was the work of the British rather than put it down to a minority of English settlers in the decades after 600. Given the reoccupation of Cadbury Congresbury it is possible that other hill forts in Avon such as Maesknoll and Stantonbury camp were also refortified. Both lie on the line of the Wansdyke. In which case the riverside pastures between Keynsham and Bath had been abandoned to the enemy.

From Dyrham Ceawlin continued to campaign to the north east. He fought in the company of Cutha. Morris made him the heir of Cuthwulf and ally of Ceawlin.[115] This Cutha was certainly the Cuthwine who fought at Dyrham. Genealogical material, later incorporated into the *Chronicle*[116], made him Ceawlin's son. In 584 Ceawlin and Cutha fought a battle at Fethan Leag. This has been identified as Stoke Lyne (Oxfordshire), as a twelfth-century charter mentioned an area called Fethelee. Stoke Lyne is some 15 miles north of Oxford.[117] The battle brought the Gewisse to the headwaters of the river Ouse and the middle Cherwell. The battle may have been against British remnants undeterred by the battle of Bedcanford. More likely the enemy were other Englishmen. Stoke Lyne (Fethan Leag) lay on the route from Middle Anglia to the Thames, the very route followed by some of the inhabitants of the upper Thames settlements. It is possible that Ceawlin blocked some otherwise unrecorded southward Anglian expansion. The account tells us that Cutha was killed at this battle but that 'Ceawlin captured many villages and countless booty' (MSS A and E). However, manuscript A also includes a very cryptic passage that reads 'and departed in anger to his own'. The passage is unexplained and has led to a number of interpretations. Did he retreat following the death of his son? Was Fethanleag really a much closer fought battle than the text suggests? Did Ceawlin face a revolt at home? And was it a revolt among his own house, the Gewisse or among the Thames valley Saxons? The text offers no assistance in deciding the matter.

In 591 an unknown chief Ceol (MS A) began a five-year reign in Wessex (six years in MS E and in a later correction of MS A, and in the genealogical preface to MS A). His relationship to Ceawlin is not made clear in the entry. In some studies he passes under the name 'Ceolric'. This is based on an error in manuscript E, in which the word 'ric' (ruled) was added to the personal name 'Ceol' giving 'Ceolric'. In this study the name Ceol will be used.

From 591 to the end of the century the genealogical material that has survived becomes dauntingly confused. The attempts to straighten it out have not made for a uniform conclusion. The story as the chronicler saw it was as follows:

591 Ceol reigned five (probably six) years (591–7)
592 Ceawlin expelled
593 Ceawlin, Cwichelm, Crida perished
597 Ceolwulf began to rule (597–611)

It would help if we knew the family connections of all the combatants but we do not. Hodgkin made Cuthwine, Ceol and Ceolwulf sons of Ceawlin. This at least made for simplicity. Copley followed an identical formula, having assumed, like Hodgkin, that Cuthwulf was Ceawlin's brother but had no heir. This interpretation was in keeping with the genealogical preface to manuscript A, which states that Ceol was the brother of Ceolwulf. If this was correct then it is likely that Ceawlin's expulsion was due to a feud within his own family. The entry for 592 records 'a great slaughter' at Adam's grave (probably Alton Priors (Wiltshire), near the vale of Pewsey) and Ceawlin's expulsion. It is likely that he was expelled from the original homeland of the Gewisse. This would have left him only the Thames valley as his base. It may have been at this time that the east Wansdyke was constructed. It stretches from Morgan's Hill near Devizes (Wiltshire) to west of the Savernake forest. It is likely that it marked the boundary between the Gewisse and the English of the upper Thames. Perhaps this latter community was also beginning to experience the activities of Anglian warbands after the withdrawal from Fethanleag. If so they had enemies at both their front and back 'doors'.

The genealogical picture of the state of affairs within the ruling house of Wessex in the late sixth century is confused by inconsistencies within the *Chronicle* itself. For example, in manuscript A (for 597) Ceolwulf is made the son of Cutha who was the son of Cynric. There is no mention of Ceawlin and this reference to Cutha would best fit Cuthwulf — the supposed brother of Ceawlin. A similar state of affairs emerges regarding the entry for 611 where a certain Cynegils is called son of Ceol, son of Cutha, son of Cynric (presumably this Ceol should be regarded as Ceolwulf). However in the entry for 688 Cynegils is made son of Cuthwine, son of Ceawlin! This kind of dynastic chaos wrecks the neat genealogies of Copley and Hodgkin. The historian P. Sawyer attempted to reconcile some of the facts by assuming that Ceawlin had two sons (Cuthwine and Cutha) and two brothers (Cutha (presumably the Cuthwulf of the *Chronicle*) and Ceolwulf).[118] He went on to suggest that Cutha (Ceawlin's brother) had two sons — Ceol (ruled 591–7) and Ceolwulf (ruled 597–611). If Sawyer is correct this may suggest that Ceawlin's conflict was with his nephews not his sons, as some have thought. This solution rests on the assumption that identical names were used in successive generations. This would help to explain some of the otherwise irreconcilable genealogies. None of this, it must be admitted though, goes any way towards explaining who were the otherwise unknown Crida and Cwichelm who died with Ceawlin in 593. We may sympathise with the translator of the Penguin edition of Bede. In the appendix he gave three genealogies, one each for East Anglia, Kent and Northumbria, but when it came to Wessex he concluded that it was '. . .too complicated to justify its inclusion here'![119]

The problems concerning Wessex after Ceawlin may have been partly explained by Sawyer. However, the source of the confusion was surely much deeper than that discussed by him. It is highly likely that in sixth- and seventh-century Wessex there existed junior members of the royal house whose exact origins were not clear to later writers. Some such as Crida and Cwichelm never rose from obscurity. Others, who did achieve greatness, had a vested interest in linking themselves to the dominant line of the royal house. As Shakespeare put it in *Twelfth Night*: 'Some are born great, some achieve greatness and some have greatness thrust upon them'. The experiences of the West Saxon princes show that those who achieve it and those who have it thrust upon them desire the legitimacy of those who are born to it. In the seventh century Somerset had its own king — Baldred — who ruled after 680. He is described as a 'patricius' in early documents but as 'king' in an eleventh-century one. Another late-seventh-century king in Wessex was named Cissa. The origins of Cissa, as of Baldred, are completely unknown. In the eighth century there were a number of such kings (whose descent from Cerdic is unknown and possibly non-existent). These include Ethelheard (ruled 725–40), Cuthred (ruled 740–56) and

Sigebryht (ruled 756–7). Such examples illustrate the looseness of the ruling house and force us to wonder whether some of the earlier rulers, with confused genealogies, had simply falsified the records in order to gain legitimacy. It is perhaps fitting that we leave Wessex as we entered it — on a note of controversy.

Regardless of whether Ceolwulf was a son of Ceawlin, a nephew of Ceawlin or no relation of Ceawlin he was a worthy successor to the bretwalda. The chronicler described how he '. . .made war either against the Angles, or against the Welsh, or against the Picts or against the Scots'. The claim that he fought the Angles may imply that he recovered the Thames valley by relieving the pressure on it from the north. The second containment of the Gewisse (behind the east Wansdyke this time) had ended.

Sussex

The *Anglo Saxon Chronicle* records that in 477 there was a landing of English warriors on the coast of what was to become Sussex, or the kingdom of the South Saxons. The leader of this expedition was named Aelle. He arrived accompanied by his sons Cissa, Cymen and Wlencing and three shiploads of followers. Aelle landed at a spot known as Cymenesora. This may have been the 'Cumeneshora' mentioned in a later Sussex charter. If it was then sea erosion has now destroyed the site. All that remains of it is the Owers Bank off the western shore of the Selsey Peninsular.[120] The *Chronicle* records that after landing the party: '. . . slew many Welsh and drove them in flight into the wood which is called Andredesleag' (MS A). (In MS E it is Andredesleg). This name for the Sussex weald preserves an archaic use of the word 'leag/leg' or 'wood'.

The *Chronicle* does not devote much space to the activities of the South Saxons. It records that in 485 Aelle again fought the Welsh. This time it was at the river Mearcredesburna (possibly the river Alun). In 491 he besieged the Roman fort at Anderida (Pevensey) assisted by his son Cissa. The siege of Anderida (or Andredesceaster as the English called it) ended when Aelle and his men massacred all those who had taken shelter within its walls. This battle indicates that the old Saxon Shore fort had provided a base for resistance even though Aelle had campaigned through its hinterland. From this it can be deduced that after landing at Selsey, Aelle moved eastwards, along the coastal plain of Sussex, striking at pockets of resistance as he encountered them.

At Pevensey Aelle reached the eastern limit of his campaign. Beyond it the Pevensey marshes prevented access to the area about Hastings. In all directions Aelle's kingdom was a limited one. To the north the forests of the Weald limited easy access to Surrey and Hampshire. The forests probably extended from Kent, across northern Sussex and into eastern Hampshire.[121] The best farming land in the little kingdom lay on the soils of east Sussex and on the coastal plain.[122]

The chronicler made no further reference to Aelle or his sons. For more clues about their activities we must look elsewhere. The warrior Cissa may have left a trace of his name in the place name of Chichester. The name is derived from Cissi an unrecorded side form of Cissa.[123] If it was not named after the Cissa of the *Chronicle* then it was named after someone else with an identical name (if subject to a little alteration over time). The place names Lancing and Linchmere contain the Old English personal name Wlenca or Wlanc.[124] These names, as with that of Wlencing, were formed from the stem 'wlanc' or 'proud'. Both place names may have arisen from the name of Aelle's son.

The archaeological clues are yet more revealing. At Hassocks and at Ringmer the early English re-used a Romano British cemetery. The fact that the majority of English cemeteries sited between the rivers Adur and Cuckmere are inhumation ones may imply that Romano British customs were influential. Alternatively they may simply point towards the late colonisation of Sussex.[125] The inhumation cemeteries include Alfriston, Brighton, Eastbourne, Ferring, Kingson by Lewes, Lancing, Portslade, Pyecombe and Selmeston. Mixed cremation/inhumation cemeteries include Glynde, Hassocks and Ringmer. In the inhumation cemeteries parallels have been noted with the Saxon remains discovered at Boulogne and in the valley of the Seine. The frequent appearance of saucer brooches indicates an original home in the Saxon Elbe Weser area. It would be incorrect, however, to conclude that the early immigrants in Sussex were a homogeneous group — they were not. Button brooches, garnet jewellery and glassware show similarities to fashions prevalent among the mixed Jute/Saxon/Frankish peoples of Kent and the Isle of Wight. Early applied disc brooches, found at High Down (cruciform type, scroll type, star type) argue for an even greater degree of cultural flexibility. These brooches have been found on a large number of sites south of the Thames.[126]

These brooches have been found in Saxon contexts on the continent but have also been discovered on the upper Elbe and on Frankish sites such as that of Krefeld Gellep.[127] They cannot be used as a definite form of cultural identification. The Frankish link is of interest, however, as more obviously Frankish items have been unearthed at the cemetery at Alfriston leading one eminent archaeologist to comment that 'early Frankish elements are present in an unusually large proportion'.[128] It is therefore likely that Aelle had campaigned on the continent for some time. As with Hengest, Aelle had gathered a culturally mixed following. Moreover after the initial landings they maintained their contacts with their allies in Kent and on the Isle of Wight. Nennius believed that Essex and Sussex were ceded to the English following Hengest's slaughter of the British notables. The trade with Kent declined after the middle of the sixth century due to fluctuations in the trading policy of that kingdom.

Despite their heterogeneous nature the invaders were conscious that they were primarily a Saxon folk (or at the least that their rulers were Saxons).[129] This said it is not surprising to find that there were connections between the Saxons in Sussex and those in Surrey. We have already noted that the expansion of Sussex was limited by the Weald forest. In the eighth century *Life of Wilfrid* the ecclesiastic Eddius described how Sussex had '. . . resisted the attacks of other districts owing to the difficulty of the terrain and the density of the forests'. Despite this, too much should not be made of this isolation. Three Roman roads cut through the Weald and linked Sussex to Surrey. Many must have travelled these, at least to begin with. There are similarities between the Thames-side cemeteries of Croydon and Mitcham and the Sussex ones of Alfriston and High Down. At Guildown and at Hassocks there are parallels (in both brooches and pottery) with sites on the Thames.

Having looked at something of the early expansion of Sussex it is now appropriate to turn to the writings of Bede. He listed those English rulers who had 'held sway over all the provinces south of the river Humber'.[130] The first one was Aelle of Sussex, the second one was Ceawlin of Wessex and the third one was Ethelbert of Kent. In all Bede listed six such overlords. (The mention of Aelle stands in stark contrast to the paucity of *Chronicle* entries regarding Sussex.) However, under the year 827 the *Chronicle* does give a version of Bede's list. To it the chronicler added an eighth name, that of Ecgbert of Wessex. In this entry the title of these overlords is given as 'bretwalda'. This title was translated by Garmonsway as 'ruler of Britain'.[131] The original spelling of the title was probably 'brytenwealda' which meant 'wide ruler'.[132] Over time it came to have the more specific meaning of 'Britain ruler'. This change led the compiler of manuscript A of the *Chronicle* to amend the spelling to that of bretwalda. In this form it resembled the new meaning. In some texts the old spelling continued to be used although it was presumably read in the context of the new definition. In this title the word 'Britain' meant the English lands south of the river Humber. There is a strong possibility that in its original form it was a Germanic title. In the form brytenwealda it may have been used to the face of a monarch such as Aelle. It was a statement about martial skill and expressed the homage due to a great king from lesser warriors and rulers. It may of course have also have been used by poets to flatter less notable kings. The difference is that their opinions were not endorsed by later historians, most notably Bede. In a similar way Bede totally ignored Mercian kings who in their time had achieved success as great as any of 'his' overlords. The chroniclers did the same thing. In other words it was not a constitutional title. It was less an objectively recognised office and more a subjectively perceived status.[133]

It is no longer possible to detect why Aelle was listed as a bretwalda. It may have been that the other English rulers thought that he possessed tactical genius. It is particularly curious when contrasted with the later insignificance of Sussex. It is difficult to believe that Aelle could have acted on a scale comparable with the later bretwaldas. In the absence of firm evidence this may seem unfair but may in fact contain the germ of an important idea. It may have been that in the early years of the conquest actions could have been less dramatic than later ones yet have succeeded in earning similar accolades to those awarded the later ones. The lack of ready comparisons available to the early settlers must have assisted this.

The cultural similarities between Sussex and the lower Thames sites may have been brought about by the military expansion of Sussex. There may have existed a short lived 'Greater Sussex' which straddled the Weald. The similarities in Buckelurnen pots found at Feering (Essex), Northfleet and sites in Sussex may have been caused by campaigns of Aelle as opposed to the fifth-century eruption from Kent following the revolt of Hengest and Horsa. A route to the Thames from Sussex may well provide something of a balance to the argument in favour of the Nene, Ouse, Cherwell route discussed earlier with regard to Wessex. The study of a number of clues (Buckelurnen pots Groups 1–4, horned urns, Group 1 cruciform brooches, equal arm brooches, saucer brooches decorated with five running scrolls) may indicate the extent of this pre-Badon Saxon empire.[134] The distribution[135] suggests a converging movement onto the upper Thames from the north east *and* from the south east.

Whatever the exact nature of this folk movement that which it created did not survive long. Some force halted the hegemony of Greater Sussex. Indeed not only halted it but actually reversed it. After the last mention of Aelle (in 491) Sussex lapsed into obscurity. There is no further mention of the kingdom until 675 when its king, Ethelwealh, was baptised. Sussex fell, never to rise again. It provided a salutary lesson in the fragility of the office of bretwalda. An institution built on military success could be swiftly destroyed by sharp reversals. The career of Ceawlin offers a similar lesson. As P. Wormald put it: '. . .it [that is, the bretwaldaship] does not necessarily reflect a constitutional principle that could be transmitted from one people to another and force does not equal political manners'.[136] Like the legendary crown of Richard III, the bretwaldaship was left hanging on the thorn bush of defeat, to be picked up by the victor.

In Sussex itself this reversal has left traces as discontinuity in a number of cemeteries around the year AD 500: Alfriston and Highdown were not used after the late fifth century; Hassocks, Glynde, Moulscombe, Pagham and Saddlescombe tend to begin later in the sixth century. It seems that some force caused a massive dislocation in South Saxon society. If it was English in origin no candidate is known. If it was British then the most persuasive candidate is of course Arthur. We should not be surprised to learn that no English source analysed so crippling a defeat.

There is evidence to support the contention that due to the disruption outlined above, the kingdom of Sussex was never fully consolidated. For example, after the death of Ethelwealh, at the hands of Caedwalla of Wessex (685?), the kingdom of Sussex passed into the control of two princes. This may reflect the fairly common practice of two relatives ruling together. Alternatively it may point to the existence of two provinces, or even kingdoms, within Sussex. There is reason to think that Sussex included at least three cultural areas — Hastings/Eastbourne area, Lewes area and the Brighton area with the region west of the river Adur. This cultural division may well have led to political divisions. In the eighth century this was particularly pronounced. In one charter, of this period, Offa of Mercia recognised two kings in Sussex — Aldulf and Elhwald. In another charter he recognised a king named Osmund. Other rulers of Sussex in the seventh and eighth centuries included Nothelm, Watt, Ethelstan (and his queen Ethelthryth) and Ethelbert. They probably do not represent a single dynasty but several. Suffice it to say that there are substantial reasons for doubting the organic unity of Sussex.

Before Sussex is left it should be noted that the political development of the area around Hastings was particularly peculiar. It preserved something of its political independence into the eleventh century. This little enclave was cut off from the rest of Sussex by the Pevensey marshes. It was separated from Kent by the marshes and shingle banks about Romney and Dungeness. Despite this it seems to have possessed similarities to Kent. It may have had a field system similar to that used in Kent and the dialects may have been related as well. This in itself is not surprising. The south east of England enjoyed a stable pattern of trade until the middle of the sixth century. What is striking is the fact that Hastings was not absorbed into Sussex. It is a vivid example of the failure of Aelle's line in unifying the kingdom. In 1101 the *Chronicle* recounts the negotiations between the English and the Viking host of Thurkil (Thorkell 'the tall'). The entry lists those areas overrun by the host. The list, south of the Thames, includes '. . . all Kent and Sussex and the district around Hastings'. This is very revealing as in theory all of Sussex should have included Hastings! Instead the chronicler deliberately differentiated Hastings. This was not an isolated case as in 1052 the *Chronicle* again records '. . .the district of Hastings . . .' as being in some way separated from '. . . the people of Sussex . . .' (MS C) It is not possible to tell whether or not Hastings once had its own dynasty but it was clearly an area in which the usual political evolution had broken down, due to geographical and military factors. Its name shows it to be an 'ingas' place name (in this case formed from 'Haestingas' or 'the people of Haesta'). In normal circumstance social evolution would have caused this group of settlers to be absorbed into a kingdom. This was the pattern to be found again and again in England in the sixth and seventh centuries as the phases of settlement, colonisation and political consolidation gave way to that of kingdom building. At Hastings this process was deformed from the start. The combination of the geographical position of Hastings and the early collapse of the central dynasty meant that the larger unit failed to absorb the smaller one. Hastings continued to exercise some degree of independence and cultural self-assertiveness. As an exception it proves the rule which applied elsewhere. It was a type of social grouping which would not normally have survived elsewhere to this extent. It was a cultural Coelacanth.[137]

Kent

The kingdom of Kent was formed from the fusion of several cultures. This was not unusual of course. It was a feature of a large number of the early English kingdoms. Initially though this fact would seem to contradict Bede's statement that Kent was settled by the Jutes. Such a simple conclusion appears to be at variance with the evidence that suggests a heterogenous community. However, Bede's account can be defended for two reasons. Firstly, it must be remembered that the Jutes were a heterogenous people. On their travels they mingled with many peoples and acquired great cultural diversity we may be sure. Secondly, Bede may have been referring to the initial warband under Hengest and Horsa. It would have been fairly typical to have let the ruling class 'speak for' the whole community. If we accept these points we can then add to Bede's account without doing any damage to his material or questioning its authenticity. It now remains to consider the evidence for Kentish cultural complexity.

Kent did not receive German immigrants before the fifth century. The considerable Teutonic presence noted in East Anglia and eastern England, from the fourth century, has not been noted in Kent. In other words, Kent did not lead the way in English settlement whatever the literary evidence says. As we have already seen there is probably a very simple reason for this contradiction. The migration of Hengest and Horsa initiated a new phase in the English settlement in Britain. It was not the first phase but it was a key one. It marked a watershed in Anglo British political relations. The Roman and post Roman settlement policy collapsed and was replaced by uncontrolled settlement and land seizure. Hengest and Horsa were not the first English warriors to land in Britain but by their actions in Kent they made sure that they would not be the last. These early Kentish settlers included many non-Jutes (even allowing for the flexibility of this term!). In the north cremating Saxon communities established themselves along the Thames at Northfleet and Sturry by the middle of the fifth century. These settlers were related to those further west at Croydon and Shepperton. The Northfleet and Sturry sites have produced Anglo Frisian pottery of a type known in Frisia and in the Netherlands. Saxon type saucer brooches have been found at Northfleet and an early fish-shaped brooch reveals Frisians at Sturry. Other Kentish sites indicate a Saxon element in the population: at the cosmopolitan site of Faversham 2 (King's Field), Saxon saucer brooches have been discovered; at Folkestone 1 (the Bayle) the cremation was of a Saxon type reminiscent of fifth-century rites carried out in East Anglia and Northamptonshire; a saucer brooch (early scroll patterned type) found at Higham suggests a Saxon inhumation; the mixed cemetery at Hollingbourne (Whiteheath) contained saucer brooches decorated with anthropomorphic designs; a cremation at Milton next Sittingbourne may have been in a Saxon Buckelurn pot but it is difficult to be sure in this case as the excavation took place in 1824.

Faint traces of other tribes have also been unearthed: at Northfleet some of the pots were Anglian; characteristic Angle girdle hangers were found at Faversham 2 (King's Field); at Buttsole one burial may have been Swaefe; a mid-fifth-century cruciform brooch found at Lyminge is similar to ones found in Scandanavia and Schleswig as well as examples found at Kempston, in Bedfordshire and Empingham, in Leicestershire[138]; mid-fifth-century cruciform brooches — typical of Anglian sites in Cambridgeshire and Suffolk — have been found at a number of places in Kent.

These examples considered above suggest an English cultural mix found in a number of the early Kingdoms. More controversial, however, has been the consideration of the evidence for Frankish settlers. At Strood the grave of a Frankish warrior has been dated as probably from before 520. Other Frankish remains have been discovered at Dover (a Frankish style spear and glass from northern Gaul) and at Lyminge (Frankish buckles, two Frankish axes, an inlaid spear and a glass bottle). On Thanet glasswork (known to German scholars as 'sturzbecher' and English experts as 'bell beakers') of Frankish manufacture has been excavated and dates from the late fifth/early sixth centuries. The identification of the glasswork's place of origin was reinforced by the presence of a Frankish buckle and gold jewellery. An analysis of the gold used has led to the suggestion that it came from melted-down Frankish gold coins.[139] These clues have not been uniformly interpreted by historians. Some have thought that they point to a large Frankish population[140] whilst others have insisted that the absence of strong, wheel-made pottery (typical of Frankish areas in Europe) means that there was no large-scale movement of Franks into the lands south of the Thames in the fifth century.[141] It must be admitted that some Franks clearly did take part in the early folk movements into southern England but they at no time constituted more than a minority group.

The clues considered above reinforce the view that Kentish culture was rich in diversity. Some early Kentishmen came from Anglian Schleswig, others came from the Saxo Frisian colonies such as Beetgum, Ezinge and Hoogebeintum. The fact still remains that many of them came from the villages of western Jutland, such as those that existed at Drengsted, Fourfeld, Herredsbjerget and Rubjerg Knude. It was these early Jutish settlers who were placed around Canterbury, Faversham and Sarre in the mid fifth century. Some probably reinforced slightly earlier settlements. The colony at Hanwell, in Middlesex, was probably an outlier of this group. For all the problems concerning exact chronology and sequence the record left by ceramics and literature dovetails to a surprising degree. The overall impression left by the evidence is that Jutish immigrants led a culturally mixed group of settlers into Kent. These settlers continued to be reinforced until the early sixth century. It was in this period that the square-headed brooches (found at Biffrons[142]) became popular in Kent and in East Anglia. The ultimate home of this ornament was in southern Scandanavia. Some were clearly made at the Swedish production centre at Helgo. Continued Scandanavian influence can also be detected by the study of bracteate jewellery. These round pendants of hammered gold were popular in Denmark but from the late fifth/early sixth centuries were also popular in Kent. At the inhumation cemetery at Finglesham (Northbourne) there was a particularly strong Danish element in the population. This site has yielded up bracteates from Jutland and a great square-headed brooch probably manufactured in Kent by a craftsman from Jutland in about AD 500. It should be remembered that these items could have been brought to Kent by trade more than by actual migrations. Nevertheless there is the very real possibility that Scandanavian reinforcements continued to bolster the English population for at least 50 years after the initial landing of Hengest and Horsa.[143]

Until the middle of the sixth century Kentish fashions were closely related to those of Sussex and the Isle of Wight. Although Kentish rulers did not succeed in expanding Kentish territory (in this period) north of the Thames, there *was* a cultural expansion. Pedestral pottery found in north-east Kent is similar to pots found on the coastal plain of Sussex, the lower Thames, the Cambridge area and East Anglia. Group 1 cruciform brooches — of the kind found at Canterbury and Reculver — have been recovered from sites in East and Middle Anglia. Pots known as 'long boss urns, with feet' have been discovered in north-east Kent as well as in southern Sussex, the lower Thames, East and Middle Anglia. These cultural connections were at their strongest from 450–500 and may have been caused by the eruption of Kent following the revolt of Hengest and Horsa or the later establishment of Greater Sussex under Aelle. The applied disc brooches (cruciform type) found at Howletts in Kent — as well as Guildown, High Down, London, Long Wittenham, Luton, Mitcham, Wallingford — date from this period.

In the middle of the sixth century the cultural pattern in the south east of England began to change (except among the cremating folk living on the Thames estuary whose impoverished lifestyles were not altered). The pair of Frankish radiate brooches found at Finglesham indicate the way that trade was going. By the 560s Kent was '. . .no longer part of a southern group, closely related to Sussex and the upper Thames'.[144] Kent had shifted into an eastern rather than a southern trading system. Both it and East Anglia increased trade with the continent at this time. At a time when other English areas kept up their traditional links with the European peoples of the North Sea and the Baltic the eastern system turned increasingly to the Frankish Neustrian kingdom of Charibert of Paris. This began to alter the kinds of commodities available in Kent as Frankish entrepreneurs made the most of this expanding market. This shift in trade began in the last years of the reign of the Kentish king Eormenric. He ruled from 512 (*Chronicle* MS A) or perhaps 522 (MS E). The date 522 is the more likely of the two. The confusion seems to have arisen over a problem in calculating the length of the reign of Oisc, which began in 488. Manuscript A gives him a reign of 24 years but manuscript E credits him with one lasting 34 years. The difference was undoubtedly caused by the compiler of manuscript E conflating two sets of dates (one set concerning the reign of Oisc, the other that of Octha) in order to produce one set of dates for one monarch (that is, Oisc). We can correct this error by assuming that Oisc ruled 488–512, Octha ruled 512–22, Eormenric ruled 522–63. This last king was succeeded by his son Ethelbert. The accession date of 565 is given in manuscripts A and E. However in these entries he is credited with a reign of 53 years. This does not fit the date of his death, given in manuscripts A, E and F as 616. To further confuse matters manuscript E records his death with the words '. . .he reigned for 56 years'. Some of the problems may be resolved by assuming that the entry for 616 provides us with a fixed point. This is reasonable as by this time there were literate churchmen in Kent. Working back 53 years (the figure quoted in three manuscripts) gives the year 563 for the accession instead of 565.[145] Why the compiler of manuscript E placed the start of the reign in 565 is unknown. The entry for 565 in manuscript A is less problematic. A later scribe erased the original text and added the information regarding Ethelbert and the length of his reign instead. In choosing to add it to the entry for 565 he may have been following another text (a common ancestor to that of E?) rather than working from an independent tradition. The choice of the 565 entry may have been helped by the fact that this entry already contained an account of the Christian missionary work of Columba and the sending of a missionary team from Rome in order to preach to the English (MS E contains both accounts). Ethelbert's conversion to Christianity was a result of this Roman mission.

The growth of trade with the Franks can be detected in the distribution of wheel-made bottles found in southern England. Some 91 per cent of these bottles have been found in Kent. Sites such as Dover, Faversham, St Peter's and Sarre had a surprising concentration of these items. Finds of these bottles have not been confined to Kent but the uniqueness of Kent lies in the large number of such finds in the county relative to other areas. The Kentish sites at Dover and Sarre were ideally placed so as to benefit from trade with Frankish Europe. This also applied to London and the Essex sites of Mucking, Prittewell and Rainham. The bottles may originally have contained oil, or perhaps wine, from the Pas de Calais. Such a trade must have been assisted by the marriage of Ethelbert to Bertha, daughter of Charibert. This dynastic union must have been followed by increased commercial contacts between Kent and Belgium, northern France and the Rhineland. Such contacts would have been assisted by the presence of a Frankish minority in the population of southern England. Similarly in the area from Calais to

Boulogne (and in its hinterland as far as Lille) the village names of Hardenthun, Ledinghem and Mazinghem suggest English settlers in Frankish territory. Other English communities existed at Anderlecht, near Brussels and around Arnhem on the river Rhine.[146] The flowering of Anglo Frankish trade has left clues in the form of English cruciform brooches found at Castelnaudary Aude in southern France, Kentish style brooches found at Hardenthun, Herpes and Preures and, finally, pottery decorated with English pendant triangle stamps found in the Rhineland and as far afield as the valley of the Danube.[147]

Trade was clearly the main source of the continental ceramic styles popular in Kent from the mid sixth century onwards. However, it is possible that an embryonic industry was starting to produce similar material in Kent itself. There is some possibility that this was the case with regard to some of the wheel-thrown pottery used in the kingdom by the early seventh century.[148] There is some evidence to support this assertion with regard to some of the 200 Frankish-style glass vessels found in England. This possibility was, some while ago, explored with regard to narrow-necked wheel-thrown bottles known as 'Asthall type bottles' (after the seventh century burial mound at Asthall (Oxfordshire) in which such a bottle was found). The results of this exploration were inconclusive.[149]

The case for an innovative indigenous industrial base can be made, more persuasively, with regard to metalworking. Kentish craftsmen did more than receive inputs of different styles. They took them and from the fusion of various traditions produced items unique to Kent or stamped with peculiar characteristics. This tendency may be traced back into the fifth century. This is if we reject Frankish, Jutish or Scandanavian origins for the quoit brooches found in Kent and instead interpret them as products of Kentish workshops influenced by late Romano British practices. This style of brooch — decorated with concentric rings of crouching animals — may have been the result of an amalgam of two traditions. It would then be another example of Celto Saxon art, or more exactly speaking — Celto Kentish. Clearer examples of such fusions date from the sixth century when Frankish jewellery inspired Kentish craftsmen to produce their own distinctive disc brooches. These items, made of gold and inlaid with garnets, became more elaborate as the century progressed. Fifty such brooches were unearthed at Faversham 2 (King's Field) and this site was probably in the vicinity of a major production centre. By the early seventh century the inlays became more extravagant and this form of decoration was further enhanced by filigree work. The concentric patterns became more involved. Experimentation with gold plate and cloisonne work produced classic pieces of art. The process reached its pinnacle in the gold, garnet, glass and shell composite brooches of the mid seventh century, the most famous of which is the 'Kingston brooch' discovered in 1771 by the Revd B. Faussett. There may also have been other expressions of Kentish inventiveness. It is possible that by the late sixth century English craftsmen were experimenting with a development of the existing stylised animal patterns used in Germanic art (known as Style 1). This Kentish experimentation may have taken place independently of other similar work taking place on the continent. It is at least permissible to say that Kentish metalsmiths (such as the one who worked on the decorated Combe Sword) may have made their own contribution to the rising fashion known as Style 2 ornamentation, made up of '. . .animals with ribbon like bodies (usually with interlacing limbs and jaws). . .'[150]

An interesting example of imitation of existing styles comes from excavations at Canterbury 2 (St Martin's churchyard). Digging in this cemetery turned up some interesting items. Alongside Frankish jewellery set with precious stones were half-a-dozen coins minted in the 580s. Made in England they were copied from Frankish and Byzantine originals. One of them was stamped with the words 'Leudardvs eps'. It was undoubtedly meant as a reference to Bishop Liudhard who was the chaplain to Bertha, the Christian queen of Kent and wife of Ethelbert.

Art work was not the only expression of Kentish individuality. Many of its social structures differed from those found in other kingdoms. The title of a nobleman — 'leode' — was a Frankish one. In legal documents some Kentish noblemen were termed 'eorl' or 'eorlcundman'. These terms may have been used to differentiate a nobility by birth from a nobility by service to the king, dominant in other English kingdoms. In other kingdoms this type of nobility by service was called by the name 'gethiscundman' or 'companion man' and represented those in the royal comitatus. If this is the correct interpretation of the Kentish material it can be fairly safely said that such a system of independent nobles did not last long after the year 600. Within 138 years of the date, the term 'king's companion' was being used for the men of outstanding wealth and martial power in

Kent.[151] The process of kingdom building had once again absorbed an independent nobility with its independent power base.

In Kent the lower class of 'ceorl' enjoyed a higher status than that accorded to this class in Mercia and in Wessex. Some ceorliscmen were independent free men in early English society, although the class also seems to have included (according to the law codes of Ethelbert and Hlothhere of Kent) rent paying tenants, 'esne' or half free men and possibly unfree men too. In Wessex his worth (expressed by his wergild) was one-sixth of that of a nobleman. In Kent the seventh-century wergild of a freeman (some of which were presumably drawn from the top strata of ceorliscmen) stood at 100 golden shillings. This sum (the equivalent of 2,000 silver pennies) was one-third of the wergild of a nobleman. This made the Kentish free peasant a fairly substantial member of the community — at least in the early period under scrutiny here. This relatively high status was probably due to the nature of the English conquest of Kent. Those who seized control were the first generation of Teutons in the region. There was not a drawn-out period in which Germanic troops first defended and then over-awed an area, as in the case of East Anglia. In Kent sub-Roman institutions continued until the Germanic mercenaries swiftly seized control within one generation of their arrival. Such a situation must have assisted the rapid transfer of British villa estates to German ownership. The lack of destruction of old institutions must have been one of the factors that led to the Kentish ruler making the Roman Durovernum Cantiacorum '. . .the chief city of all his realm. . .'[152] Even given the possible abandonment of the site for a period in the late fifth century,[153] the choice suggests a deliberate attempt to adopt previously legitimised ruling structures and forms. It was economics that made such an attempt problematic not English vandalism and destructiveness. In the countryside such a rapid seizure of power must have meant the capture of fertile land as well as the British labouring population. The three classes of inferior cultivators — or 'laets' — found in Kent were unique to that kingdom and were probably made up of British peasants who had been absorbed into the English agrarian class structure. The capture of estates and peasants must have led to the social elevation of the lowest class of English people since others could, in the short run at least, carry out the most menial and exhausting tasks.

Kentish agriculture employed forms of landholding scarcely known elsewhere. The dividing of land between co-heirs ('gavelkind') may have been a Jutish contribution to Kentish farming as to the agricultural system used in the Meon valley in Hampshire (Bede's 'province of the Jutes').[154] The administrative division of Kent into 'lathes' was peculiar as was the measurement of land known as a 'sulung' and made up of four 'jugum' or 'yokes'. Attempts have been made to find an origin for these in the lands of the Ripuarian Franks of the middle Rhine. This is not without its problems as it assumes a large-scale Frankish migration into Kent, an idea not supported by the ceramic evidence. Such a hypothetical folk movement is not supported by literary evidence either. The first Christian missionaries to Kent relied on 'interpretors from among the Franks'[155] but this proves nothing more than trilingualism. This is hardly surprising given the wide-ranging trading activities of the Franks. A rather stronger case can be made for a limited sixth-century migration into Kent from the lower Rhine.[156] Frankish objects found in Kent could have arrived as much by trade as by immigration in the period after 550 as in the period before that date. Frankish agricultural customs could have reached Kent via that mongrel people, the Jutes. Frankish claims to authority in Kent may have been encouraged by an unrecorded oath of loyalty sworn by Ethelbert to the father of his bride or by his father-in-law assuming that such an oath of fealty existed. The reiteration of these arguments (previously touched on earlier in this section and in an earlier exploration of Frankish claims on Britain in Chapter 1) may appear repetitive but is necessary due to the constant pressure from some academic sources to overstate the influence of Frankish settlers in southern England.

The name of Ethelbert has already been mentioned. He was the greatest king of Kent after Hengest. Indeed between Oisc and Ethelbert the rulers of Kent are but names to us. We know nothing about the reign of Octha or that of Eormenric. In his *History of the Franks* Gregory of Tours wrote about a Frankish princess who married 'the son of a certain king of Kent' but gave no extra information concerning this king, who must have been Eormenric. The only scrap of material that has survived concerning Octha (apart from the work of Nennius) is to be found in the Welsh poems *How Culhwch won Olwen* and *The Dream of Rhonabwy*. By the time of the construction of the framework of the latter in about 1200 he had become Arthur's enemy at Badon. In the former he is described as able to carry the sword called 'Bronllavyn Short Broad', which is so large it

. . .would be bridge enough for the three armies of the island of
    Britain
and the offshore islands with all their plunder.[157]

Clearly to use such sources as a means by which the details of
Octha's life may be discovered is like using the story of the Pied
Piper of Hamblin in order to discover medieval methods of pest
control! This is not an attempt to claim that there are no germs of
truth within these legends. It is simply to admit how inappropriate
these are as a basis for historical discussion. Such material is too far
removed from the primary sources. More than this it has become a
vehicle for the poetic conveying of national myths and legends.

 Against such a background of obscurity exploded the person of
Ethelbert. The *Chronicle* (MS F, entry for 552) named his father as
Eormenric. Bede (2.5) named his father as Irminric, a variant
spelling of the name Eormenric. The *Chronicle* entry for 827 names
Ethelbert as the third 'ruler of Britain' after Aelle and Ceawlin.
Bede described him as 'the most powerful king' in Britain 'whose
dominions extended northwards to the river Humber . . .'[158]
Ethelbert could not have achieved such a position before Ceawlin's
set back at Fethanleag in 584 or perhaps Ceawlin's expulsion from
Wessex in 592. The battle of Wibbandun (in the year 568) may have
represented an earlier attempt to assert his authority which was
crushed by Ceawlin and his allies. The *Chronicle* describes how
Ceawlin and Cutha 'drove him into Kent'. The implication is that
Ethelbert had tried to seize Surrey but had lost the region to the
Gewisse. By the 590s Ethelbert had fully recovered from his earlier
defeat. He married the daughter of the king of the Franks and gave
his own sister in marriage to Sledd(a) the king of Essex. He was
clearly building up a considerable power base in the south east
through careful dynastic unions. The fact that by 604 a church had
been built in London (the capital of Essex) on the order of Ethelbert
illustrates the extent to which Essex had lost its autonomy.
According to Bede, the East Saxon King Sabert (son of Sledd(a)
and nephew of Ethelbert) held the kingdom under the suzerainty of
his powerful uncle.[159] The *Chronicle* entry for 604 (MS E) states that
Sabert was 'appointed as king' by Ethelbert.

 It was in Ethelbert's kingdom that the first missionaries from
Rome landed in 597. They were sent by Pope Gregory 'the Great'.
It was this pope who, according to the legend, met the Angle slave
boys in the market in Rome in the 570s and created the pun, based

on their tribal name, that they were angels not Angles. The story is a charming one and bears the familiar stamp of a well-remembered tradition. If sceptics find this difficult to accept then it is up to them to disprove the historicity of the story. Until then it stands as a delightful cameo.

The mission to convert the English was finally dispatched in 596. Its leader was Augustine from the monastery of St Andrew, on the Coelian Hill in Rome. He was commissioned to '. . .preach the word of God to the English nation'.[160] After some initial doubts — which led to a request that the mission should be abandoned — the team finally landed in Thanet in 597 (MS F). The dates 596 and 595, found in manuscripts E and A respectively must have arisen due to a confusion with the date of the start of the enterprise in Rome. Ethelbert received them politely as he already had some contacts with the church, through his wife. A stipulation of their marriage had been that Bertha should be free to worship God without hindrance.

Some days after the arrival of the mission the king met Augustine and his 40 monks. He met them out of doors as he feared that in a confined space they might have been able to put a spell on him! The result of the meeting was that Augustine was allowed to reside in Canterbury although the king would not immediately commit himself to the faith. Augustine was also free to use the church of St Martin which had stood in the city since Roman times. Queen Bertha had used this building for her worship since she had arrived in Kent. From this it is clear that the church cannot have been in ruins. Indeed it may have been in continuous use by British Christians who had stopped it from decaying.

In time the king himself accepted the faith and was baptised. Manuscript F of the *Chronicle* claims that this took place in the tenth year of his reign. According to this manuscript's chronology this would have been in 573. This is clearly incorrect. The compiler may have meant that he was baptised in the tenth year of his holding the position of bretwalda. This would then imply that he assumed this undisputed position in the late 580s. Since the bretwaldaship was a statement of military might, not constitutional right, this date would fit excellently as it lies after Ceawlin's débâcle following Fethanleag.

The conversion of the king accelerated the progress of the missionary team. Following it permission was given for the restoration of old churches and the building of new ones.[161] Bede indicated that among these restored churches were St Martin's and Christchurch in Canterbury. No clear proof of this has yet been discovered at the latter but at the former the chancel may be of Roman construction. Another church which may have been raised over a Roman one is that of Lydd. In this case the area in question is that of the small basilican building, now part of the church. However, the evidence is not yet conclusive.[162] A fairly definite example is that of the church at Stone by Faversham. This did re-use a small square Roman building which had fallen into decay. There is no proof that it was formerly used as a church but it would seem to fit the general picture of the Augustinian revival. The identification of Roman churches is not made any easier by uncertainty as to the exact lay out of such early places of worship. Excavations at Littlecote Manor (Berkshire) in the early 1980s have uncovered a mid-fourth-century pagan sanctuary showing architectural styles usually associated with sixth-century Byzantine churches in Turkey. We clearly have a lot left to learn concerning the significance of many early buildings. Nevertheless modern research suggests that Roman Christian centres may underlie a number of modern churches in central London.[163] A cautious conclusion has been advanced by Bridget Cherry who wrote (in an article already referred to):

> The case for the influence of Romano British ecclesiastical buildings on Anglo Saxon churches is not yet proved, although the conversion of Roman secular buildings or the reuse of building materials is indicted in several cases.

Whilst the Littlecote Manor discoveries buttress this call for caution in the swift identification of buildings as 'definite' Roman churches, there is still increasing evidence to support the basic account to be found in Bede's writings.

The growth of church membership was not accomplished by any kind of force, but by persuasion. Some historians have taken this as more evidence for the early English preoccupation with things Roman and associated with imperial authority. The church being the repository of learning and the last surviving expression of western Roman government. This may have been a factor but it should not be assumed that it was the only one. Such a conclusion arises from too secular an interpretation of historical events. In the late sixth century the English were in a state of 'spiritual crisis': their belief in the old gods had been reduced to confused and threadbare superstitions; the rites practised by their ancestors had become dislocated; their society was in a state of flux. A description possibly all too familiar to modern students of history. Into this situation came the Christian Gospel: it offered a persuasive explanation of the human condition; it brought the idea of God into direct contact with ordinary men and women through the person of Jesus; it offered hope in a resurrected eternity coupled with a strong moral code for this life. In short the very content of the message preached by Augustine demands to be evaluated. It would be short sighted indeed to *only* consider its socio-economic and socio-political context. It was this message which, for all set-backs and problems, the ordinary men and women of early England accepted through conversion. In 598 when Pope Gregory wrote to the Patriarch of Constantinople he was able to tell him that 'At the feast of Christmas last year more than ten thousand English are reported to have been baptised.' For some of these their sincerity may be questioned, at least in Essex.[164] When the client king Sabert died his sons expelled Christians from the kingdom. Elsewhere the experience was more firmly rooted.

In 603 Augustine met the native British clergy at a place later called Augustine's Oak. It lay somewhere on the border between the territory of the West Saxons and that of the mixed Angle/Saxon peoples of the Hwicce (probably somewhere north of Bath). The meeting place illustrates the kind of authority enjoyed by Ethelbert: he could install a client king in Essex; he could sanction construction work in another king's capital and in 603 he could ensure safe passage for the ecclesiastical party far into the provinces of other rulers. This was the reality of the bretwaldaship in action. In 616 he died and the overlordship passed to Raedwald of the East Angles who had already risen to prominence during the last years of Ethelbert's reign. When Ethelbert was king, southern England had seen increased contacts with Europe and Kent had seen the consolidation of its monarchy and the growth of its own cultural genius; the church had been established in England and for all future crises it was to prove a lasting foundation. Its establishment was to have vast repercussions and it would eventually help lead to the cultural unity of England. Bede summed it all up very concisely: 'King Ethelbert of the Kentish folk died after a glorious earthly reign of 56 years and entered the eternal joys of the kingdom of Heaven.'[165]

Northumbria

The kingdom of Northumbria was formed out of two earlier kingdoms. These were the kingdoms of Bernicia and Deira. Both of these names were derived from British originals. The name Deira appears in Welsh sources as 'Deur' which developed into 'Deifr'. This area lay between the rivers Humber and Tees. Its name was derived from the Celtic for 'waters'. The name Bernicia appears in Welsh sources as 'Breennych', Brennych' and 'Birneich'. Despite a long accepted convention it can no longer be safely thought of as derived from the British tribal name 'Brigantes' (by way of a later form 'Briganticia'). Work by philologists such as K. Jackson, A. L. F. Rivet and C. C. Smith suggest that the name of the English kingdom may well have had an original British form such as 'Bernia' or 'Berniae'(rooted in a Celtic word 'berna' or 'birna' meaning 'mountain pass' or the like).

To the south of these kingdoms lay the great riverine routeway of the Humber system. The use of this as a frontier had no real meaning in the period before 600. It was later English politics which turned it into a dividing line and separated those English living north of it from those living to the south. It was dynastic disputes which made such a unifying element into a division. Northumbria knew many such conflicts from the late sixth century onwards. Many of its crises were internal feuds between the rival houses of Bernicia and Deira as they struggled to gain control over the whole of the kingdom. In these disputes Bernicia was the more successful of the two until 617. However, violence was not only caused by English civil strife. The Welsh kingdoms of northern Britain attempted to exterminate the English settlers but were too divided to ensure a long-term concerted response to the English penetration. Much of Northumbrian history was played out against this dramatic and violent backdrop.

The first English immigrants arrived in the Wolds of Deira when Britain was still part of the Roman empire. As late as the time of Bede the woodlands in the Plain of Beverley were called 'Dera Wudu' — 'wood of the Deirans' — and must have been the home of some of the first immigrants. Characteristic wheel-made Romano Saxon pottery implies a mercenary presence at Aldborough, Heworth and in the Roman city of York. In this last example English settlers used the Romano British cemetery. In one area of this city a row of solidly built late Roman buildings may have been used as living quarters by fifth-century Germanic troops. It is clear from this that German troops were used to guard Roman communication routes and key strategic sites in Yorkshire as they had been in other areas north of the Thames. The early presence of such troops can be demonstrated by reference to pots of Germanic manufacture as well as late Roman ceramics. At Sancton, on Humberside, some urns are similar to ones unearthed from fourth-century contexts on the Baltic island of Fyn.[166] Other parallels with pots found at Sancton have been noted at Borgstedt, in Anglian Schleswig.[167] Anglia peoples seem to have been dominant from the start in Deira. Many came to eastern Yorkshire and Humberside (as to Caistor by Norwich) direct from Schleswig. However, it would be wrong to conclude that there were no tribal minorities in Deira. Some of those buried at Sancton came originally from the Saxon dominated settlement at Wehden, some came from the Saxon site at Quelkhorn. Swedish pottery has also been discovered at Sancton along with evidence which has led some experts to suggest the presence of Alemanni, Boructuarii and Rugini in the population. The evidence is in the form of sherds resembling fourth-century pieces from Landsachsen Anhalt and other sherds which were clearly produced as handmade imitations of sixth-century Frankish wheel-made pots.

The compiler of the *Historia Brittonum* named Hengest's relative Octha as the commander of the English troops in the north. In one source the name 'Oessa' (Oisc?, Octha?) is linked to the founding of Bernicia.[168] This seems highly unlikely for reasons which will be discussed below. As usual the recording of the deeds of the troops invited by Vortigern have obliterated all literary references to earlier troop deployments. Octha was obviously not the first English warrior north of the Humber. Fellow Germans had been defending the area from Pictish intruders for at least a century. As elsewhere the policy which led to disaster had obscured a previous policy which worked. Despite the silence of the literary sources it is clear that the users of pure Anglian and Anglo Frisian pottery who appeared in the north in the mid fifth century were reinforcing earlier settlers.

The Anglian genealogies/king lists appended to the compilation of Nennius record an otherwise unknown character named Soemil. His name can be found six places above the name of Edwin (a king of Deira) in the place reserved for Saefugel in English versions of the genealogy.[169] The Welsh list is a faulty one. It intrudes Beldeyg and Brond into the places reserved for Waegdaeg and Sigegar in the English version of the Deiran material. There are other confusions in the Welsh version which make it of dubious value as a piece of evidence. Despite all of this the reference to Soemil may be of some value. He, it is stated, 'first separated Deur o Birneich'. This corrupt statement is false as the kingdom of Bernicia was not founded until 547. The seperation of Deira from Bernicia (the intended meaning of this statement) was clearly not possible and the entry is a puzzling anachronism. The compiler (as has been discussed previously) probably meant that Deira rebelled against the authorities in York. It was British power *not* Bernician control that they separated themselves from. It was a counterpart to the revolt of Hengest and Horsa in Kent.

The revolt in Yorkshire achieved only a limited success. Myre's distribution maps for stehende Bogen (standing arch decoration) pots[170] and for later Buckelurnen (bossed pots) of the second half of the fifth century[171] reveal that with the exception of Saltburn (Cleveland), on the coast, no great land seizure took place. The expansion of Buckelurnen users, noted in the south of England, was not mirrored in the north. Here there was no great influx of people from the Elbe Weser region, although the established sites of Heworth and Sancton did continue into the era of bossed ceramic fashions. Some historians have attributed this slow start and the later violence of northern English history to the large presence of military units on Hadrian's Wall and throughout the northern military zone that had been established in Roman times. This is not a satisfactory answer. The field army had been withdrawn from Britain in the early fifth century and the static units which garrisoned the forts on the wall were by 410 more of a peasant local militia. Some of these may have joined the armies of British rulers. The majority must have melted back into the indigenous population. The reason for the slow start to the English conquest of the north is better sought in the smallness of the Teutonic population. This is not to say that the northern revolt was a total failure. The Anglian settlers were not dislodged. It is possible that they succeeded in gaining control of the Roman fortress and colonia of Eburacum. Deira experienced a slow but steady growth from the late fifth century onwards: at Catterick a stone building, with an impressive entrance, built close to a timber structure may have served as the headquarters of an English chief; at Elmswell (Humberside) and at Staxton (North Yorkshire) pits, floors and domestic objects have been found; at Sewerby a circular ditch in a cemetery may mark the position of an English shrine; at the appropriately named Wykeham (North Yorkshire) some 24 SFBs spread over two hectares. As well as domestic sites and buildings, the cemeteries began to slowly multiply: inhumation rites predominated at Catterick, Garton on the Wolds (Humberside), North Newbald (Humberside), Seamer (North Yorkshire) and in the sixth-century cemetery used alongside the larger cremation cemetery at Sancton; cremation was the practice at Broughton (North Yorkshire) as well as in the older sites mentioned earlier; mixed rites were practised at Driffield (Humberside), Nafferton (Humberside), Robin Hood's Bay (North Yorkshire), Saltburn and Upper Dunsford (North Yorkshire). Exactly how this area was touched by the British revival of the late fifth century is difficult to say. There is a possibility that the English hold on York was temporarily loosened. A British tradition insists that the Celtic kings Gurci (or Gwrgi) and Peredur (or Pryderi) ruled at York until their defeat at the hands of the Bernicians, at the battle of Caer Greu, in 580. It was this Peredur whom later Welsh writers knew as Peredur son of Evrawg (Peredur son of York!) and who eventually appeared, as the Arthurian knight Percival, in the grail legends of Chretien de Troyes and Wolfram von Eschenbach. The tradition of the British kings may not disprove the English presence at York. Given the confused politics of the times the troops who defended the city may have been German, whether they mastered the place or were made to serve a British ruler until the late sixth century.

The first recorded king of Deira was named Aelle. The *Chronicle* records that he began his reign in 560 (MSS A and E). Manuscript E (and a later addition to MS A) adds that he ruled for 30 years. Later, in both manuscripts, his death was entered under the year 588! It was this Aelle who was mentioned by Bede in his retelling of the story of the Angle boys in the slave market in Rome. When Gregory asked the name of their king they replied — Aelle. '"Then", said Gregory, making play on the name, "it is right that their land should echo the praise of God our creator in the word alleluia."'[172] Nothing more is known about the life of this king. The chronicler gave his genealogy under the year 560 (MSS B and C) and it is noteworthy for its 'S' alliteration and for the fact that the name Waegdaeg (first under Woden) is the same as that name in the same place in the genealogy of Kent,[173] in the *Cotton Vespasian* manuscript (the *Chronicle*, Aethelweard, and Bede preferring the name Wecta or

Withar for this position in the Kentish list). The dynasty may have been founded by Sigegeat who would have been in his prime in the 470s or by Saebald in the 480s or 490s.

Shortly before Aelle came to the throne the kingdom of Bernicia was founded to the north of Deira. Under the year 547 the *Chronicle* notes:

> In this year Ida, from whom sprang the royal race of the North-umbrians, succeeded to the kingdom and reigned 12 years [that is, 547–59]. He built Bamburgh which was first enclosed by a stockade and thereafter by a rampart.(MS E)

The mention of the length of his reign and the reference to his fortifications were not in the original text of manuscript A but exist in E. (The original text (with only the mention of his accession) survives in MSS B and C. The material from E has been added to A after the original material in A was erased. The original material also contains a genealogy.[174]) The length of his reign may have been borrowed from the chronological summary in Chapter 24 (Book 5) of Bede. There are similarities between the genealogies of Benicia and Wessex and minor similarities with East Anglia, Kent and Lindsey.

Ida founded his fortress far to the north of Deira. It lay north of Hadrian's Wall and faced Bewick Moor and the Cheviot Hills. The landing came too late in the migration period to be regarded as a fresh penetration from Germany. Ida's origins were probably in Deira or northern Lindsey. There is though no relationship, mythical or otherwise, between his genealogy and the English versions of that of Deira. The place names Lindisfarne, near Bamburgh (Northumberland) and Lindsey are related, however. The name Lindisfarne meaning 'island of the Lindsey People' or 'island of the people who have been to, or who regularly go to, Lindsey'. The first element of the name being 'Lindis' (the old name of north Lincolnshire) and the second 'faran' or 'travellers'.[175] If Ida came from Lindsey the presence of established English colonies immediately north of the Humber would have forced him to go even further north in order to carve out a kingdom for himself. His descendants were to be the bitter rivals of the Deirans for generations.

The compilers of the *Chronicle* did not grasp this early division among the northern English. If they did comprehend it then they chose to ignore it. They pretended that when Aelle became king in 560 he succeeded Ida. In the original text of manuscript A this was not the case. Only the accession and genealogy of Aelle was entered. However, a later writer erased the genealogical material (preserved in MSs B and C) and substituted the line '. . .Ida having died and each of them reigned 30 years' so that it followed on from the note regarding Aelle's accession. This created a false sense of continuity and royal succession. This censored entry is all that remains in manuscript E, the compiler of which may either have copied from or alternatively influenced the thinking of the later censor of A. All of this implies that they ruled a united kingdom which they definitely did not. The basic independence of Bernicia was recognised by the compiler of the Anglian genealogies appended to Nennius. Two places after Woden he placed Beornec (a personification of the kingdom name) as one of the heroic ancestors of Ida.[176]

The band of settlers led by Ida did not constitute a huge group. It was probably only a small warband and their families. The remains of this sixth-century settlement are scarce. In the construction of a Gazeteer of Anglo Saxon Domestic Sites,[177] Philip Rahtz listed only one early site in Bernicia — West Whelpington (Northumberland), where a rock cut drain and post holes lay beneath a deserted medieval village. Other finds have been as scanty. In total they amount to two inhumation cemeteries — Darlington (Durham) and Howick (Northumberland); one secondary inhumation in a barrow- Barrasford (Northumberland); five inhumation burial sites with up to three burials — Capheaton (Northumberland), Corbridge (Northumberland), Galewood (Northumberland), Great Tosson (Northumberland) and Hepple (Northumberland).[178] These burials were poorly furnished. At Corbridge only early cruciform brooches identified the dead as English and at Howick the grave goods consisted only of beads and knives, of Anglian type. As David Wilson has concluded: 'There are . . . only eight sites in Bernicia which have produced pagan Anglo Saxon graves and only one of these (Howick Heugh) can in any sense be called a cemetery.'[179] This lack of evidence may be due to an earlier spread of Christianity (from the northern British) than has been recorded in the literary sources. Alternatively the answer may be that 'Bernicia consisted of a small Anglian aristocracy ruling a largely native population'.[180] In time this latter point may have helped Bernicia to become a regular channel for cultural exchanges between the British and the southern

English. To begin with though the contact was violent.[181]

Ida and his descendants faced bitter opposition from the northern British. To the west lay the powerful kingdom of Rheged or Reget. To the north was the kingdom of Manau Gododdin, with its fortress at Edinburgh and territories that spread around the head of the Forth of Firth and southwards through Lothian. To the north west lay the Irish colonies of Dalriada, in Argylle (ruled after *c.* 574 by Aedan Mac Gabrain who was eventually defeated at the battle of Degsaston in 603 after having launched a long range expedition against Bernicia). It was from these Celtic rulers that the resistance to the founding of Bernicia came.

The information regarding these campaigns cannot be found in any detail in the *Chronicle*. They are recorded in the work of Nennius. These records are made up of English material which has passed through Welsh hands, probably at the ancient scriptorium at Bangor in the Welsh kingdom of Gwynedd. In the process elements of Welsh history were grafted onto the original to create an Anglo Celtic hybrid document. The lengths of the reigns mentioned in this source can be cross-checked by reference to a twelfth-century manuscript from Durham.

The first British king to fight against Ida was Dutigern (or Outigern). This may represent a confused form of Eudeyrn a member of the royal house of Kyle, in the southern uplands of Scotland, about Strathclyde. Traditionally the war broke out over the fortification of Bamburgh by Ida. The results of the war are not recorded in any source.

According to the Nennius compilation (the *Northern British History*) Ida was succeeded by Adda, his son, who ruled for eight years.[182] However, the Durham manuscript indicates that in the year 559–60 Bernicia was ruled by, an otherwise unknown, Glappa. If this was so then Adda ruled from 560–8. It may have been this king who killed Gurci and Peredur. Adda was succeeded by his brother Ethelric. According to the *Chronicle* (MSS A and E) he came to power in 588 and ruled for five years (that is 588–93). This clashes with the Durham manuscript which implies that he ruled 568–72.[183] The reliability of the *Chronicle* is not enhanced by its claim that Ethelric succeeded Aelle, who was of course king not of Bernicia but of Deira. This error may have been caused by the chronicler's persistent refusal to recognise the sixth-century division of Northumbria! In this case he may have substituted the name of Ethelric for that of Edwin the actual son and successor of Aelle of

Deira. The dates given by the chronicler for this reign (588–93) may give the game away. In 593 a powerful ruler came to the throne of Bernicia–Ethelfrith. He overawed Deira and eventually annexed it and expelled its king Edwin. After escaping to East Anglia Edwin eventually regained his throne in 617. He then ruled from 617 until his death in battle in 633. During this time he became the fifth bretwalda, following the death of Raedwald of East Anglia. Edwin's troops conquered 'all Britain except Kent alone' (*Chronicle*, MS E). This later and outstanding reign may have eclipsed references to his earlier one. This may have caused the chronicler to insert another name into Edwin's reign up to 593, to fill the gap (that is, Ethelric). This may have been particularly tempting if the threat to Deiran independence had begun under Ethelric and culminated in Ethelfrith's later triumph. The matter is further complicated by the author of the *Northern British History* who at one point named Ethelric (in the form Aedldric) as a son of Ida and then later, in the same work, listed him as a son of Adda. This latter claim is clearly an error. When Ethelric died the crown of Bernicia passed to his brother Theodoric. He appears as Deoric and perhaps as Decdric in the British source. He ruled for seven years (572–9). In this period he faced fierce opposition from Urbgen, or Urien, the king of Rheged. The war did not go easily for either side. '. . .at that time sometimes the enemy, now the citizens [that is, the British] were being overcome'. This account was clearly meant to be a paraphrase of Gildas' account of the struggle in the fifth century. In this instance it was quoted to show that it was the English who were now on the defensive. According to this same British tradition Theodoric was besieged for three days and nights on the island of Metcaud. Since the Irish name for Lindisfarne was Inis Metgoit it is not difficult to identify the location of the siege. It would seem that Theodoric evacuated the bridgehead of Bamburgh and withdrew over the causeway — across Holy Island Sands — to take refuge on the island. Theodoric 'fought bravely with his sons'. The source does not name them but we may assume that they included the Frithuwald (Friodolguald in the Welsh text) and Hussa who reigned after him (their dates, as king, being 579–85 and 585–92, respectively). This is likely as Hussa is said to have fought against Urien and the latter did not outlive Theodoric. In addition there is other evidence which suggests that Hussa, at least, was of the legitimate royal line. When the Bernicians fought against the Irish of Dalriada in 603 'Hering, son of Hussa, led the host thither.' (*Chronicle* MS E)

Clearly Hussa and his family were of the royal house. The enemies of the English formed a formidable confederation. The dominant member of it was Urien. The Welsh bards later remembered him as:

> Great sovereign, all high ruler
> Refuge for strangers a strong defender in battle.
> The English know this when they tell their stories —
> Theirs was death, theirs was rage and grief
> Their homes are burnt, their bodies are bare.

Taliesin was not the last bard to recount the great deeds of Urien. Alongide Urien fought Ridec Hen of Dunbarton, Guallanc and Morcant of Kyle.[184] This confederation broke up through treachery when Urien was murdered at the siege of Lindisfarne. The Welsh *Triad* poems name his killer as Llovan Llaw Dino[185] who was in the pay of Morcant who was jealous of the prowess of Urien. Perhaps he feared that Urien would grow too powerful if he defeated the English. Urien's head was carried home to Rheged. His body was left in Bernicia. With his death the confederation collapsed although his son Owain continued to make war on the English. It was his campaigns which inspired Taliesin to write:

> 'The great host of England sleeps
> With the light in their eyes.'

Despite this his victories could not match those of this father. As with Arthur, British hopes had collapsed through internal divisions and small-minded rivalries.

In 593 Ethelfrith, son of Ethelric, son of Ida, came to power in Bernicia. He ruled until 617 when he died at the hands of Raedwald of East Anglia. He married Acha the daughter of Aelle of Deira and expelled her brother Edwin (known to the British as Eoguin or Aedgum). The *Northern British History* tells how he ruled for twelve years in Bernicia and twelve years in Deira. Presumably he united the two in 605. Perhaps Edwin had been a client king for some time prior to this. Ethelfrith was known to his Celtic enemies as 'Flesaurs', the 'twister', and he embodied the more extreme hegemonistic dreams of the English. He overran British areas '. . . exterminating or enslaving the inhabitants, making their lands either tributary to the English or ready for English settlement'.[186] It was after this unlovely man's wife that Bamburgh took its name.

Prior to this it had been called (if the Welsh sources are to be trusted) Dinguoaroy. It is likely that Ida had captured an existing Celtic promontory fort and had enlarged its defences. By his wife– Bebbe — Ethelfrith had seven sons — Eanfrith, Oswold, Oswy, Oslac, Oswudu, Oslaf and Offa. It is an interesting example of 'S' alliteration. He also had a brother, named Theodbald, who died at the battle of Degsaston.

It was against Ethelfrith that Mynyddog of Edinburgh sent the army known as 'the Gododdin'. This force of warriors was accompanied by the poet Aneirin who recorded their exploits in the poem known as *Y Gododdin*. The poem was composed in the late sixth/ early seventh centuries although the earliest written form that we now have dates from the thirteenth century. In this manuscript 42 stanzas (called Version B) when judged by their spelling and language seem to have been copied from a document dating from the ninth or tenth century. The warriors of *Y Gododdin* rode out to do battle with the 'men of Lloegr' (the English). The later *Triads* described this army as 'the generous host' because 'every one marched at his own expense without waiting to be summoned and without demanding either pay or reward . . .'[187] Aneirin expressed their hatred of the English. An emnity such as that of Tudfwlch Hir who 'slew Saxons at least once a week'. Others of the warriors he described as 'shouting for battle' and he recalled 'many the women that they widowed and many the mothers who cried'.

No English source mentions the battle of the Gododdin but the Welsh annals place it in the year 598. The Gododdin met the English at Catraeth (Catterick). By the time they reached this place they had already penetrated some 70 miles into Anglian territory. They threatened not only Bernicia but Deira as well. They represented one of the last serious attempts to throw back the Northumbrians. Had they succeeded Bernicia might have been crushed and Deira crippled. The plans of Ethelfrith would have been frustrated and those of Edwin (still nominal ruler of Deira at this time) would have been still born. Instead it was the British army which was destroyed. As Aneirin put it 'they were killed, they did not grow old'. Welsh tradition insists that only Aneirin survived the catastrophe. The British had sought to inflict another Badon on, at least, the northern English. They failed and with their failure the British hope collapsed. It was many more years before this was realised. The great events of history often need the passage of time for their full significance to be realised but Aneirin realised something of the scale of the disaster. Looking at the events from an even greater distance we may well ask whether even the battle of Catraeth could possibly have turned such a tide. Perhaps Catraeth and the campaigns of Urien were merely echoes of past possibilities. After all by the end of the sixth century the English had been established for over 200 years. Even had victory been secured in the north would it really have made all that much difference in the end? There was not to be a repetition of Badon and even that great victory, it will be remembered, did not expel the English. The poet Aneirin caught something of the hopelessness of the British cause. His words may stand as a melancholy reminder of the destruction of Celtic hopes. Concerning one warrior, named Gwawrddur, Aneirin wrote: 'He glutted black ravens on the wall of the fort — but he was not Arthur.'

Arthur was dead and so was the Roman diocese of Britannia.

Notes

1. That is, place names ending in -ham and -ingaham.
2. E. Ekwall, *Concise Oxford Dictionary of English Place Names* (Oxford, 1960), p. 130.
3. See Appendix 1.C.
4. G. Speake, *Anglo Saxon Animal Art and Its Germanic Background* (Oxford, 1980) p. 31.
5. J. N. L. Myres, *A Corpus of Anglo Saxon Pottery of the Pagan Period* (Cambridge, 1977), p. 4.
6. D. Hill, *An Atlas of Anglo Saxon England* (Oxford, 1984), p. 16.
7. See Appendix 1.D.
8. Bede, *A History of the English Church*, 4.11.
9. See Appendix 1.B.
10. J. Morris, *The Age of Arthur*, (London, 1973) p. 296.
11. Who have left traces in the place names Ealing, Mimms and Yeading.
12. An area lost early on to Kent or possibly Wessex (probably to Wessex, see *Anglo Saxon Chronicle*, entry for 568).
13. A. Burnett, *The Coins of Roman Britain* (London, 1977), p. 15.
14. P. Salway, *Roman Britain* (Oxford, 1984), p. 459 and p. 495.
15. Bede *A History of the English Church*, 2.3.
16. Ibid, 2.6.
17. J. Sydney, 'Sceattas and Their Place in Numismatic History', *Coin Monthly* February 1985, pp. 5–10.
18. D. V. J. Fisher, *The Anglo Saxon Age, c. 400–1042* (London, 1973), p. 110
19. By 672 in the *Acts of the Council of Hertford*.
20. This eventually gave rise to the area name 'Northhymbre' (867) and 'Northhymbralond' (895) and eventually 'Northumbria', and 'Northumberland'.
21. Bede, *A History of the English Church*, 2.5.
22. *British Museum MS Harley 3271 fol. 6.v.*
23. Bede, *A History of the English Church*, 2.14.

24. See Appendix 1.G.

25. Ekwall, *Concise Oxford Dictionary*, p. 365.

26. Bede, *A History of the English Church*, 3.21.

27. Of some 600 graves, 241 were inhumations.

28. Above Woden the names (Frealaf, Fin, Friothulf, Geot, Godwulf) were clearly borrowed from a source common to both Bernicia and Wessex.

29. Bede, *A History of the English Church*, 2.16.

30. See Excavations at Lincoln. Second Interim Report', *Antiquaries Journal*, 59 (1978), pp. 50–91 and M. J. Jones (ed.), 'Third Interim Report', *Antiquaries Journal*, 61 (1981), pp 83–114.

31. Bede *A History of the English Church*, 5.21.

32. Hill, *An Atlas of Anglo Saxon England*, p. 76.

33. M. Gelling, *Signposts to the Past* (London, 1978), p. 157.

34. M. Wood, *In Search of the Dark Ages* (London, 1981), p. 46 and p. 48 for sketches of this site 'reconstructed' by an artist. Also R. Jackson, *Dark Age Britain* (Cambridge, 1984), pp. 31–6 for photographs of the site.

35. P. Rahtz, 'Gazeteer of Anglo Saxon Domestic Settlement Sites' (Appendix A) in D. Wilson (ed.), *The Archaeology of Anglo Saxon England* (Cambridge, 1976), p. 450.

36. R. Jackson, *Dark Age Britain* (Cambridge, 1984), p. 38.

37. P. Rahtz in Wilson (ed.), *Anglo Saxon England*, p. 423.

38. Ekwall, *Concise Oxford Dictionary*, p. 212. In this work he offered a definition of the word 'halh' as it was used in the south of England and in the Midlands.

39. Wocansaetna — 'settlers by the Wrekin'. Also Stepelsaetna — 'settlers by the steep place'; Temesaetna — 'settlers by the river Teme'.

40. Abingdon, Bledlow (Buckinghamshire), Brighthampton (Oxfordshire), Fairford, Frilford, Hampnett (Gloucestershire), Long Wittenham, Reading, Souldern (Oxfordshire), Wallingford.

41. Excavations at the Dyke Hills, Dorchester on Thames, produced one burial so old that it might have been that of a fourth-century immigrant. Later evidence has also come from this town.

42. I. A. Richmond, *Roman Britain* (Harmondsworth, 1963), pp. 95–6.

43. J. Wacher, *Roman Britain* (London, 1978), pp. 107–9.

44. Gelling *Signposts*, p. 118.

45. J. N. L. Myres *Anglo-Saxon Pottery and the Settlement of England* (Oxford, 1969), p. 102.

46. R. G. Collingwood and J. N. L. Myres, *Roman Britain and the English Settlements* (Oxford, 1937), 2nd edn, p. 408.

47. J. R. Kirk in H. M. Chadwick (ed.), *Studies in Early British History* (Cambridge, 1954), p. 126.

48. K. Rutherford Davies, *Britons and Saxons in the Chilterns Region* (Chichester, 1982), pp. 58–9.

49. Myres *A Corpus of Anglo Saxon Pottery*, vol. 1, p. 127.

50. This is assuming that Ceawlin, the sixth-century overlord of the southern English, was not a Thames valley Saxon.

51. L. and J. Laing, *Anglo Saxon England* (London, 1979), pp. 72–3.

52. J. Morris, *The Age of Arthur*, pp. 322–3.

53. S. Taylor (ed.), *Anglo Saxon Chronicle*, vol. 4 (London, 1983).

54. G. N. Garmonsway (trans.), *The Anglo Saxon Chronicle* (London, 1954), 2nd edn, p. 15.

55. V. Evison *The Fifth Century Invasions South of the Thames* (London, 1965), pp. 84–6.

56. Other historians have considered the possibility that the landing on the Solent took place as late as *c*. 550. See D. P. Kirby's article in *English Historical Review*, 80

(1965).

57. Morris, *The Age of Arthur*, pp. 103–4.
58. Ibid., p. 225.
59. J. Chant, *The High Kings* (London, 1983).
60. A. J. Young, *The Swords of the Britons* (London, 1984), pp. 49–53.
61. Ibid., p. 52.
62. Ibid., p. 14. It is surprising to find a version of this concept in G. Ashe, *The Discovery of King Arthur* (Appendix) which attempts to prove that Cerdic was son of Arthur(!) and grandson of Vortigern. There seems to be not a shred of evidence (excepting a phrase of Geoffrey of Monmouth's about Vortigern being duke of the Gewissae) to support this unlikely assertion.
63. Bede, *A History of the English Church*, 3.7.
64. Ibid., 4.15.
65. Ibid., 5.19.
66. Morris, *The Age of Arthur*, p. 294.
67. Bede, *A History of the English Church*, 1.15.
68. Ibid., 4.16.,
69. See Appendix 1.H.
70. D. Whitelock (ed.), *English Historical Documents*, vol. 1 500–1042 (London, 1979), 2nd edn, footnote on the regnal list in question.
71. D. Whitelock, (ed.), *English Historical Documents*, (vol. 1). The confusion over a 24-year reign or a 32-year reign may have arisen out of a confusion over the actual year in which Ceawlin fell from power. The 32-year reign is the one best supported by the surviving literary evidence.
72. The argument for Badbury Rings (Dorset) can be found in a number of books and articles, for example, D. Bicheno, 'Mons Badonicus — Badbury Rings', *East Dorset Antiquarian Society Journal*, vol. 1 (1983), pp. 7–12.
73. Evidence exists to suggest secondary inhumation burials on Martin Down (Dorset). I am also grateful to Mr. R. Briggs who informed me about another (seventh century?) English secondary inhumation in the Bronze Age Bradford Barrow (Dorset) and for allowing me to examine the skeletal remains recovered from a chalk pit cut into the side of the barrow. Another isolated (sixth century?) barrow burial took place at Hardown Barrow, Morecombelake, containing shields, axes, small long brooches etc.
74. Just as school children in Avon were taught the myth concerning the foundation of the town of Keynsham by a Welsh princess named Keyna who turned local snakes to stone. I am grateful to my father, Mr J. M. Whittock for this tradition.
75. Morris, *The Age of Arthur*, p. 104.
76. Ekwall, *Concise Oxford Dictionary*, p. 336.
77. F. Stenton, *Anglo Saxon England* (Oxford, 1971), 3rd edn, p. 22.
78. A. Campbell (ed.), *The Chronicle of Aethelweard* (London, 1962), p. 11.
79. Ekwall, *Concise Oxford Dictionary*, p. 95.
80. J. Campbell, 'The Lost Centuries' in J. Campbell (ed.), *Anglo Saxon England* (London, 1982), p. 12.
81. Bede, *A History of the English Church*, 4.16.
82. As over the kings of Sussex after Aelle.
83. Morris, *The Age of Arthur*, p. 225.
84. Myres, *A Corpus of Anglo Saxon Pottery*, pp. 122–3.
85. See M. Biddle in Wilson (ed.), *Anglo Saxon England*, Chapter 3.
86. M. Biddle, 'Excavations at Winchester', *Antiquaries Journal*, 55 (1975), pp. 295–337.
87. Myres, *Anglo-Saxon Pottery*, p. 113.
88. The date of his death was discussed by Alcock, *Arthur's Britain*, pp. 22–3 and pp. 53–5.

89. See work by J. F. D. Shrewsbury, *A History of Bubonic Plague in the British Isles* (Cambridge, 1970).

90. W. McNeill, *Plagues and Peoples* (Oxford, 1977), p. 123.

91. A number of rats were drawn in the company of two cats.

92. J. F. D. Shrewsbury, *A History of Bubonic Plague in the British Isles*.

93. *The Plague Reconsidered* (Local Population Studies, 1977) p. 38.

94. P. Ziegler, *The Black Death* (London, 1969).

95. R. L. Gottfried, *The Black Death* (London, 1983).

96. V. Evison, *Wheel Thrown Pottery in Anglo Saxon Graves* (London, 1979), p. 8.

97. Cannington, Cheddar, Ilchester.

98. V. Evison, H. Hodges and J. Hurst, *Medieval Pottery from Excavations* (London, 1974), Ch. 5.

99. Ordnance Survey map of *Britain in the Dark Ages* gives a distribution.

100. H. P. R. Finberg, *The Formation of England* (St Albans, 1976), pp. 21–2.

101. D. J. V. Fisher, *The Anglo Saxon Age c. 400–1042* (London, 1973), p. 36.

102. Bede, *A History of the English Church*, 2.5.

103. Morris, *The Age of Arthur*, p. 226.

104. Ibid., p. 293.

105. Ekwall *Concise Oxford Dictionary*, p. 137.

106. Rutherford Davies, *Britons and Saxons in the Chilterns Region* (Chichester, 1982), p. 55.

107. P. Salway, *Roman Britain* (Oxford, 1984), p. 459 and Wacher *Roman Britain* (London, 1978), p. 265.

108. J. Morris, 'Dark Age Dates' in M. Jarrett and B. Dobson (eds), *Britain and Rome: Essays Presented to Eric Birley* (Kendal, 1965), p. 172.

109. P. Hunter Blair, *Anglo Saxon England* (Cambridge, 1956), p. 32.

110. H. P. R. Finberg *The Formation of England*, p. 22.

111. The pot was in the process of being reconstructed when I examined it in the spring of 1985 and I am grateful to the Director of the Corinium Museum, Cirencester for allowing me to see this item.

112. J. Haslam, *Anglo Saxon Towns in Southern Britain* (Chichester, 1984), p. 347 (for the state of Bath).

113. B. Cunliffe, 'The Excavation of the Roman Spring at Bath', *Antiquaries Journal*, 60 (1980), pp. 187–206. For the reference to votive offerings see B. Cunliffe, *Roman Bath Discovered* (London, 1971). For reference to Abbey Gatehouse see p. 215, and p. 219 for an admission that it is not possible on present evidence to assess the state of town life in Bath in 577.

114. J. Wacher, *Cirencester Roman Amphitheatre* (HMSO, 1981), p. 7.

115. J. Morris, *Londinium* (London, 1982), p. 347.

116. *Chronicle* entries for 688, 728, 855.

117. Morris (1973), identified it as having taken place near Tintern, on the river Wye, against Mouric the Welsh king of Glevissig (east Glamorgan), pp. 227–8. No other historian seems to have followed him in this identification and it is not regarded as a serious alternative in this study.

. 118. P. H. Sawyer, *Roman Britain to Norman England* (London, 1978), p. 44. For the other ideas see Hodgkin, *History of the Anglo Saxons* (Oxford, 1952), vol. 2, table 3 and G. Copley, *The Conquest of Wessex in the Sixth Century* (London, 1954), p. 157.

119. L. Sherley Price (trans.), *A History of the English Church and People* by Bede (Harmondsworth, 1968), Appendix, item 6.

120. Ordnance Survey map *Britain in the Dark Ages*.

121. Hill, *Anglo Saxon England*, p. 16.

122. Ibid., soil map. p. 7.

123. Ekwall *Concise Oxford Dictionary*, p. 102.

124. Ibid., p. 298.

125. Nevertheless Sussex has a high rating of '-ham' place names and an average rating of '-ingaham' names. However, its rating for the later '-ingas' type place names is very high and this is another factor pointing to late colonisation in Sussex.

126. V. Evison, 'Early Anglo Saxon Applied Disc Brooches, part 2, in England', *Antiquaries Journal* 58 (1978), pp. 260–78.

127. Ibid., 'Early Anglo Saxon Applied Disc Brooches, Part 1, on the Continent', *Antiquaries Journal*, 58 (1978), pp. 88–102.

128. Evison, *Fifth Century Invasions*, pp. 36–7.

129. Myres, *A Corpus of Anglo Saxon Pottery*, Ch. 5.

130. Bede, *A History of the English Church*, 2.5.

131. Garmonsway, *Anglo Saxon Chronicle*, p. 60.

132. E. John, *Orbis Britanniae* (Leicester, 1966), p. 7.

133. R. Collins, 'Bede, the Bretwaldas and the Origins of the Gens Anglorum' in P. Wormald and D. Bullough (eds), *Ideal and Reality in Frankish and Anglo Saxon Society* (Oxford, 1983), p. 118.

134. Myres 'The Phase of Uncontrolled Settlement, 450–500', *Anglo Saxon Pottery*.

135. Myres, *Anglo Saxon Pottery*, map 8.

136. R. Collins, 'Bede, the Bretwaldas and the Origins of the Gens Anglorum' in P. Wormald and D. Bullough (eds), *Ideal and Reality in Frankish and Anglo Saxon Society* (Oxford, 1983), p. 109.

137. A reference to the 'fossil fish' thought extinct until its rediscovery in 1938 off the coast of east Africa.

138. B. M. Ager, 'An Anglo Saxon Cruciform Brooch from Lyminge', *Archaeologia Cantiana*, 99 (1983), pp. 59–65.

139. S. Chadwick Hawkes and A. C. Hogarth, 'The Anglo Saxon Cemetery at Monkton, Thanet', *Archaeologia Cantiana*, 89 (1974), pp. 49–89.

140. Evison *Fifth Century Invasions*.

141. Myres, *Anglo Saxon Pottery*,.

142. The Kentish and East Anglian types differ in various ways: the Kentish types, for example, tend to have undivided feet.

143. For further study see S. Hawkes and S. Chadwick, 'The gold Bracteates from Sixth Century Graves in Kent in the Light of a New Find from Finglesham', *Fruhmittelalterliche Studien*, 15 (1981).

144. V. I. Evison *Wheel Thrown Pottery in Anglo Saxon Graves* (Chichester, 1984), p. 5. p. 64.

145. Confusingly Bede gave him a reign of 56 years (Book 2, Chapter 5) and this is echoed in the entry of the *Chronicle* (MS E) for 616 which contradicts *its own* entry for 565! It is likely that MS E took its 616 calculation from the work of Bede. If Bede had a reliable source on this matter, the reign should be dated from 560.

146. In addition to these colonies, there were also colonies between the mouths of the rivers Seine and Somme and on the Cotentin Peninsular in Normandy.

147. Myres *A Corpus of Anglo Saxon Pottery*, p. 117.

148. Evison, *Wheel Thrown Pottery*, p. 58 (with regard to pottery found at Dover and Margate).

149. V. I. Evison, 'The Asthall Type of Bottle' in Evison, Hodges, Hurst, *Medieval Pottery*, pp. 77–94.

150. Wilson *Anglo Saxon England*, p. 26 (on the classification work of Bernard Salin in 1904).

151. A charter of king Eadbert (738) referred to his companions as 'commites'. Earlier than this the term 'gesith' was used in the writing of a law code of king Wihtred (reigned 690–725).

152. Bede, *A History of the English Church*, 1.25.

153. Haslam, *Anglo Saxon Towns*, p. 5.

154. Bede, *A History of the English Church*, 4.16.

155. Ibid., 1.25.

156. Fisher, *The Anglo Saxon Age*, p. 26–7 (for an overview of the debate).

157. *Mabinogion*, J. Gantz (trans.) (Harmondsworth, 1978), p. 143.

158. Bede, *A History of the English Church*, 1.25

159. Ibid., 2.3.

160. Ibid., 1.23.

161. Ibid., 1.26.

162. B. Cherry, 'Ecclesiastical Architecture' in Wilson (ed.), *Anglo Saxon England*, pp. 156–8.

163. Biddle in Wilson (ed.), *Anglo Saxon England*, p. 111.

164. Here the king was baptised in 604 through the preaching of Mellitus, Bishop of London. Mellitus, Justus (Bishop of Rochester) and Paulinus (later the missionary to Northumberland) were dispatched from Rome in 601 to assist Augustine in England.

165. Bede, *A History of the English Church*, 2.5

166. For an overview of the use of this site see M. Lindsay Faul, 'The Location and relationship of the Sancton Anglo Saxon cemeteries', *Antiquaries Journal*, 56 (1976), pp. 227–33.

167. Myres, *A Corpus of Anglo Saxon Pottery*, p. 115.

168. D. N. Dumville, 'A New Chronicle Fragment of Early British History', *English Historical Review*, 88 (1973), pp. 312–14.

169. See Appendix 1.B.

170. Myres, *Anglo Saxon Pottery*, map 3.

171. Ibid., map 4(a).

172. Bede, *A History of the English Church*, 2.1.

173. See Appendix 1.E.

174. Ibid.

175. Ekwall *Concise Oxford Dictionary*, pp. 298–9.

176. These surviving Anglian genealogies/king lists include a list for each of the following kingdoms: Bernicia, Deira, East Anglia, Kent and Mercia. The lists were probably compiled in eighth-century Mercia. Later they were transmitted to Welsh writers. These scribes interpolated them into a history of Ida and the relationship between the northern English and the northern British. In the process some of the genealogies were undoubtedly expanded and additional material added to them.

177. Rahtz in Wilson (ed.), *Anglo Saxon England*.

178. To these may be added a barbed spear (an angon?) found at Carvoran and a trefoil headed brooch found at the Roman fort of Birdoswald on Hadrian's Wall.

179. Wilson (ed.), *Anglo Saxon England*, p. 5.

180. Ordnance Survey map *Britain in the Dark Ages*, p. 22.

181. On the subject of the population ratio see L. Alcock, 'Quantity or Quality: the Anglian Graves of Bernicia' in V. I. Evison (ed.), *Angles, Saxons and Jutes. Essays presented to J. N. L. Myres* (Oxford, 1981), pp. 168–86.

182. The *Northern British History* credits Ida with 12 (should be 6?) sons who it lists as Adda, Aedldoric (the Welsh form of Ethelric), Decdric, Edric (one of these must have been the Theodoric of the English sources — also known to the Welsh as Deoric), Deothere and Osmer.

183. Morris, *The Age of Arthur*, accepted the date as recorded in the *Chronicle* (pp. 234–6). This then forced him to reduce the kings of Bernicia, until 593, to mere local lords as he assumed that Ethelric was king until 593.

184. Morris (1973), located them as rulers of the upper Forth and eastern Cheviots respectively.

185. *The Triads*, W. Probert (trans.) (London, 1977), p. 39.
186. Bede, *A History of the English Church*, 1.34.
187. *The Triads*, p. 53.

APPENDIX 1: KING LISTS/GENEALOGIES

In these king lists the fullest form is shown in the left-hand column. Above it, as above all the columns, is the title of the source from which the material has been taken. A year after 'MS' indicates which *Anglo Saxon Chronicle* entry has been used. Columns to the right of the fullest list show major variations on that list, regarding names, spelling or order of names. Information in brackets provides more details about that particular item.

The primary sources for these lists include the *Anglo Saxon Chronicle*, Bede's *A History of the English Church and People*, the Anglican genealogies appended to the *Historia Brittonum*, the ninth-century document known as *Cotton ms. Vespasian B.6 fol.108.foll* which gives lists of kings and bishops, and the ninth-century document known as *Ms. Add.23211* in the British Museum and consisting of two leaves — one a martyrology fragment, the other king lists for Essex and Wessex.

Notes on the lists

A. Nennius' work gives the Welsh form of some names but confuses the order by intruding 'Beornec' into the list.

B. Once again Nennius' work confuses the order and his list is out of step with the English ones. 'Beldeyg' and 'Brond' are intruders. Nennius overcame this problem by omitting 'Swefdaeg' and 'Sigegeat' and by further intrusions (for example, 'Soemil'). He also misplaced 'Sguerthing' (a Welsh form of 'Saefugel').

C. The third name is a garbled form of 'Caesar'! Nennius combined his form of 'Wilhelm' with his form of 'Wehha'. Hence the doubled-barrelled 'Guillem Guecha'.

D. This list is famous for its origin in Seaxnet.

E. Note the confusion in the ordering of names above 'Hengest' and the intrusion of 'Wegdaeg' and 'Frealaf' into the list in *Cotton Vespasian*. Note also the confusion after 'Hengest'.

F. This list has been included, although it stretched far beyond AD 600, in order to show how the Lindsey list lacks synchronisation with even the rough chronology of other lists. It is likely that this dynasty was founded late in the sixth century.

G. Note the confusion in Nennius.

H. Note the number of names above 'Woden' and the omission of 'Creoda' from some sources.

I. This list has been extended well beyond AD 600 but is worthy of study for its alliteration alone, as is the list J.

K. This outlines just two of the options regarding the genealogically confusing period that followed the death of Ceawlin of the West Saxons. It should be noted that there are more options than these two!

THE LISTS

A. Bernicia

MS B,C (547)	Nennius
Geat	
Godwulf	
Finn	
Frithuwulf	
Freotholaf	
Woden	Woden
Baeldaeg	Beldeg
Brand	Beornec
Benoc	Gechbrond
Aloc	Aluson
Angenwit	Inguec
Ingui	Aedibrith
Esa	Ossa
Eoppa	Eobba
Ida	Ida

B. Deira

MS B,C (560)	Nennius
Woden	Woden
Waegdaeg	Beldeyg

Sigegar	Brond
Swefdaeg	Siggar
Sigegeat	Sebald
Saebald	Zegulf
Saefugel	Soemil
Westerfalca	Sguerthing
Wilgils	Giulgils
Uscfrea	Usfrean
Yffe	Iffi
Aelle	Ulli

C. East Anglia

Cotton Vespasian MS	**Nennius**
Frealaf	
Woden	Woden
Care	Casser
Tyttwian	Titinon
Trygil	Trigil
Hrothmund	Rodmunt
Hryp	Rippa
Wilhelm	Guillem Guecha
Wehha	
Wuffa	Guffa
Tyttla	Tydil

D. Essex

MS Add. 23211
Seaxnet
Gesecg
Antsecg
Swaeppa
Sigefugl
Bedca
Offa
Aescwine
Sledd(a)
Sabert

E. Kent

Cotton Vespasian MS	Bede	MS E (449)	Aethelweard's Chronicle	Nennius
Frealaf				
Woden	Woden	Woden	Woden	
Wegdaeg	Wecta	Wecta	Withar	
Wihtgils	Witta	Witta	Wihta	
Witta	Wictgils	Wihtgils	Wihtels	
Hengest	Hengest	Hengest	Hengest	Hengest
Ocga	Oeric (Oisc)			Octha
Oese	Octa			Ossa
Iurmenric	Irminric			Eormoric
Ethilberht	Ethelbert			

F. Lindsey

Cotton Vespasian MS
Geot
Godulf
Finn
Friothulf
Frealaf
Woden
Vinta
Cretta
Cueldgils
Caedbaed
Bubba
Beda
Biscop
Eanferth

G. Mercia

Cotton Vespasian MS	MSS B,C (626)	Nennius
Fr(ea)laf		
Woden	Woden	Woden

Watholgeot		Guedolgeat
Uihtlaeg	Wihtlaeg	Gueagon
Uermund	Wermund	Guithleg
Off	Offa	Guerdmund
(An)g(en)geot	Angeltheow	Offa
Eamer	Eomer	Ongen
(Ic)il	Icel	Eamer
Cnebba	Cnebba	
Cynewald	Cynewald	
Crioda	Creoda	
Pypba	Pybba	Pubba
Penda	Penda	Penda

H. Wessex

MSS A,B,F (855) and some variants	Aethelweard's Chronicle	MS Add. 23211
Sceaf		
Bedwig (Beowi in MS D)		
Hwala		
Hathra		
Itermon		
Heremod		Scef
Sceldwa		Scyld
Beaw		Beow
Taetwa		Taetwa
Geat		
Godwulf		
Finn		
Frithuwulf (MS A)		
Frealaf		
Frithuwald (MS A)		
Woden		
Baeldaeg		
Brand		
Frithugar		
Freawine		
Wig		
Gewis		

Elsa (not in MS D)
Elesa
Cerdic   Ceardic
Creoda (not in MS A,   Criodo
genealogical preface or
main text, but given as
son of Cerdic in this
entry in MSS B,C,D)
Cynric   Cynnric
Ceawlin   Ceaul(i)n

I. Alliteration in the full king list for Essex

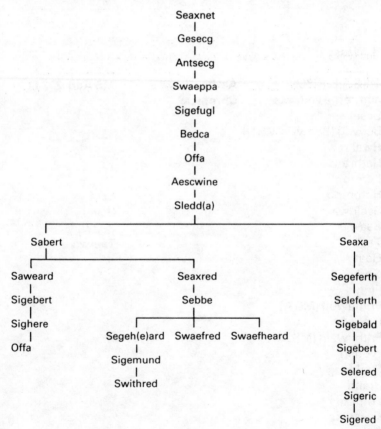

Seaxnet
|
Gesecg
|
Antsecg
|
Swaeppa
|
Sigefugl
|
Bedca
|
Offa
|
Aescwine
|
Sledd(a)

Sabert   Seaxa

Saweard   Seaxred   Segeferth
| | |
Sigebert   Sebbe   Seleferth
| |
Sighere   Segeh(e)ard Swaefred Swaefheard   Sigebald
| | |
Offa   Sigemund   Sigebert
           | |
           Swithred   Selered
                                          |
                                          Sigeric
                                          |
                                          Sigered

J. 'C' alliteration in the West Saxon royal house

Names include Cerdic, Cynric, (Crioda), Ceawlin, Cuthwulf, Cuthwine, Ceolric, Ceolwulf, Cynegils, Cuthgils, Cadda, Cutha, Ceolwald, Cenbryht, Ceneferth, Cwichelm, Cenwalh, Centwine, Cuthred, Cenfus, Cadwalla, Cenred.

K. Alternative genealogies for Wessex after the death of Ceawlin

(i)

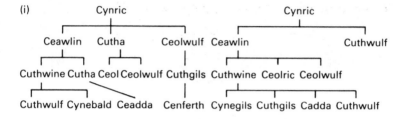

APPENDIX 2. THE TRIBAL HIDEAGE

This document may date from the seventh century and can be found in an eleventh-century manuscript known as *Harleian MS 3271, fol.6.v.* The tribal names are given below in the left-hand column. Place names derived from them are given in the right-hand column. If no place names have survived a simple identification is given where this is possible.

Myrcna landes	Mercia
Wocensaetna	Wrekin settlers
Westerna	An alternative name for the tribe called the Magonsaetna
Pecsaetna	Peak (District) settlers
Elmedsaetna	Elmet settlers
Lindesfarona/ Haethfeldland	Lindsey/Hatfield Chase
Suth Gyrwa	From the Fens
North Gyrwa	From the Fens
East Wixna	Uxbridge, Uxindon Avenue in Harrow, Waxlow (all ex-Middlesex)
West Wixna	Whitsun Brook (Warwickshire), Wisbech (Cambridgeshire)
Spalda	Spalding (Lincolnshire), Spaldingmoor, Spaldington (both Humberside); Spalford (Nottinghamshire)
Wigesta	?
Herefinna	Hurstingtone Hundred (Cambridgeshire)
Sweord ora	Sword Point, in Whittlesea Mere (Cambridgeshire)
Gifla	River Ivel (Buckinghamshire), Northill, Southill (Bedfordshire)
Hicca	Hitchin (Hertfordshire)
Wihtgara	?
Noxgaga	?
Ohtgaga	?
Hwinca	Hwicce tribe. Edgecote (Northampton-shire), Whichford (Warwickshire), Whiston (Northamptonshire), Wichenford (Oxford-

	shire), Wichnore (Staffordshire), Wychwood (Oxfordshire)
Cilternsaetna	Chiltern settlers
Hendrica	?
Unecungga	?
Arosaetna	Arrow settlers. River Arrow (Warwick-shire)
Faerpinga	Phepson (Warwickshire)
Bilmiga	?
Widderigga	?
East Willa	?
West Willa	?
East Engle	East Angles
East Sexena	East Saxons
Cantwarena	Dwellers in Kent
South Sexena	South Saxons
West Sexena	West Saxons

APPENDIX 3: EARLY ENGLISH PERSONAL NAMES

Diagrammatic Representation of Early English Personal Names

(1) Migration names (for example, Haest)
(2) (a) Compound names (for example, Sigegeat)

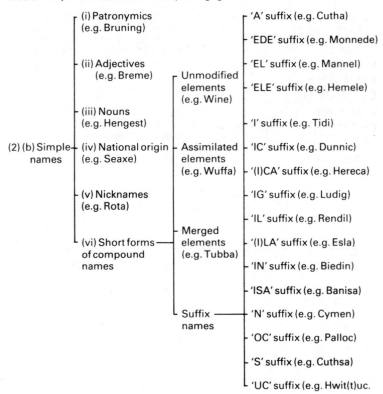

INDEX